Traditional
Newfoundland
English

UPDATED AND EXPANDED

Traditional Newfoundland English

The Lost Language of New Founde Lande and the First English of the Americas

R. A. BRAGG

NIMBUS
PUBLISHING

Nimbus Publishing Limited
3731 Mackintosh St, Halifax, NS B3K 5A5
(902) 455-4286 nimbus.ca

Printed and bound in Canada

NB1345

Design: Jenn Embree
Cover photo: The fishing outport of Diamond Cove on the southwest coast of Newfoundland. ©Russell Bragg

previous ISBN: 978-0-9918947-0-3

Library and Archives Canada Cataloguing in Publication

Bragg, R. A., 1945-
[Traditional Newfie talk] Traditional Newfoundland English : the lost language of New Founde Lande and the first English Language of the Americas / R.A. Bragg. — Updated and expanded.

Revision of: Traditional Newfie talk : the first English language of North America / R.A. Bragg. — Halifax, NS : Nimbus Publishing, 2015.
Includes bibliographical references.
Issued in print and electronic formats.

ISBN 978-1-77108-514-4 (softcover).—ISBN 978-1-77108-563-2 (HTML)

1. English language—Dialects—Newfoundland and Labrador—Dictionaries.
2. English language—Newfoundland and Labrador—Dictionaries.
 I. Title. II. Title: Traditional Newfie talk.

PE3245.N4B73 2017   427.9718   C2017-904133-9
                                                     C2017-904134-7

Nimbus Publishing acknowledges the financial support for its publishing activities from the Government of Canada, the Canada Council for the Arts, and from the Province of Nova Scotia. We are pleased to work in partnership with the Province of Nova Scotia to develop and promote our creative industries for the benefit of all Nova Scotians.

Dedicated to the memory of
Arthur George Farrell
1881–1973
grandfather and superlative Victorian Newfoundland English speaker

Contents

Illustrations

Contents

Preface

There is tremendous language domination from outside the traditional area of Newfoundland English from "mainland" radio, TV, Internet, videos, and movies, not to mention effects of travel and residence relocation into and out of the province. These influences have occurred over several decades and are increasing. Their cumulative impact threatens to reduce pre-Confederation Newfoundland English to little more than a few surviving, genuine, and isolated words and phrases, or eventually to merely a distinctive accent—especially in larger population centres. This is an ages-old, worldwide "prestige language syndrome" phenomena. A typical example is Xhosa, the "click" language of the late Nelson Mandela, whose speakers now prefer *iradiyo*, from English "radio," at the expense of the quaint but more poetic mystery of their earlier *unomathotholo*, "voices channelled from the healer ancestor spirits by a box." World English itself has been both a product and an instigator of this process.

However, in every case, a language gains prominence only after it gains literary status, an impossibility without having first gained a system of symbols—an orthography—to put itself into words on clay, hides, bone, stone, parchment, or paper. The ancient language of the indigenous Iron-Age Xhosa herdsmen first appeared in print in 1823 and is now the major language (80 percent) of Eastern Cape province and the second language of South Africa. World English was first put into print in the mid-600s AD. Newfoundland English never gained its own spelling system.

Using established nineteenth century orthographies of its ancestral West Country dialects as a guide, *Traditional Newfoundland English* reconstructs Newfoundland English spelled and systematised the way it could have been to represent its traditional speech under the umbrella of "many dialects, one language." We propose that, had it acquired its own spelling system, Newfoundland English language publications, including translations of the Bible, would have gained Newfoundlanders more than the barest remnants of a credible ethnic literary heritage. Instead, the casually uninformed or indifferent references to it today as "slang," "lingo," "Newfinize," or waggish "accents" are disparaged in facetiously satirical "joke" publications for opportunistic mercenary profit.

The learnéd *Dictionary of Newfoundland English* preserves for posterity several thousand entries on its seven hundred pages. *Traditional Newfoundland English* can hope to offer just a teaser of Newfoundland's very rich linguistic tradition (although we *do be* listing many items not yet in the DNE). However, this book in your hands does take Newfoundland English outside the context of the cultural extremes of "Newfie jokes" and obscure academic dissertations in a layman's twenty-first-century glimpse of the first English language of the Americas in the first colony of the British Empire and the last province of Canada. Here you will learn that Newfoundland's traditional English language is as capable of detail, subtlety, abstraction, and precision as any other and certainly as interesting, funny, *wunnerfo*, poetic[25], and as historically and culturally relevant as other aspects of Newfoundland heritage—as well as being endangered.

Having grown up and lived decades in the previous and oldest colony of the British Empire gives one a unique opportunity to recognize and appreciate one of the most traditional incarnations of the English language. However, for their contributions to this decades-long project, specific appreciation must be given to past relatives, friends, acquaintances, and several thousand former senior Newfoundland students now scattered worldwide. Jonathan Archibald of Blue Griffin Books in Middleton, Nova Scotia, deserves much gratitude for his encouragement towards the initial realization of this project into earliest print. And to my patient, persevering expat Newfie *townie*, Linda, who lost me for days at a time to the computer: an official thank you!

A dictionary, even one with "traditional" in its title, is a work in progress. Readers are invited to Like, Comment on, and Share the frequent entries on the interactive "TNT—Traditional Newfy Talk" pages on Facebook and Twitter.

—Russell A. Bragg
Annapolis Valley, Nova Scotia

Introduction

"It is an amazing place, and it is unbelievably remote, you know. They don't even get Toronto TV there."
—Actress Julianne Moore, fresh from the Newfoundland movie
The Shipping News, 2001[1]

In the course of mutual commensurations on the state of Central
London traffic, a casual fellow pedestrian once unintentionally complimented me with, "An' what part of Irrrland would ye be after comin' from?" Not surprisingly, that ex-pat Dubliner was unaware that the last great wave of settlers, generations ago, to the rugged first outpost of the fledgling British Empire, New Found Lande, were Irish adventurers in search of a new life or escapees from the despotic rule of Irish landlords.

Nine thousand years before them, the very first Newfoundlanders were the Maritime Archaic people, followed by the Dorset or Palaeo-Eskimo. Those earliest peoples are represented by later Inuit, Innu, Beothuk, and Mi'kmaq. Early Viking island settlers of L'Anse aux Meadows between 1001 and 1011 AD preceded visiting Basque whalers on island shores colonized half a millennium later by fishers, merchants, and rogues from England, France, the Channel Islands, and southeast Ireland. Although for centuries a British colony, French place names along vast stretches of the coastline attest to the "French Shore" of a forgotten war. A third of Channel–Port aux Basques phone book surnames derive from Napoleonic French, *langues de famille* also long forgotten. For the few thousand early Newfoundland *livyers* of the 1500s and 1600s, survival in a harsh land[2] superseded considerations for the future of their West Country speech.

Italian archives allege that explorers from Bristol, England, had visited lands in the western Atlantic before 1470 and Bristol letters of late 1497 or early 1498 confirm landfall there by Italian Giovanni Caboto ("John Cabot") in June of 1497, but did not define where. The University of Bristol "Cabot Project," begun in 2009, in collaboration with the Archaeology of Historic Carbonear Project begun in 2011, continues research to clarify details of Caboto's expeditions, including hints of a mission set up at Carbonear.

Bristol was a preferred departure point for the later West Country seasonal fishermen to Newfoundland, some of whom began overwintering in the late 1500s. Iceland's stringent regulations of 1580 encouraged fishing activity in Newfoundland. Coastal enclaves grew in defiance of England's Western Charter of 1634 and of the rough governance meted out by "fishing admiral" controllers hired to take commercial advantage of the abundance of Newfoundland cod. Settlement was encouraged by King William's Act of 1699 giving naval commanders superior rank over commercial captains, by the ceding of French Shore claims to Great Britain in the 1713 Peace Treaties of Utrecht, and by the assignment of the King's governor to the island in 1729.

It was a West Countryman of Devon, Sir Humphry Gilbert, who had first claimed Newfoundland for Elizabeth I in 1583, while his colonizing half brother, Sir Walter Raleigh, declared in Parliament that the Newfoundland fishery was the "stay and support of the West Counties of England." In 1610, a West Country merchant of Bristol, John Guy, formed a company, enrolled settlers, chartered a vessel, and, as governor, set up Newfoundland's first colony at Cupids. The influential Bristol and other West Country merchants continued lobbying the English home government to control fishing and settlement to their advantage into the 1800s. By then, new *planters* from Ireland were migrating to St. John's and the southeast Avalon Peninsula.

Young Irish Catholic fishermen (and women) from southeastern counties Wexford, Kilkenny, Tipperary, Waterford, and Cork appeared on the Avalon Peninsula as early as 1536. Ireland's economic collapse increased their numbers after 1790 and doubled the resident Newfoundland population by 1830. The influence of Munster Irish speech on the West Country dialects of Newfoundland English, especially on the Avalon, was predictable and pervasive. Nevertheless, for various reasons, many similar to today's general decline of Newfoundland English, the Irish Gaelic (*Gaeilge*) of this still distinctive Newfoundland subculture faded into history. Bitter division over the use of Irish Gaelic exists even today in Ireland where anti-Irish bigotry is not unknown.

The mainland Mi'kmaq, who hunted and fished for generations before settling, and other visitors—Portuguese, Spanish, Norman, and Breton French—have left traces, but Newfoundland English is the result of long-term migration from southwestern England and, later, southeastern Ireland. Bits of their original dialects still linger—dropping initial "h," switching "v" for "f," items of vocabulary, the rhythm and accent of speech—and subsequent melding over several centuries, modified by the influences of local conditions and lifestyle, has produced a distinctive speech of a unique ethnic group. Or, as linguists would put it, an independent set of lexical, grammatical, phonological, and orthographical conventions.

But is it a language? A "language" may be proclaimed for the least linguistic reasons, or none at all; the speech of 20,000,000 speakers of former Yugoslavia became the separate "languages" Serbian, Croatian, Bosnian, and Montenegrin from 1991 to 2006 for reasons of religion, politics, and pride. The Visayan languages of the Philippines are also mutually intelligible to a high degree but are classified as distinct "languages." Afrikaans and Dutch speakers may converse with no obstacle to communication. Contrasting the Afrikaans sentence, *My hand is in warm water* with a bayman's *Me an bes een warm wadder* should at least cause hesitation about uninformed claims that the latter is just "slang" English! Many other examples worldwide serve to show why serious linguistic researchers avoid an absolute definition for "language," using it instead as the colloquial, general-purpose word it is. Here we will consider Newfoundland English a convenient umbrella term for the various historic dialects of Newfoundland and the most fundamental expression of its common history, culture, heritage, and ethnicity.

THANK ALEXANDER THE GREAT

The many varieties of today's World English have been spun from a fifteen-hundred-year history beginning with the migration of West Germanic peoples from northwestern Europe into England after its Roman occupation ended in the 400s AD. The previous Celtic-speaking Britons were gradually overwhelmed and pushed west and north by the sheer numbers of these Anglo-Frisian-speaking newcomers (also called "Angles", "Jutes" and "Saxons"). Over time, Anglo-Frisian developed into the Anglo-Saxon ("Old English") dialects (see the "Newfoundland English Tree" diagram below), the two most influential being Anglian of the English Midlands and West Saxon of the Wessex southwest. By the 800s AD, through successful military campaigns and wise government, progressive leaders such as King Alfred the Great (849–899), his son Edward, and grandson Aethelstan made Late West Saxon into the first official and prestige literary dialect of English. At this time, the Mercian and Northumbrian Scots varieties of Anglian lacked such guidance or tangible literary expression, in most part due to disruptive Norse Viking invasions and settlement which disabled their northeast, midlands, and northern kingdoms. Norse and Mercian English had a high degree of mutual intelligibility and Mercian-Norse intermarriage was widespread. Because of this

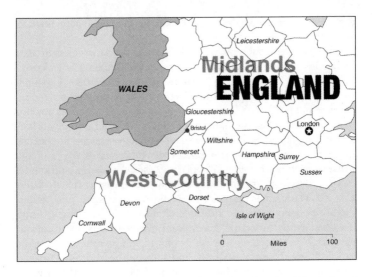

today there is a degree of convergence between a Standard English and Scandinavian. However, West Country English preserved the most representative features of Anglo-Saxon, and, in particular, of King Alfred the Great's West Saxon. Thus, as a descendant of West Country English, traditional Newfoundland English became a beneficiary of the speech of King Alfred the Great.

Sentence structure and many proper words in the Standard Englishes have a decidedly Scandinavian edge and the modern Standard Englishes are basically different from Anglo Saxon in grammar and structure, so much so that some have claimed that World English is a Scandinavian language influenced by Anglo Saxon.[3] True, many Norse words now absent from modern Scandinavian languages (Danish, Norwegian, Swedish) have survived intact in modern worldwide English (and Icelandic). And modern World English exhibits heavy Viking Norse influence before and after the Norman French conquest, but Newfoundland English is more a product of the prestigious Late West Saxon, the dialect that became the first standardized written "English" (the "Winchester standard"). Linguistic conservation in Newfoundland preserved into the twentieth century archaic West Country English characteristics, many now lost to its original speakers.

The initial ancestral dialects of Newfoundland English—the West Country dialects of Cornwall, Devon, Dorset, Hampshire, and Somerset—originated from Late West Saxon. However, royal alliances, marriages, and related events led to an eventual shifting of

Wessex power eastward from Winchester to the previous Roman colonial capital of London until all social and literary prestige for West Saxon ended with the invasion in 1066 by the Norman French from across the English Channel. London and the Mercian Midlands and East Anglia became the more prosperous parts of England, areas which corresponded to the Norse settlement areas, the "Danelaw."

Geographical features favour conservation socially, culturally and linguistically while, unlike dispersed settlements, cities foster contact and linguistic change. Under the Normans' 200-year feudal influence from their political power base of London it was a melding of the Norse-influenced London-Mercian dialect infused with Old French expression that gradually became a virtually new English language we call "Middle English". Thereafter, relatively isolated Late West Saxon and its West Country descendants were marginalised. The later West Country speech of the immigrant *planters* and *livyers* of Newfoundland inherited this loss of prestige. The subsequent influx of Irish migrants did not improve negative attitudes which have persisted into modern times with unfortunate results, as we shall see.

Newfoundland was the eventual destination for disgruntled West Countrymen, but much earlier in 1169 several hundred West Saxon-speaking emigrants crossed to County Wexford, southeastern Ireland. Their dialect of English, under some local Irish influence, became *oure yola talke* ("our old language") and represented the Forth and Bargy Baronies of Wexford for seven hundred years. We will meet this "sister language" to Newfoundland English again, below.

Over three centuries of settlement of West Countrymen along several thousand miles of Newfoundland coastline and of later Irish immigrants on the Avalon peninsula produced a settlement pattern

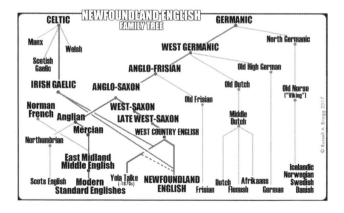

usually reflecting the quest for fishing opportunities, but it isolated many dialect speakers for generations and preserved Newfoundland English well into the twentieth century. More than enough time for the language to flower into serious prose, poetry, book publications, newspaper editions, Bible translations, other print literature, and even road signs.

Well, not quite. In fact, not at all.

NEWFOUNDLAND ENGLISH IN PRINT. NOT.

While the ancestor dialects of Newfoundland English back in England's West Country persisted in devising their own spelling systems and thereby enabling literary works and translation of the Bible, the Newfoundland English of the colony received no such consideration. Although Britain had more than enough resources to clothe, feed, and house all of its population, it was focused on colonisation to build a greater British Empire and on its colonies to absorb Britain's mass of unemployed. Local matters of ethnic concern were considered comparatively insignificant and irrelevant. Unlike England, no great separation of the social classes was evident in Newfoundland English; the task of survival, for the most part, took precedence over such idle sociolinguistic niceties. The social distance between His Britannic Majesty of the United Kingdom of Great Britain and Ireland and of the British dominions beyond the seas and Emperor of India, and the humble *livyers* of the Newfoundland colony was immeasurably vast and deep.

Ongoing prejudice towards West Country and Irish-derived speech of colonial British administrators did not encourage positive attitudes towards the common Newfoundland vernacular through 1949 and into Confederation of Newfoundland with Canada. In the 1950s and early 1960s the only university of the new province allegedly pursued a subsequently undocumented policy of "English elocution" for its prospective day-school teachers and others to rid them of their traditional Newfoundland English.[4] This ill-informed precedent was ameliorated by later praiseworthy efforts from the same institution to record Newfoundland English for posterity in a scholarly manner resulting, after thirty years of research, in a prodigious dialectal dictionary with thousands of early print references, but without pronunciation guides or etymologies and judiciously avoiding official support for its legitimacy as an ethnic language, which is deserving of its own orthography.

Newfoundland English Timeline

© Russell A. Bragg 2017

PRE-COLONIAL WEST COUNTRY ENGLISH IN NEWFOUNDLAND (153 years)	**1560s** (first West Country fishing crews over-wintering) **to 1713.**
TRADITIONAL NEWFOUNDLAND ENGLISH DEVELOPMENT PERIOD (227 years)	**1713** (Treaty of Utrecht, Britain assumes sovereignty) **through 1792** (Irish immigration; public recognition of NE by trader, explorer, glossarist and Royal Navy Captain George Cartwright) **to 1941.**
RECENT NEWFOUNDLAND ENGLISH PERIOD (75+ years)	**1941** (first US troops in Nfld.; WWII era and Confederation with Canada) **to present.**

In the natural order of things, languages are divided by distance and evolve through time, but the trend is often deliberately accelerated to achieve the vested interests of prestige language speakers. Oligarchic empire-building tramples on cultures and local traditions; eliminate the language to control the culture and you then control the people. The trend has dramatic worldwide examples as you go back in time: Arab suppression replaced Aramaic, South Arabian, Coptic, Nubian, and Berber languages. The Romans eliminated Etruscan, Iberian, and Gaulish. The Greeks trampled the ancient Paleo-Balkan, Phrygian, Thracian, and Dacian languages. Turkey has only recently begun to grudgingly allow Kurdish to be taught and broadcast; today's hostilities may well reverse that trend. It is a historic fact––remove the language from community life and you have automatically removed cultural identity from its speakers as evidenced by the indigenous peoples of the Americas and today's Tibetans under Chinese rule.

British political unification of the 1500s onward eventually subordinated other languages and colonial English dialects to the East midlands and London speech of English which, by the 1700s and 1800s, was intentionally sanctified to reflect the greatness of the growing British Empire, promote British imperialism, and immortalize the empire's achievements for posterity. Linguistically puritanical sensibilities were seen as an indication of Georgian and Victorian social and moral worth. "Home" English represented that imperialism and worth at the trivial expense of any colonial considerations, beginning and continuing with the already discredited West Country babble of Newfoundland fishermen. Subsequent Irish influences into the New Founde Lande colony were merely further troublesome babble from a troublesome "race."

Newfoundland English was first publicly recognized as a separate dialect in the 1792 by trader, explorer, glossarist, and Royal Navy Captain, George Cartwright, an East Midlands native. But dialect spellings, where attempted, remained unofficial, and, just as Newfoundland never achieved eventual nationhood, so too no formal, literary version of Newfoundland English ever developed. Without its own orthographic standardization, no language can be properly expressed in print or foster greater cultural and social legitimacy. Although not a guarantee of recognition, without access to printed publication no language can properly represent the unique culture of its speakers and is effectively starved to death. In the words of Irish hero-poet-politician Pádraig Pearse, *Tír gan teanga, tír gan anam*—"A country without a language is a country without a soul."

The British Elementary Education Act of 1870 served to deprecate regional varieties of English everywhere. Typical of the generally prevailing autocratic attitude of the vast British Empire were the highly regarded Royal School Series texts produced in Britain from the 1870s and used in Newfoundland and other colonial schools of the Victorian world and elsewhere—even Panama[5]—as late as 1965. The series covered, among a variety of other British-oriented subjects, the preferred reading, spelling, and pronunciation in its process of promoting to its juvenile audience the virtues of the Empire. Typically, *Royal Readers No. VI*, first appearing in 1885, says of Great Britain: "There the circle of European—nay, of universal—civilization and industry has its centre. By her colonies she has diffused the influence of her spirit and the energy of her sons throughout the world..." (p. 126). And, under a piece titled "Colonial Loyalty," quoted "a distinguished

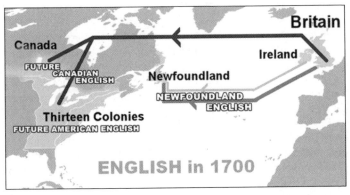

Map[11]

American statesman," otherwise unnamed, to assert that "The proudest Government that exists upon the face of the Earth is that of Great Britain" (p. 175). To expect official concessions to be given to the legitimacy of local colonial speech systems under such overwhelming indoctrination would have been considered unprecedented absurdity. All official print material was resolutely in British English, the language of "the Empire upon which the sun never sets."

English, once the linguistic property of one island, has become the world's international language with over five hundred million speakers in every country on Earth, most of them speaking it not as their "mother tongue," but as a second language. It is also the language with the most words—as many as 1,022,000 by Harvard University's count––the majority "borrowed" from other languages. For the initiation of the tremendous proliferation of English we can thank the language priorities of the British Empire.

But those priorities have had their collateral casualties. One of those is Newfoundland English.

A DECLINING BASELINE

English-speakers everywhere speak it a little differently. There are hundreds of varieties of "English." Mutual understanding is achieved by way of World English made up of the major "Standard" Englishes including British, American, Australian, and South African. This is not unique to English—all major languages have varieties and standard versions. But speakers of a standard version claiming greater prestige sometimes decide that speakers of another variety are substandard in some way and insist that the rules and spelling system, the orthography, of the prestigious Standard version should be applied to all "lesser" varieties of their language.

There is no factual logic to this. All languages, and their varieties, are equally complex, and are as equally useful to their speakers. To claim otherwise, or to portray speakers of other varieties as stupid or pretentious, is merely a reflection of the emotional prejudices, or lack of knowledge, of the claimant. Languages do not degenerate, they evolve. All languages were once varieties or "dialects" of an earlier language.

Adopting the orthography of the prestige version of a Standard English in a misguided attempt to "legitimize" dialectal speech merely hastens the demise of the minority language. Emulating British or Canadian English spellings for Newfoundland English in print not only implies subordinate and derivative status, but blurs the historic distinction of, and even spurns the separate existence of Newfoundland English.

By the mid-twentieth century, any official recognition of Newfoundland English had become a bleak prospect. The 1941 influx of thousands of Royal Canadian and American troops to Harmon, Goose, Argentia, Torbay, and St. John's military installations foreshadowed the many intrusive and disruptive influences into Newfoundland English (and culture) which continued through Confederation with Canada into the present. Prevailing negative attitudes and ill-informed assumptions ensured no agency of government, education, culture, or the media would actively or officially support the viability of Newfoundland English as a bona fide language of print or broadcast media or propose its serious study in the schools of the province. "Accent" has a social value judgement aspect as well as a phonetic definition; as late as 1982, a formal survey[6] among St. John's *townies* ranked local non-standard outport accents last in social prestige.

Although 97.6 percent of residents reported Newfoundland English as their mother tongue in the 2006 census, ignorance, neglect, and outright suppression of Newfoundland English have permitted its misrepresentation into current times as "slang," a mere "accent" and bad Canadian English. This is ironic since Newfoundland English not only has a separate and different history from Canadian English, but predates the very settlement of mainland North America by English-speaking people. In fact, only present-day Northumbrian Scots has an older history than Newfoundland English outside England's borders and shores.

MANY ENGLISH DIALECTS

Serious attempts were made by the mid-1800s to translate the Holy Bible into the many dialects of England which had evolved over the centuries. Those of southwestern England, the West Country English (WCE) dialects whose examples of *King James Bible* translations are illustrated below, are representative of the historical origins and ancestral contributors to Newfoundland English. The onslaught of popular Modern English, itself arising from a dialect of East Midland, has since eroded the credibility and incidence of WCE and other regional dialects of the British Isles.

3.11 *Go foathe, Aw you dafters of Zion, and behowld King Solamun weth th' crown weth which hes mother crowned un in the day of hes espousals, and in th' day of th' gladness of hes heart.*

—SS 3.11 in the **Cornish English** dialect, WC England; first published in London, 1859, by George Barcley

3.11 *Go vore, Aw ye daters uv Zion, an behold King Zola-min way tha crown wareway es moather crown'd'n in tha day uv es espowsils, an in the day uv tha gladniss uv es hart.*
—SS 3.11 in the **Devon** dialect, WC; translated by Henry Baird, first published in London by George Barcley

3.11 *Go voäth, eu yeue maid'ns o' Zion, an leuke at king Solomon crown'd as ez meuther'd a-crown'd'en th' day ee was married, th' day when ez hort was za glad.*
—SS 3.11 in the **Devon East** dialect, WC; translator George P.R. Pulman, first published London, 1860, George Barcley

3.11 *Goo vwo'th, O you da'ters o' Zion, an' look on King Soloman, a-wearen the crown that his mother zet on en the day ov his wedden, the day ov his gladness ov heart.*
—SS 3.11 in the **Dorset** dialect, WC; translator Rev. William Barnes, first published London, 1859, by George Barcley

3.11 *Goo voäth, ye darters o' Zion, an' zee King Zolomin crown'd wi' th' crown hiz mother crown'd un wi' i' th' day o' hiz weddin, an' i' th' day o' th' gladness o' hiz heärt.*
—SS 3.11 in **Somerset** dialect, WC; translator T. Spencer Baynes, LL.B., first published in London by George Barcley

3.11 *Gwo vwo'th, aw ye da'ters o' Zion, an' zee King Zolomon wi' th' crown az huz mother crowned un wi' in th' day o' huz weddun', an' in th' day when huz heart wer' glad.*
—SS 3.11, **Wiltshire North** dialect, WC; translator Edward Kite, first published by Strangeways & Walden, London

3.11 *Goo foorth, O ye dâhters of Zion, and look at king Solomon wud de crown what his mother crowned him wud de dee of his weddin, de dee of de gladness of his heart.*
—SS 3.11, **Sussex** dialect; translator Mark Antony Lower, M.A., F.S.A., first published London, 1860, George Barclay

The actual wording of the *King James Bible* may have been deliberately artificial to the advantage of James I and the Anglican Church of England, but no other single piece of English literature has influenced the English language to such a degree. Shakespeare's thirty-six plays produced more new words than the *King James Bible*, and the language of that 1611 *Bible* represented no specific regional speech in print, parliament nor pub. Nevertheless, despite its deliberate archaisms, word-for-word Hebraic translations, and generally elevated vocabulary, the *King James Bible* inspired or greatly influenced the English regional dialects. For comparison's sake, here is the original version of the Song of Solomon, verse 3.11, from the *King James Bible* of 1611:

> 3.11 *Goe foorth, O yee daughters of Zion, and behold king Solomon with the Crowne wherewith his mother crowned him in the day of his espousals, and in the day of the gladnesse of his heart.*

Although never attempted, this example of holy text, put into traditional Newfoundland English, may have looked like this...

> 3.11 *Gwan out, O yiz dau'ers o' Zion, an luh a' kayng Sawlermon wid d' Crown dat es mudder crowned en wid on d' day ov es weddin, an on d' day o' d' gladness ov es eart.*

Any Bible verse could have been so translated; a popular verse from the Gospel of John:

> 3.16 *God luvd da wurl lashins an fer dat e geevd op es onny barnd son, so dat whoaer ud clum to e ud naer doy, an e ud leev verver.*

Natural language is casual spoken speech, not written composition. By definition, all dialects, English or otherwise, are consistent in those characteristics that can be used to describe them. That is, speakers in the same speech area, social level, and historical era speak alike. Although we lack universally accepted criteria for distinguishing them from languages, related dialects are considered somewhat mutually intelligible, but languages are usually not. Everyone speaks a dialect. A bunch of similar dialects grouped as a language represents a distinct ethnic population. It is a matter of varying degrees of mutual intelligibility. Although dialectal differences existed among the isolated coastal **outports**, a *Newfoundland English Bible* may have further united an ethnic group th it number over half a million today. Newfoundland English speakers are still unintelligible to many **Mainlanders**[7] and, inversely, Standard English is readily recognised in outports as **opalonger** talk, a separate language of textbooks and of the urban print and broadcast media.

NEWFOUNDLAND ENGLISH

Newfoundland English is now increasingly viewed as a valuable herit-age. Nevertheless, today's planet-wide network of the most influ-ential prestige English dialects, loosely referred to as the "Standard World Englishes," is considered the language norm. But its perva-sive influence makes it the elephant in the room of English speakers. Contrasting Newfoundland English to that norm encourages popular but negative perceptions. Contrary to opinions arising from casual, if misinformed interest, and despite the representation in print of trad-itional Newfoundland utterances using Standard English spellings in a misguided attempt to "legitimize" dialectal speech, Newfoundland English is not "slang" nor a mere "accent" and is not a substandard subset of contemporary Standard English which its speakers are trying unsuccessfully to speak.

Step back in time again to the ancient Saxons, fifth-century tribal warriors crossing to England from today's Lower Saxony in Germany. West Country dialects are descendants of Late West Saxon, a promin-ent literary and political dialect of eleventh-century England. But to-day's Standard Englishes were distilled from the East Midlands speech of the London-Oxford-Cambridge triangle, a survivor of the Norman Conquest of 1066. They also derive from the earlier Saxon speech, thus making any standard English a cousin to Cornish English[8], Dorset, Somerset, Devon, Wiltshire—and to their descendant tongue, Newfoundland English!

Traditional Newfoundland English is thus as valid a member of the greater English world language family as Australian, American, or British Received English of Whitehall and as rich in expression. None has an older heritage. Only when Newfoundland English is taken into consideration does English Canada display anything like the linguistic diversity of the United States or Great Britain. It is, by far, the most colourful English in Canada; the lilting accent of Shakespeare's *King Lear* can still be heard in island outports, and its words hint at its an-cient Old Country and sailing-ship origins.

Most of Newfoundland's language inheritance, preserved in mu-tually isolated settlements by a scattered immigrant population without road links, represent Elizabethan era or older speech patterns of the West Country English of Cornwall, Devon, Dorset, Somerset, Bristol, and Wiltshire. Not until two centuries later did the southeastern Avalon Peninsula absorb migrants from southeastern Ireland. Limited Highlands Gaelic also came to the southwestern coast, but influential New England migrants and later Loyalist refugees never did reach Newfoundland. Hence, traditional Newfoundland English speakers adhered more strongly to aspects of older West Country English than did their UK cousins. Ninety percent of descendant speakers of Newfoundland English still live along the island's 9,655 kilometres of coastline. Its stubborn, hardy persistence over time has assured its place as North America's earliest version of English as well as its oldest surviving representative of "The Rock" and of the distinct ethnic group who have lived on it in relative seclusion for hundreds of years.

And seclusion, born out of necessity, was the norm for *inshore* fishermen. *The Encyclopedia of Newfoundland and Labrador* mentions that "three or four families of Lomonds were engaged in the inshore cod fishery and small farming at Rocky Barachois for about 100 years." Rocky Barachois, now long abandoned and its oldest graveyard washed out to sea, is about five kilometres north of Port aux Basques. One of those families was my maternal great-great-grandparents, George and Sarah Lomond. The "Lomond" surname is rare in Newfoundland. As a new *planter*, and a Lomond, George was an immigrant (or a clan-warfare Lamont fugitive) from Argyll on Scotland's Cowel Peninsula, the home of the Lamont [LAW-muhnt] clan (but not the French Lamont [law-MOH?]). Such generations-long isolation preserved old speech habits as well as old lifestyles until disrupted by outside intrusion. For the Lomonds of Rocky Barachois, that critical and liberating "intrusion" was the *make'n'break* motor boat engine.

This isolation pattern, though not arbitrary, tended to scatter the original dialects widely so that usage varied and word choice was geographical. Using only the perplexity of *comefomaways* as a criterion, one may easily conclude that Newfoundland English is indeed a language! Although it can be heard in Yellowknife, Fort McMurray, Cambridge (Ontario), and even in coastal villages of the Basse-Côte-Nord shore of Quebec, subtitles must occasionally be dubbed over Newfoundland English in televised media for the wider North American and world viewing audience[7]. However, due to ever-increasing social integration and for the general practical purposes of this book we refer only in a very broad manner to Central (White Bay to Trinity Bay), Irish (St. John's to Argentia), South (Burin Peninsula to Port aux Basques), West (south of Corner Brook where French is also spoken and Aboriginal (Mi'kmaw is seeing a revival), and North (Northern Peninsula and southern Labrador) where it may be of interest in the following Newfoundland English word list.

Interestingly, in all four determining criteria, vocabulary, grammar, usage (meaning), and pronunciation[9], Newfoundland English matches Lowlands Scots in its distinctive linguistic identity, if not in its nationalism.

LOWLAND SCOTS, AN EXISTING TRADITIONAL LANGUAGE

The beginning of Modern English in the mid-1500s—the time of Shakespeare, the *King James Bible*, and the British Empire's earliest colonization of foreign territory, including Newfoundland—may also be considered the point of divergence between Newfoundland English and today's World English. Such it also was for Lowland Scots of eastern Scotland (political prerequisites of Lowlands social identity aside).

> 18. *And walking by the Loch o' Galilee, he saw twa brithers, Simon (ca'd Peter), and Andro his brither, castin aboot a net i' the Loch, for they war fisher-folk.*
>
> 19. *And quo' he to them, "Follow ye me ! and I'se mak ye fishers o' men!"*
>
> 20. *And they, withoot ado, left the nets, and gaed eftir him.*
>
> 21. *And gangin forrit tharawa, he saw ither twa brithers, James, son o' Zebedee, and his brither John, in a smack wi' Zebedee their faither, workin on their nets: and he bad them "Come!"*
>
> 22. *And they, forsakin the boat, and their faither, gaed eftir him.*

—Matthew 4:18–22 in **Lowland Scots**, by Reverend William W. Smith, *The Four Gospels in Braid Scots*

By 1945 Lowlands Scots, or "Lallens," was nicely summed up by a Scots writer who said, "Of the Lallens many genteel Scots used to be ignorant and ashamed…But there is now a realization, especially among the younger Scottish writers, that this is a powerful and, in many ways, beautiful language deserving a fate far kinder than preservation in a literary museum. A gifted and many-tongued Scot like Douglan Young writes poetry in Lallens just as much, and just as well, as he does in Gaelic, English, Latin, Greek, French, and German. Such men regard Lallens…as a surviving and valuable member of a comity of tongues."[10]

Lowland Scots (not to be confused with Highland Scots Gaelic) is composed of four regional dialects. It was recognized as a language by the Scottish and UK governments under the European Charter for Regional or Minority Languages, and ratified by the United Kingdom in 2001. Cornish English was so recognized in 2003, but Scouse, Cockney, Geordie, the West Country dialects, and the rest are still otherwise officially defined as English dialects of pronunciation rather than of grammar or vocabulary.

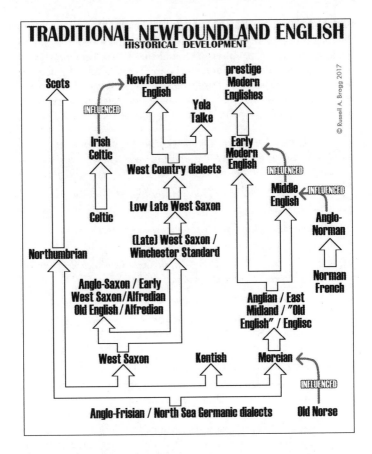

TRADITIONAL NEWFOUNDLAND ENGLISH
HISTORICAL DEVELOPMENT

© Russell A. Bragg 2017

NEWFOUNDLAND ENGLISH, AN EXISTING TRADITIONAL LANGUAGE

A hundred pages or so cannot hope to detail all relevant criteria issues, let alone counter contentious arguments of social relevancy or status. *Lashins* (plenty) of unique vocabulary items—*bogie, janny, livyer, longers, scoff, stepeens, tickle, touton,* and many more—are pervasive and appropriately and thoroughly useful in the context of the traditional Newfoundland lifestyle.

Newfoundland English grammar is unique in North America. The case-stripped present verb form of *be,* using only *is* ('s) or *'m,* is Scandinavian-like in its invariable simplicity: *oi is, you is, e/she is, we is, yiz is, dey is,* and *oi'm, you'm, we'm, dey'm.* Simplicity also rules in general present tense usage: *oi goes, you goes, e/she goes, we goes, yiz goes, dey goes*—simple yet not simplistic! The use of *do, be*, and *ave* may seem atypical to Standard English speakers as in *Dey **doos** deyr work*, *Oi **aves** lashins o' silver* (pocket change), *She* (it) ***bes** co* (cold) *on da wadder yere een summer*, except in questions, ***Ave** Marty finished op es toime* (work period) *een Wabush?* ***Do** e live dere now?* and the habitual and also invariable ***do be***: *E **do be** late f' work on toimes, but e **don' be** late fer es pay.* Then we have ***sot*** for sat, ***knowed*** for knew, and ***buildeed*** for built, and four ways to show completed action: ***oi've done**, **oi've a-done**, **oi ben done**, **oi'm after doin***. Some negative forms are derived from WCE: ***baint'e*** are you not, ***oi idden*** I am not, ***you idden*** you are not, ***e idden*** he is not, ***tidden*** it is not. Some NE expressions from Irish-English sound like Yoda of *Star Wars* fame: *T'is she **wha' pays d' bills**, so t'is ersauf **wha' droives deyr car.*** Unlike the do-it-all "you" of a Standard English, Newfoundland English displays a half dozen options: ***ya/you/dee/ye/yous/'ee***, plus ***you***, a pragmatic marker amounting to a vocative pronoun[12] with no common Standard English equivalent.

Pronunciation differences are distinctive in Newfoundland English, as it is in its ancestral West Country dialects. Sound differences between Newfoundland English and other versions of world English are not random and are easily distinguished in corresponding words of Standard English. Compare the vowel sounds of Standard English *in* and Newfoundland English *een*, *beans* and *bayns*, *orange* and *arnge*, *dirty* and *darty, boil* and *bile*, *night* and *noight,* and *awful* and *aavo* and you have the keys to the pronunciation of other corresponding word sounds as well.

As with related West Country English dialects, Newfoundland English already exhibits the familiar **t/d** substitute for "th," and T-glottalization[13] in the likes of ***bo'le*** (bottle), ***bu'er*** (butter), ***wa'er*** (water), ***ke'le*** (kettle), and ***wha'*** (what). Even a short "street" stretches to a long **straayt** in Central. "Sometime" is heard as **sometoime** or, more likely, as **bumbye** in South—unless it means "a great party!" Initial "**h**" may be added before stressed vowels or conveniently dropped, as in the often quoted, *E draps es "h" een Olyrood an picks en op een Havondale* (Avalon towns, Holyrood and Avondale). And some Newfoundland English speakers still share the "Gaelic Gasp" with the Maritimes and downeast Maine, a gender-specific pulmonic ingressive (inhaled) aspirated ***yeah*** and ***no*** in chatty girltalk, a unique feature traceable to ancient Scandinavian influence.

Somewhat surprisingly, Newfoundland English shares at least three characteristics with an increasingly popular version of east London English related to Cockney called Estuary, which is claimed to have affected the speech of Prince Edward and even Her Majesty, Elizabeth II[14], and has been predicted to eventually replace the prestigious Received Pronunciation. As in Newfoundland English, Estuary uses the "-s" to end present tense verb forms (*I sees, you sees, we sees*, etc.), shows glottalized **t** as in *lots of* [LOH?-zuhv], and sounds the Standard English [AI] diphthong more like [OY] giving *proize* for prize, *noice* for nice, *toie* for tie, etc.

But don't expect everyone you meet on *The Rock* to know that *fish* [FEESH] means only "cod." Today's Newfoundlanders function at any point between a traditional dialect of the outports (*Ow bes ya, b'y?*) and the Americanized media English of the urban centres (*Wha's up, dude?*). The operative word here is ***traditional,*** and the approximately 1,500 main entries listed in this choice collection typify several speech regions, age groups, levels of change, and historical eras in Newfoundland's five-hundred year history. Despite major changes elsewhere, Newfoundland remained relatively unaltered into the twentieth century.

Newfoundland and Labrador, Great Britain's oldest colony, became Canada's newest province in 1949. The advent of television, the historically recent influence of ***out-migration,*** and then the Internet have taken their toll, and many expressions that grandparents used are ones that their grandchildren will never know. One of the unfortunate consequences of cultural globalization trends is that people worldwide tend to assimilate their appearances, behaviours, and speech patterns to a uniform standard. Language diversity often varies inversely with general socioeconomic success and economic growth, along with globalization trends, to result in the loss of minority languages.[15] Still, despite dire past predictions, even where "standard" urban English has gained ground, the irrepressible Newfoundland English accents remain. On a jaunt *roun d' Bay* west of St. John's, an **opalonger** may be delighted by the diction of Bay Roberts [WAW-buhts], but will be completely mystified by "Wif" (Wilfred) of nearby Island Cove!

YOLA TALKE, AN EXTINCT "SISTER" LANGUAGE

Centuries before The West Country of Cornwall, Devon, Dorset, Hampshire, and Somerset produced Newfoundland's first English speakers, it had been "Wessex," home to original "Old English" speakers, the Anglo-Saxons. West Saxon, the Wessex dialect of this early English and official language of King Alfred the Great, dominated southern England after 800 AD to achieve the social prestige and political authority to become England's written literary language until just after the Norman French conquest of 1066. But not everyone in Wessex remained to experience the new order of the Norman overlords.

Yola Talke (Yola: *oure yola talke,* "our old speech") was the language of English immigrant settlers to southeastern Ireland from Somerset or Devon in the 1160s. They were called "Wessexmen" because of their noticeably slow-spoken West Country English speech in their new homeland of Forth and Bargy in County Wexford. As with Newfoundland English dialects, geographic isolation preserved and shaped Yola Talke to such a degree that by the 1300s it had become distinct from the mainstream spoken English language. Also like Newfoundland English, Yola Talke assimilated features of the surrounding Irish speakers, as well as from regional Manx and Flemish traders.

The general similarities of history and development between Yola Talke and "Newfy talk" don't end there (see "Newfoundland English Tree" diagram). Wexford is the third county along the southeastern coast from Cork and Waterford from which thousands of Irish shipped across the Atlantic to eastern Newfoundland in the 1700s and later. Not all those opportunistic Irish immigrants spoke an Irish Gaelic dialect. Keeping in mind that Yola Talke also originated from West Saxon English, a representative sample of words indicate a recognizable relationship of the Yola Talke (YT) of County Wexford to traditional Newfoundland English (NE):

aam — YT "them," as in NE *Give **em** a cup o' tea.*

aar — YT "there," as in NE ***Aar!** Bain't dat wha' oi ben sayin aa long, eh?* and Standard English "There! Isn't that what I've always said?"

angish — YT "poverty," as in NE *angish* "poverty."

barm — YT "yeast," as in NE *barm* "yeast."

be — YT "by," and "near," as in NE *down **be** d' lanwash* and Standard English "down by the beach."

bibber — YT "shiver with cold," as in NE *biver* and Standard English "shiver with cold."

bibereen — YT "trembling," as in NE *bibberin/bibbereen* and Standard English "shivering."

bile — YT "boil," as in NE *bile-up,* an outdoor meal with tea.

brazon — YT "impertinent," as in NE *brazen* "impertinent."

breed — YT "bread," as in NE *bread* [BREED] "bread."

bye — YT "boy," as in NE *b'y* and Standard English "boy, pal, buddy, guy, chum, or dude."

deed — YT "dead," as in NE *deed* "dead."

dole — YT "an amount, a deal," as in NE *dole* and Standard English "living allowance."

faace — YT "face," as in NE ***faace** [FAAYS]* "mouth."

fashoon — YT "fashion," as in NE *fashion* "idiosyncrasy."

gom — TY "fool," as in NE *gom, gommy, gommil* "gaping fool."
heiftem — TY "weight, burden," as in NE *eft* "weight."
keen — TY "sharp," as in NE *keen* "cold, crisp, clear (day)."
knap — YT "knob," as in NE *knap* "small rounded hill."
mizleen — YT "misting," as in NE *misky* "misty."
oer — YT "over, above," as in NE *oer* "over, above."
ov — YT "of," as in NE *ov* "of, from."
rusheen — YT "rushes," as in NE *rushy* "dense brambles."
sleeveen — YT "deceitful," as in NE *slieveen* "deceitful person."
starm — YT "storm," as in NE *starm* "storm."
talke — YT "speech," or "language," as in NE *flat **talk*** "vernacular."
yer — YT "your," as in NE *yer* and Standard English "your."

The generalized judgmental attitudes that assume a connection between vernacular speech and social positioning, educational status, and material success are recognized, but are not a consideration in focused linguistic analyses. However, barring unrelated disruptive influences (invasion, pandemics, economic collapse, or other *forces majeures*), such non-linguistic features of a dialect or language determine the level of social credibility it receives and, as a result, its eventual fate. Such was the case with Yola.

Much like the past and ongoing situation of Newfoundland English, the lack of a thriving literature, negative influences of non-speakers, and official disinterest and eventual outright discouragement—in this case "Stanley's Irish Education Bill of 1830" promoting English literacy throughout Ireland—have shoved Yola Talke into decline from the six-hundred-year-old language of a distinct ethnic group to a mere accent and a few remnant words and phrases still heard in Kilmore, Lady's Island, and Rosslare.

Yola Talke would have taken its place among Modern Standard English, Newfoundland English, Scots English, Frisian, Dutch, and other surviving Germanic tongues. However, it was visited by the four horsemen of the minority language apocalypse––outside intrusion, official neglect, social stigma, and speaker attrition––and Yola Talke went extinct by the 1870s. Its sister (or perhaps stepsister) language, Newfoundland English, after a run of over four hundred years, has gained no greater prestige, has endured similar negative influences and, today, barely represents its former usage in accent, scattered words and phrases, and currently popular, traditional-sounding expressions, usually to elicit a humourous reaction.

Flat Talk

"Yes you have! You got that real Canadian twang. Some words you says I can't hardly understand you a-tall. I s'pose Newfoundland talk is not good enough for you now, after bein' away so long." —*The House of Hate* by Percy Janes

Newfoundland English orthography would resemble that of West Country Dorset, Devon, or Somerset had it not been subordinated to the subsequent effects of a Standard English spelling. The spoken word is judged in terms of the written word. Without its own consistent, official, or recognized spelling conventions and no extensive, established dialectal literary tradition from which to extract a coherent, harmonized system, Newfoundland English has become an orthographic mongrel. Its spelling reflects historical, regional, accidental, and idiosyncratic variations, some originating before a time when there was any demand for standardization. While there is no reason why Newfoundland English orthography should be entirely modelled on Contemporary Standard English in attempting to give the written form historic continuity from centuries of British colonization, it is sensible to recognize the influence of the Standard Englishes in representing the spoken word. Meanwhile, such a system must also offer spelling for the convenience of native speakers as well as the *opalong* learner or the curious page-turner. This is a daunting task and compromises are unavoidable.

Increasingly speakers routinely mix Newfoundland English with a Standard English, either Canadian or American. Existing tentative spelling conventions have been sometimes exhibited as a unique, if somewhat random, feature of Newfoundland English. While *Traditional Newfoundland English* gives few concessions to such jocular "Newfinese" spellings, as an established, senior, and enduring member of the worldwide English speech community, Newfoundland English deserves its own exclusive representation in print.

Incidental and obvious loanwords of a specific technology or profession—radar, cam shaft, helicopter, meteorite, cardiogram, microchip—keep their original spelling, but pronunciation may vary somewhat with dialect (i.e.: 'elicopter). Other Newfoundland English items share their spelling and pronunciation with recognizable Standard English words, but vary from them in usage and meaning, sometimes widely. **Abroad** (scattered), **arse** (posterior), **bakeapple** (a berry), **blossom** (snow flake), **brazen** (impertinent), **case** (rascal), **charm** (noise), **clamper** (ice pan), **clobber** (litter), **contrary** (irritable), **faggot** (fish bundle), **fish** (cod), **ice candle** (icicle), **jigger** (unbaited hook), **juice** (electricity), **machine** (thingamajig), Friday [FRUEH-dih], Thursday [TURZ-dih], Saturday [SAHD-duh-dih], months of the year, and **wop** (wasp) are a few examples.

Coincidental Newfoundland English terms that appear familiar to Standard English speakers will usually differ in pronunciation, quite often in meaning, and sometimes in origin. Examples are **aavo** (very), **affer** (verb tense indicator), **babby** (baby, "dear"), **baccy** (tobacco), **blong** (resident of), **bumbye** (bye and bye), **budder/bu'er** (butter, Margarine), **crump** (cramped), **co/cood** [KOH/KOHD] (cold), **da/dem** (the), **deed** (dead), **dere** (there), **drectly** (soon), **e** (he), **faace** ([FAAYS] mouth), **fer** (for), **hawl** (awl), **naer** (never), **ov** (of), **offen** (often), **skoo** (school), **tree** (three), **yesday** (yesterday), **wadder /wa'er** (ocean, sea), **wunnerfo** (awesome), **you'm** (you are/have).

Fundamental words that have no recognizable equivalent in contemporary Standard English and are unique to Newfoundland, or are preserved from West Country (or Irish) ancestry, have earned traditional spellings over time. Examples are **angishore** (sluggard), **bannikin** (tin cup), **bes** (be), **besom** (broom), **brewis** (boiled hard biscuit), **b'y** (boy, fellow, "dude"), **clum** (clutch), **conner** (fish species), **dwall** (dozing), **emmet** (ant), **en** (him/her/it), **frapes** (dress up), **kinkarn** (throat), **livyer** (settler), **mauzy** (misty), **nish** (delicate), **slieveen** (rogue) and **yarry** (athletic).

Short function words (pronouns, prepositions, etc.) and others represented by no traditional spellings are recorded here in a systematic format arrived at by compromises involving easily recognized spelling convention, phonetic interpretation, and analogy with West Country English equivalents: **oi** (I/me), **yiz** (you, pl.), **en** (he/him), **deyr** (their), **ud'n/wud'n** (was/were/would not).

Pronunciation guidance in *Traditional Newfoundland English* has been kept to the simplest expediency. Some attention to the following, much simplified **PRONUNCIATION KEY** will become helpful.

AH as in b**a**t	**OW** as in b**ow** (of boat), ch**ow**
AW as in b**ou**ght	**OH** as in b**o**ne
AY as in b**ay**	**UH** as in b**u**t
EH as in b**e**t	**OO** as in b**oo**t
IH as in b**i**t	**J** as in **j**u**dg**e, pi**ge**on, wa**ge**
AI as in b**i**te	**CH** as in **ch**ur**ch**
EE as in b**ee**t	**G** as in **g**oat, to**gg**le, fro**g**
OY as in b**oy**	**NG** as in si**ng**, fi**ng**er
Y as in **y**ou, **y**oke	**W** as in **w**ing, **w**ay, **wh**y

AAY as in prolonged [AY], **hey** or **hay** sounded long
UEH between ch**ewy**, b**uoy** and French *oui*, *huit*, *lui*
TH as in **th**ick, **th**in, **th**ought, **th**ing, **th**ree
DH as in **th**en, **th**an, **th**e, **th**ey, **th**em, **th**at
KH as in Gaelic *loch*, German *Nacht*, Russian плохо (*ploko*)

ʔ — voiceless glottal stop as represented in Standard English by the hyphen of *uh-uh*, the apostrophe in *Hawai'i*, or the "t" in Britney [BRIHʔ-nee], but not otherwise specifically represented in the English (Roman) alphabet, is seen as T-glottalization and indicated in this text by an apostrophe. See dialectal variants **wa'er** (water), **men'al** (mental), **bu'er** (butter), others.

Newfoundland English initial [H] sound may not appear where expected by a Standard English speaker (*ave*, have) or may show up as [Y] (*yere*, here). The listing gives established traditional spellings or reasonably likely eye-dialect representation for initial [H].

Stress (accent) is shown pronounced as [KAH-PIH-TUHLZ], unstressed as [loh-ehr kays]. Stress affects pronunciation: **by, dat, da, fer, ov, to, ya** usually revert to **b', da', d', f', o', t', y'** in unstressed position except before vowels and glides [**w**], [**y**]. See *OTHER SMALL WORDS* and *CONTRACTIONS* below.

Within the word listings, **Also** further references a synonym or related word, **See** indicates a word of related meaning or more information, **Note** compares another relevant or cognate word, and **From** offers available word sources. Borrowed loanwords are designated **Lnwd**.

Abbreviations for repeated etymological sources are:

NE — original to Newfoundland English
WCE — West Country English of southwest England
SEI — Southeastern Ireland
OF — Old or Norman French (800–1300 AD)
MF — Middle French (1340–1611 AD)
FR — French, and from the "French Shore" era
OE — Old English (Anglo Saxon, 400–1150 AD)
ME — Middle English (1150–1500 AD)
London Cant — street English of the 1600s[16]
Brit — British colonial era usage and later
SE — Standard English
Irish Gaelic — Gaeilge
Yola — Forth and Bargy ME dialects (1169 to mid-1800s) of Wexford county, southeastern Ireland
Leics., — Leicestershire dialect representative of influential mid-1800s East Midlands UK speech, and others by name.

All terms further referenced in **bold** print are also separately listed under **Newfoundland English** word list. In addition to meanings and where necessary for clarity, SE transcriptions or literal meanings of some words, phrases or sentences are given within quotation marks. As indicated, significant regional usage may be only occasionally noted by Central, Irish, South, West, and North.

This *Traditional Newfoundland English* annotated compendium is a sampling of a continuum over several speech regions, age groups, levels of change—and of society—and different times in the long history of Newfoundland. The result must of necessity be both proscriptive as well as impressionistic since it cannot individually represent all such regions, changes, generations, or historical periods, nor all casual variations in spelling. Expect any native Newfoundlander to argue his or her own differing point of view. And, of course, exclusiveness to Newfoundland is not claimed for all items; many Maritimers and New Englanders also share West Country and Irish ancestry.

Small Words

through the mists of history and the fogs of the *outports* resembles herding cats at night in a *stroife o' ween!* Newfoundland English lacks redundancy to some extent and so depends more heavily on context for meaning, but is highly regular with fewer grammatical exceptions than a Standard English. Following is a list of regularized, basic function words; the smallest, most hard-working little words of traditional Newfoundland English.

PERSONAL PRONOUNS usual non-subject forms are in *italics*

	SG	PL
speaker (I/me, we/us)	**oi**, *oi*	**we**, *we*
hearer (you, you all)	**ya, you, dee** ('ee)	**yiz**, *yous/ye*
topic, masculine (he/him, they/them)	**e**, *en*	**dey**, *dem*, *em*
topic, feminine (she/her, they/them)	**she**, *she*	**dey**, *dem*, *em*
topic, neutral (it)	see **it** in main listing	

you, *yous/ye*   stressed or emphasized forms of **ya/yiz**: *Oi'm shor dat* **you** *knows d' bess rental car t' get.* (**Ye**, Irish influence.)

dee ('ee)   See **dee, 'ee**, Newfoundland English wordlist.

en, em   also subject forms in some dialects: ***En** bes ome on d' weykends .* "**He** is usually home on the weekends."/***Em** give we aur pay Friday, but narn fer dey.* "**They** gave us our pay on Friday, but [there is] nothing for them."

    Unstressed subject pronouns may be dropped: *Buildeed a gert smack, e did.* "He built a big in-shore fishing boat."

VOCATIVE PRONOUN[12] (no Standard English equivalent in non-command, casual speech)

hearer	***you***	***you**s*

Comin een fer yer supper, ***you?*** "Will you be coming in for dinner?"

PERSONAL POSSESSIVE MODIFIERS

speaker (my, our)	**me/*moy***	**aur**
hearer (your, your)	**y'/*yer***	**yeer**
topic, masc (his, their)	**es**	**deyr**
topic, fem (her, their)	**er**	**deyr**

moy, ***yer***   stressed forms: *Dey bes* ***yer*** *cuffs, dese bes* ***moy*** *cuffs.*

Unstressed *yer* may be also heard before a vowel-initial word.

PERSONAL POSSESSIVE PRONOUNS

speaker (mine, ours)	**moyn**	**aurs**
hearer (yours, yours)	**yers**	**yeers**
topic, masc (his, theirs)	**es**	**deyrs**
topic, fem (hers, theirs)	**shes**	**deyrs**
topic, neuter (its)	see **it** in main listing	

REFLEXIVE PRONOUNS
Possessive adjective forms +-**sauf** ("-self"): **mesauf, yersauf, essauf, ersauf, oursaufs, yersaufs, dersaufs** myself, yourself, himself, etc. **Essauf, ersauf, dersaufs** may be heard in place of **e, she, dey** as in ***Ersauf*** *wants a word wid ya 'bout dem fippers ya promised.* "She wants to discuss those seal flippers you promised."

OTHER SMALL WORDS (articles, demonstratives, interrogatives, relatives, conjunctions, prepositions):

aa ands [AW AHNZ]	everyone, everybody
aer [EH-uhr]	ever; that…ever
affer [AH-fehr]	after; a verb tense marker
ar; nar (adj.)	any, either; no/neither
ar'n; nar'n (pron.)	one, some; none, no one
at (a')	at
av [AWV]	off
by, b' [BUEH]	by, before, by way of
da (d')	the (*definite article*)
dan ('n)	than
dat (da'); **dose**	that; those
dat ('at)	that, who; so
dem	them; plural article the
den	then, at that time
dis; dese	this; these
een	in, into, inside
eider, neider, er	either, neither, or
fer (f')	for
fom [FUHM]	from
fore, afore	before (time)
longsoide	beside, next to
naer [NEH-uhr]	never, didn't
oer; unner [OHR]	over; under, underneath
op	up, upward
ov (o')	of
ow	how
to (t')	to; until
trou [TROO]	through, from side to side
tween, mongst	between, among
way	so that, in order that
wha' [WAWʔ]	what; that (*conj., rel. pron.*)
wha'…fer [wawʔ fehr]	why;
Wha'fer? [wawʔ-FEHR]	Why?
Whaaer [waw-AH-uhr]	whatever
when; whenaer; den	when; whenever; then
wher; wheraer	where; wherever
who?, whoer [OO-ehr]	who?, whoever
whoile	while, during, until
yere; dere [YUHR], [DUHR]	here; there

CONTRACTIONS and other abbreviated forms:

y' (**ya, yer,** your), **d'** (**da, dis,** the, this), **f'** (**fer,** for), **t'** (**to,** to), **o'** (**ov,** of), **ar'n** (**ar one,** any one), **nar'n** (**nar one,** not any one), **'s** (**is,** am/is/are), **'m** (**is/aves,** am/is/are, have), **a'n't** (am/is/are not), **bain't, a'n't** (am/is/are not, has/have not), **t'id'n** (is not), **da's** (that is), **usen't** (didn't used to), **t'noight** (tonight), **em** (**dem,** them), **d'mar** (tomorrow), **see'n** (because), **b'roights** (rightfully), **'at** (**dat,** that), **a'** (**at,** at), etc.

Newfoundland English

See previous pages for **PRONUNCIATION** and **ETYMOLOGICAL** sources keys. In connected speech, [H] may be heard sounded before words beginning with a stressed vowel, depending on speaker and dialect area. As in West Country English, Newfoundland English word-final [L] is sometimes heard as [OH] as in *aavo* awful, *boo* bull, *cando* candle, *carjo* carjel (accordion), *macro* macherel, *teo* tell. Numbers in superscript refer to **Endnotes**.

A

a [AH], [AY], [UH] a, an. *Peter bought **a** o ouse.* "Peter bought **an** old house."

aa [AW] all, everything.

aa ands [AW AHNZ] everyone, everybody. Literally, "all hands."

Aaat! [AH?] (prolonged [AH]) expression of frustrated impatience. ***Aaat!** Oi drapped me paintbrush een d' can!*

aa d' same [AW duh SAYM] unimportant. *Ar diff'rence, t'is **aa d'same**.* "It is of little importance"; acceptable, okay. *Eef 'tis **aa d' same** t' you, oi ull barry yer wheelbar.* "If you **don't mind**, I'll borrow your wheelbarrow." Also **aa loike**, **no odds**. Note NE **wha' odds.**

aa op een slings [AW OHP een SLEENGZ] in disarray, in chaos. *Ousecleanin toime evyting bes **aa op een slings**.*

aal [AWL], [AIL] oil (cod oil, fuel oil, engine lubricant, etc.). South.

aal clot [AWL KLAW?], [AIL–] type of thin, impermeable canvas table cloth decorated with coloured patterns. South.

aa loike [AW LUEHK] of little importance. Also **aa d' same, no odds**.

aamos [AW-mohs] almost, nearly. Also **goin fer**.

aa oer [aw OHR] characteristic of, not surprising for, as in *Da's Debbie, **aa oer!*** "That is only what is to be expected of Debbie."

aa qualls See **talqual**.

aar [AWR] assent, "yes". *Aar, now!* [AWR NOW] expression of satisfied corroboration. *Aar, now! Wha'd oi teeo ya! Bain't oi roight, eh?* "So there! What did I tell you! Wasn't I right?" WCE, from *arr* "yes." Note Wexford Yola *aar* there.[17]

aaroight [aw-RUEH?] expression of agreement or pleasant discovery, "Ah-ha!" "Eureka!" or "Okay!" Lnwd from American English *all right*![18]

aaveez, aaweez [AW-veez], [AW-weez] always. See **verver**.

aavo [AW-voh] very, exceedingly, excessively. See **some, wunnerfo**.

aavo___fer [AW-voh...fehr] has the personal habit or idiosyncrasy of, habitually. *Benny do be a **aavo** feller **fer** d' boddle.* "Benny is a **habitual** drinker." *Oi bes a **aavo** one f' choc'late!* "I **just love** chocolate!" Also *wunnerfo___fer, ___***got d' fashion ov***.

abroad apart, scattered: *E wopped me bite **abroad** d' planken.* "He **scattered** my share of money **over** the floor."

adurt [ah-DEHRT], [ah-DEHR?] motion across from one place to another: *Dey rowed **adurt** da arbour.* Athwart. WCE, from Dorset *athirt*. Note Devon *come athort*, to perceive, note. Note NE **tawt**.

accent an indiscriminate reference to local NE dialect usage. Lnwd from SE *accent*. Also *Newfy talk*. See **slang, flat talk**.

aer [EHR] that...ever...*D' firs teevee **aer** I seen was black an whoite.* "The first TV **that** I **ever** saw was black and white."

aff [AHF] rear, back, or aft end of a boat. Also *stern, back aff.*

af-cut [AHF KUHT] partly ("half") intoxicated, tipsy. SEI. Note Irish *cut* drunk, embarrassed, London Cant *cut*, "Drunk." See NE **sousht, pluteed**.

affer [AHF-fehr] afterwards, later, as in *She come ome **affer**.* "She came home later."

affer, be/ben- [AHF-fehr] verb tense: has/have just completed. *O Jonah **ben affer** aulin es traps d' marnin.* "Old Jonah **has just** checked his cod traps this morning." SEI. Irish.

agin [ah-GIHN], [GIHN] against, opposed to. *D' minster bes **agin** gardin parties on Sundays.* Note Dorset *agean* [ah-GEH-ahn] against.

agin [ah-GIHN] again, once more, anew. *Yere comes d' rain **agin**.*

airsome [EHR-suhm] drafty; fresh, bracing, or cool ambient temperature.

all [AWL] a social gathering place as in *church all*, "church hall."

alley [AHL-lee] a "marble" toy used in *chip-chip* or *allies* child's game. WCE. Note Leics. *alley.*

amper [AHM-pehr] infection, a sore; *ampered* infected, purulent. WCE, from Dorset *amper.*

an [AHN] and; but, as in *Sam come t' d' scoff,* **an** *got too sousht t' scuff.* "Sam attended the dinner, **but** became too drunk to dance." SEI. Irish.

an aa [AHN AW] too, also, included, in addition; even. *Willy got d' job, grub found* **an aa.** "Willy was hired with free meals **included**."

and [AHND] pass to s.o., as in ***And*** *oi d' salt an pepper, f'ya playse.* "**Pass (to)** me the salt and pepper, if you please."

ands [AHNZ] available help; crewmen aboard ship. *Aa* **ands** *is affer leavin d'* Sadie J, *cap'in an aa.* "All **crew members** have abandoned the *Sadie J,* even the captain."

andy [AHN-dee] near and ready for use. Note **ome to, longsoide**. Note Dorset *handy,* Leics. *handy,* near, close by.

andy to/bout resembling, close to, equal to: *D' Fisherman's Paint, dere bes nodding* **andy to** *dat*; nearly, approximately: *She's noine er tan moile t' Bakeapple Cove fom yere,* **andy bout.** "Bakeapple Cove is **approximately** nine or ten miles from here." Also **noigh (on)**.

angishore [AHNG-uh-shohr] sluggard, lazy or unambitious fellow. SEI. From Gaelic *ain dei seaoir* or *aing cei seoir,* wretch, unfortunate pitiable person or thing; influenced by local "hang ashore." Irish. Also *hangishore.* Note NE **nunnyfudgen**.

an so ardly barely, almost did not, nearly not: *Oi makes enough t' pay me bills,* **an so ardly.** Also...*an da's aa.*

a'n't [AHNT], [AHN?] contraction for "has not," "have not." *Oi* **a'n't** *got d' toime f' dis!* "I **have no** time for this!" Note **bain't**.

apse [AHPS] to fasten or lock; door latch; clothing fastener. WCE. Note Dorset, *Hapse the geate.* "Fasten the gate."

aps, apse [AHPS] trembling aspen (*Populus tremuloides*), a northern deciduous poplar. From OE *aeps* as applied in England to the English equivalent, *P. tremula.* Also *apsy,* thick with *apse* trees. WCE.

ar [EHR] any, some: *Ar duff een d' pot?* "Is **any** pudding left?" WCE. See **ar'n**. Note Dorset *a'ra*, any.

ard case [ard KAYSS] a disorderly fellow, hooligan, ruffian. Note London Cant *hard case*, "severe or deep Misfortune or ill Treatment." See NE **jeezler, ral, carner b'y**. WCE. Note Dorset *hard*, tough, as in *a hard boy*.

arder grocery list. *Ned bes affer usin d' xac same **arder** at d' shop f' yeurs.* Note **dole arder**.

ard op (fer) [awrd OHP] lacking, as in ***ard op fer** money*; unlucky. Also **stuck fer**.

ard tack ship biscuit, sea biscuit, hard biscuit (thick, oval-shaped, very hard, unsalted and leavened with baking powder or soda, then kiln-dried). A sailing ship's staple. Also *ard bread*.

arg [AHRG] argue. *E **arg'd** oer dat, roight 'r wrong.* WCE, from Dorset *arg*, argue.

ark (at) [AHRK] listen (to), as in ***Ark** wha' Jarge caas frut; 'arnges!'* "Hear what George calls fruit; 'oranges!'" WCE, ***Ark** a'ee!* Listen to him!

ar'n [AHRN] any, one. *Me racket's broke. Got **ar'n** t' len me?* "My snowshoe is broken. Do you have (**any**) **one** to lend me?" WCE, from Dorset *arn*.

arnge [AHRNJ] orange (the fruit). WCE, from ME from OF *orenge*, Italian *narancia*, Arabic *naranj*. Note Leics. *arringe* orange.

arp on pay undue attention to, make an issue of, nag about, make an exaggerated production of the topic. *Da wife **arped on** me long 'air so oi got en faired av.* Note London Cant *harp-upon*, to insist on a course of action.

arse posterior, derriere, rear. Also *arse-end* the back end of a directional object (car, boat). From WCE from OE *ærse* [AWR-suh].

arse horse. *Can 'ee sketch me **arse**?* "Would you photograph my **horse**?" Note WCE Somerset *harse*.

arse-stinger dragonfly (order *Anisoptera*). Also *devil's needle, mosquito hawk*. North. WCE. Note Dorset *hoss-stinger*, Leics. *'os-sting,* dragonfly, from the mistaken belief that they sting horses.

arse-oer-keddle [(H)AHRS ohr KEHD-duhl], [-KEH?-uhl] tripped, tumbled "head over heels."

asleep muscle numbed by sustained inactivity, "pins and needles" feeling. Also **dunch**.

article (li'l–) misbehaving child or unpredictable young girl. *E's a noice* **article***, e is*. Note Leics. *A's a noist article, a is* (a term of contempt).

ataa [ah-TAW] regardless, in any case, anyway. *Some wunnerfo stroife o' rain! Can't get outdoors* **ataa***!* Also **gardless**. Note **dat is**.

ataa [ah-TAW] expression of surprised amusement, wonder or amazement. *Bought a pink Jeep! Wa's ya loike,* **ataa***!* "You bought a pink Jeep! **You amaze me!**" *Wa's ya at, ataa?* "**Whatever** are you doing?"

August-flower [AW-guhs flawr] the fall dandelion (*Leontodon autumnalis*), resembling the dandelion, but blooms in August, frequently in pastures. Also *horse dandelion*. NE.

aul [AWL] to pull out of the water or forest; to check fish nets or traps. *Dey* **auled** *deyr traps*.

auler's bread [AWL-ehrz BREED] rich raisin bread served by the minister's wife to the volunteer "haulers" cutting winter firewood for the parsonage. Also *Methodist bread*.

aunt [AHNT], [AHN?] general term of respect to an older woman regardless of actual family relationship, used with first or full name.

Avalon, on da- [AHV-lawn], [HAHV-lawn] "on the Avalon Peninsula," the relatively higher populated eastern end of Newfoundland island and site of the capitol, St. John's. Originally named the "Province of Avalon" after legendary island of King Arthur in today's Glastonbury, Somerset, UK, once surrounded by swampy marshland.

ave [AHV] auxiliary verb (no ending). *Skipper Joe* **ave** *gone to Sin John's da weyk.* "Joe, the Captain, **has** gone to St. John's this week." Formal usage for *Skipper Joe is affer goin to...* See NE **aves, affer**.

aves [AHVZ] main verb has, have, as in *oi* **aves***, you* **aves***, e/she* **aves***, we* **aves***, yiz* **aves***, dey* **aves**. "We have, you have, he has," etc. *Froidays we aaveez* **aves** *fish*. See **ave** (auxiliary verb). Note **a'n't**.

awk (op) cough up phlegm or an obstruction. Note NE **urge**.

B

babby [BAHB-bee] woman's informal direct address to either sex *Ow bes y' t'day, me* **babby***?* Conception Bay. WCE from *babba* baby. Note Cornish English, *babby* baby. See NE **daw, ducky, luv**, and note Brit *luv, honey, sweetie, my dear*. Note NE **girl, maid**.

babbish [BAH-beesh] animal sinew or leather snowshoe plaiting. From 1800–10 French Canadian *(la) babiche*, from Mi'kmaw *a'papi'j* [AW-baw-beech] thread, twine, string, from *a'papi* "rope, fishing line."

bad cess bad luck, unlucky incident. SEI, from "(as)sess," as in apply a *cess* or "tax" in Ireland, Scotland and India. Irish.

badness See NE **devilment**.

bad job [BAHD JAWB] ill-advised course of action or circumstances. *E bought dat o car, gardless. A **bad job**, oi'd say.* London Cant *badjob*, "an ill bout (activity), bargain, or business" (enterprise).

Bacallao [baw-kaw-YAH-oh] earliest European name specifically for Newfoundland from 1400s Basques fishermen documented from 1710 at Saint-Jean-de-Luz, a Basques town of southwestern France. Note 1500s Portuguese *Tierra de Bacalaos* "Land of Codfish," 1600s French *Isles de Bacaleo* "Codfish Islands." Note present-day Basque *bakailaoa* [baw-kaw-YOW-aw], and Portuguese *bacalhau* [baw-kaw-YOW], codfish.

baccy plug tobacco (chewing) or loose tobacco (pipe). Note WCE Cornwall English *backy*.

bachelor's button ox-eye daisy (*Chrysanthemum Jeucanthemum*) and scentless chamomile (*Matricaria maritima*); various round, button-shape flower species. Brit.

back answer retort in anger or insolence. Also **yap**. See NE **guff**.

back on (to) positioned with one's back to. *Jonah was **back on t' da opm door**.*

backfarmis [bahk-FAHR-mihs] backwards, back-to-front. *Y' got y' gansey on **backfarmis**! Also *arsefarmis*. Note WCE Devon *assards*.

bafflin ween wind gusts that unexpectedly, abruptly, and sometimes forcefully blow in the opposite direction. *Drivers get blowed av d' road een Wreckhouse by d' **bafflin weens***. WCE *baffle* from Fr *bafouer* deceive, hoodwink.

bain't be not, am not, is not, are not, as in *Walt **bain't** een d' country so e ull get nar moose.* "Walt **isn't** in the backwoods so he will get no moose." WCE.

bain't em aren't they? Note **bain't**. WCE.

bait sticks sticks used to insert bait into a lobster **trap**.

bakeapple [BAYK-ah-boh] cloudberry, salmonberry or mountain raspberry (*Rubus chamaemorus*), a perennial yellow or orange, creeping, circumpolar raspberry. From Labrador Inuktitut *apik* for *R. chamaemorus* + early modern (to 1700s) English *appel* "apple, fruit" (from ME *aeppel* "any fruit or nuts"). Note OE *fingeraeppla* "dates," *eorthaeppla* "cucumbers," and SE *pineapple*.

baker's fog   a disdainful term for **store-bought** bread as compared to preferred home-baked.

ballycatter   [BAHL-lee-kahd-dehr] ice that forms from freezing salt water spray, sometimes rafted up along the seashore in winter; broken harbour ice. From Spanish *barricada*, "barricade" or rail across front of ship's quarterdeck. Also *bellycanter*. See NE **frore**, **clumper**, **copy**. Note NE **silver taw**.

ballycattered   covered by **ballycatter** ice.

ballyrag, bullyrag   tease mercilessly, pester, harass. WCE, from *ballarag*, *-rag* from Danish *rag* grudge. Note NE **vex, crossackle.**

bang   See **vang**.

bangbelly   a flapjack or pancake. Also **damper dog**, **frozie**, *grace cake*. NE.

bank   large **shoal** or **grounds** frequented by banker schnooners. Note **shoal**.

bankburry   cranberry (*Vaconium macrocarpon*). Found growing on banks by the ocean in Newfoundland. Also *bearburry*.

banker   a sail-rigged or powered deep-sea 80-120 ft (24-37 m) schooner of 24 men carrying 10 dories for cod-fishing on a fishing bank with hooks or jiggers fastened to hand lines; the banking fisherman or banker schooner owner. NE.

bannock   a round bun of bread. From Scots Gaelic *bonnach*. Also **loaf**.

bannikin   small tin cup. WCE from *pannikin*. Note NE **noggin**.

bar   two-ended hand barrow or hand cart.

bark   to preserve sails or fishing nets in liquid steeped from evergreen buds and tree bark. Note **rind**.

bark sail loaf   brown molasses bread without raisins. NE.

bark boots   dress boots from *barked* sealskin. NE.

barm   a spongey pre-bread mix of commercial yeast cakes ("Lallemands" or "Royal"), warm water (sometimes of steeped hops buds), sugar, and a little flour and left to rise in warmth before mixing with additional water, flour, and (often coarse) salt. WCE, from Dorset *barm*, yeast. Note Wexford Yola *barrm*.

barmp [BAHRMP] to blow a horn or make a similar loud sound for attention; honk a car horn. Imitative. NE.

barvel a fisherman's homemade leather or canvas apron water-proofed with linseed oil, WCE, from ME *barm fel* leather apron. Also *barbel, barb*.

barrens [BAHRNZ] as in *on d' barrens*: bogland; nearly treeless moors. Note NE **mish**.

barsway [BAHRZ-way] a sand-bar; the lagoon inside. From FR *barachois*, from Basque *barratxoa* [bah-rrah-CHOH-ah] harbour inside a gravel bar. NE.

bavin [BAHV-uhn] wood shavings to light a fire. SEI. From Gaelic *baban* tuft, tassel. Irish. See **faddle, brishney**. WCE. Note Dorset *baven*, and Leics. *bavin*, a bundle of twigs, sticks or branches for burning.

bawk greater shearwater (*Puffinus gravis*) a type of sea bird (from imitative call).

bawl weep, cry, as of children; shout out. *Dat choil bes verver bawlin*. See NE **blear**.

bawn rocky beach to dry fish. SEI. From Gaelic *babhún*, a stone inclosure. Also *barren, fish beach*. Irish.

bayman [BAY-muhn] a sometimes pejorative term for an outport resident. Also *baywop* (pejorative). NE.

be, b' [BEE], [BUH] by, as in *down be d' lanwash* "down by the beach." Note Wexford Yola *be* by.

be [BEE] auxiliary verb (no ending), as in *Dey be singin at d' church cross da arbour*. "They **are** singing in the church on the other side of the harbour." For present tense **be**, see NE **is**. Note NE **bes**. Also **do be**.

be will be, as in *Oi be workin on me ouse d'mar*. "I **will** work on my house repairs tomorrow." Note NE **bes**. WCE.

be affer [bee AHF-fehr] searching for, seeking. *Dey's got a job o' work eef dey's affer a good used car*. "They will have a difficult task if they**'re looking for** a good used car." For verb tense see **affer**, **be/ben affer**.

beat out [BEHT OWT] physically exhausted. *E was beat out fom splittin wood*. Note **fagged (out)**.

beat d' strayt [BEHT duh STRAAY?] frequent nighttime street life. *Dey young people bes beateen d' strayt aa noight long*. WCE, from Somerset *beat the streets*, run about idly.

bedflies [BAYD-floyz] bedbugs (*Cimex lectularius*). WCE, from Somerset *bedfly*, flea.

bedlamer [BIHD-luhm-uhr] young seal. WCE crazy or wild person. From London *bedlam* madness, chaos, from *Bedlam*, a London, UK, insane asylum, Bethleham Hospital, opened in 1337. See NE **young fat**.

beens [BEE-uhnz], [BEENZ] because, now that, since, considering that. ***Beens** Sarah's yere, she can put out d' warsh fer ya.* "**Now that** Sarah's here, she can hang out your laundry." WCE, from Dorset *beens* [BEE-uhnz], because. See **see'n**.

b' d' looks ov [buh duh LUHKS], [BEE duh LUHKS] it appears, seems. *A breeze is on da way **b' d' looks ov** dat skoy.*

begob [bih-GAWB] euphemistic exclamation, "by God." WCE. Note Somerset *begummers*. Note NE (**b'**) **juice**!, (**b'**) **Jingo**.

beholden (to) under obligation to, obliged. WCE, from OE *behealden*. Note Leics *beholden* obliged.

belly 'n' back(s) odd gloves or mitts; method of stacking fish.

ben [BIHN] has been, have been: *Jack **ben** on d' Labrador dese tree yeur.* "Jack **has been** (fishing) off Labrador for three summers."

Beothuk [bee-AW-thuhk], [bee-AW-thihk] indigenous, extinct (1829) tribe of Newfoundland island. The presumed Algonkian language of this tribe. From *Behathook/Behat-hook/Beathook* (from inexpert and incomplete word lists of mid-1800s) "the red Indians." Also *Beothuck*, **red Injun**.

bes [BEEZ] continual, repeated or habitual form: *Jim **bes** yere evy Sat'day.* "Jim **is** here on Saturdays." See **be** (auxiliary verb). *Gramfer **bes** paintin es dory evy chance e gets.* "Grandfather paint**s** his dory whenever he can." WCE, from OE *byð* as in *winter byð cealdost*, "winter is coldest." Sometimes not expressed: *E not fom round yere.* "He **is** not a local person." Note NE **do be, be**. See NE **'m**.

besom [BIHSS-uhm] broom of birch twigs. WCE, from OE *besum*. Note Leics. *besom*.

besom een d' fits one's hairdo on a bad hair day. NE.

bess koin (ov), (d'–) [BEHS KUEHN] expression of general approval. *She's d' **bess koin** o' boat goin.* "It is an **exceptional** boat." Positive reply to the greeting, *Ow bes ya? –**Bess koin**, b'y!* May be heard ironically: *Affer a get-t'gedder da ouse bes een d' **bess koin** o' mess.* Also **noice**.

biggedy   [BEE-gehd-dee] conceited, egotistical, pompous. WCE, from Somerset *begotty*, egotistical.

bile-op   [BAIL-ohp] an outdoor meal with tea. Note NE **mug-op**. Note Leics. *bile* boil (water). Note Wexford Yola *bile* boil (water).

bill   [BEE-oh] the check or tab as at a restaurant. Brit.

binicky   ill-tempered; difficult to control.

bird   [BEHRD] penis (a child's word).

birdin/birdeen   hunting sea birds for the table, fowling, birding. Also *gunnin*. See NE **shell bird**.

biscuit   soda cracker; sea biscuit (see **ard tack**). Brit

bite   [BAIT] a share or portion of money, as in *me **bite*** "my share". WCE, from OE *bitan* "bite, bite off" (note: OE *bita* "a piece bitten off, morsel"), ultimately from ancient root word *bheid-*"split."

biting stick   wooded stick to twist-tighten a rope to fasten a load (firewood, etc.) onto a sleigh.

biver, bibber   [BIHV-vehr] to shiver with cold; "Br-rr-rr!" WCE, from Dorset *biver, bibber*, shake as with cold or fear. Note Wexford Yola *bibber* tremble with cold. Also **snacker**.

blaggard   [BLAY-gehrd] vulgar language, swearing. WCE from *blackguard*, the lowest menial or a criminal. Note London Cant *black-guards*, unkempt, "rough boys" who serve as menials to the Royal Horse Guards. Note Leics. *black-guard* to scold, malign; a shrewish woman.

black hurts   black huckleberry (*Gaylussada baccata*), dark, blueberry-like without a bloom. Brit. (*hurtleberry* of 1400s). See **hurts**.

black jack   See **tar felt**. Note **felt tins**.

black joke, the   [blahk JOHK] a wry antidote of tragic irony or contrary circumstances, often told in defiance of a difficult situation; dark, black or gallows humour. *Trust een d' Lard, but naer dance een a dory*. Brit. Note Brit. *black joke*, a reference to female genitalia in a 1700s ribald tune. Note **Newfie jokes**.

blasty bough   dry evergreen branch that crackles and burns quickly. WCE, from *blasty* "gusty."

blather   [BLAH-thuhr] nonsense, foolish talk. From Icelandic *blaethra*. See **pishogues**. Note Leics. *blether* cry; be winded, Scots *blether*.

blay   brown, brownish. Also *duckedy-mud colour*.

blay   tie up (a boat), fasten. From Brit. sailing term *belay*.

blear   to bellow, shout loudly without consideration; a loud bellow. WCE, from Dorset *bleare*, low as a cow or cry loudly. See **bawl** (**out**).

blong (to)   be from, a native of, born at; be related to. *Jamis **blongs** t' Careless Cove.*

blony   [BLOH-nee] bologna or "baloney," a popular and economical large sausage of finely ground, cooked pork and lard. Also jocularly *Newfie steak.*

blossom   a large, fluffy snow flake.

blow on   [BLOH awn] inform on someone, betray, tell on. *Naer aer tell Noddy nar secret 'r e ull **blow on** ya.* WCE, from Dorset *blow*, tell upon one.

blowed   [BLOHD] spoiled, decomposed, as of canned or bottled meats. *Me bot'led moose meat is aa gone **blowed**.* From the often bulged condition of the can. NE.

bluddy   [BLUEHD-dee] accursed, damnable. *Oi hates dis **bluddy** wedder.* Potentially profane expletive (Central). Brit. Note Australian *bloody* intensifying adjective. Also *jeez*.

blueberry hurts   [BLOO-buhr-ee UHR?S] oval-leaved bilberry (*Vaccinium ovalifolium*), a type of blueberry. West, North. Also **mathers**. From WCE for stinking chamomile *(Anthemis cotula)* and other unrelated West Country species. See **hurts**.

blue een d' faace   […FAAYS] testing one's patience. *Aunt Sally talked oi **blue in d' faace**.* "Aunt Sally **tried my patience** with her chatter."

boarden   [BAHR-dehn] of boards, as a *boarden fence*. Note NE *glassen*, *brazen*, SE *wooden*, *woolen*.

boat   [BOH?], [BOHT] a smaller undecked or partly decked inshore fishing craft; the (harlequin) blue flag (*Iris versicolor*), a wetlands iris, light to deep blue, purple or violet, having toxic roots, skin-irritating sap and triple seed capsules resemble boat hulls, also **chirpers**, **chirpen**, *conk*. NE.

boat hook   [BOH?-ook], [BOHT-ook], long-handled gaff.

bobber   bullhead lily (*Nuphar variegata*), a spherical, yellow pond lily resembling a fishing bobber. Note Brit. *bobbins* (waterlilies *Nymphaea alba*, *Nuphar lutea*).

bogie   [BOH-GEE] small camp stove. WCE, from ME *bogge/bugge* evil spirit, gremlin. Note Scots *bogie* ghost, SE "bogeyman."

boide [BUEHD] to stay, remain, not leave, wait: *Boide wher ya's at whoile oi comes wher ya's to.* "Stay there until I get there." WCE, from Dorset *bide*, dwell, abide, stay. From OE *bidan*.

bolt to swallow one's food without chewing. Brit. 1700s, to swallow meat without chewing. See **glutch, stog**.

Bonfoire Noight [BAWN-fuehr nueht] the night of Guy Fawkes Day, November 5, in celebration of the "gunpowder plot" of a dissident Catholic against England's Protestant king, James I, in 1605. Also previously "Pope Day" by Reformation anti-Papists when the Pope was burned in effigy. Increasingly an outport community celebration disaffiliated with religious issues. *We ud be affer stackeen op tan puncheons fore we set em afoire on **Bonfoire Noight**,* "We would set up ten large barrels before igniting them on **Guy Fawkes Day night**." Brit.

bonnif a young pig. SEI. From Gaelic *banbhín*. Irish. Also *boneen*.

book a grade level in school. *Wha' **book** you een now, Jargie, eh?*

Boston States New England, a term retained from the early 1800s migration to Boston area by many Newfoundland Irish.

bostoon [baws-TOON] to complain loudly; a clumsy idiot. From Irish *bastún*. See **oonshick**, NE **chucklehead, stun po**.

boughten [BAWʔ-uhn] purchased at a shop as opposed to crafted by hand. *A **boughten** garnsey bes less trouble dan knittin yer own.* Also **store-bought**. WCE from OE *bohte* bought. (See **brazen** for -**en** ending.)

bough whiffen [bow WEHF-fehn] a trapper's or woodsman's small, temporary shelter built on site in the woods. See *tilt*.

bracers [BRAY-sehrz] suspenders to hold up trousers. Brit.

brack [BRAHK] a crack, as in a dish.

brazen [BRAY-zuhn] mischievously impertinent in action and speech. WCE, ME *brasen* of brass from OE *braesen* of brass (Note SE *wooden, woolen, leaden, leathern*: "of wood," "of wool," "of lead," "of leather"). Note Wexford Yola *brazon* bold, Also **saucy, lippy**.

brazen faace [BRAYZ-uhn FAAYS] mischievously impertinent child. WCE. Note London Cant *brazen-fac'd*, "Bold, Impudent, Audacious."

breach [BREECH] to leap to or break the surface, as of fish. WCE, from OE *breche* crack open, break apart, divide. Also *bleach*.

bream [BREEM] to heat, with fired mop of birch-rind, the bottom of a boat hauled up and turned over on the beach and ready to be tarred.

breeches [BREE?-chehz] roe of female **cod** fish within its membrane (a delicacy). WCE *breeches* [BREH-chez] from its resemblance (from OE *brec*, plural of *broc*, a leg garment). Also *britchers, britchits, britchchins,* **fish peas.**

breed See **loaf.** *Blayss yer **breed** an make en roise.* "Bless your **bread** and make it rise." Note Wexford Yola *breed* bread.

breed poultice [BREED PUHL-dihs] bread soaked in hot water (or hot linseed oil) as a medium to apply a common heat treatment, held in place by gauze or a clean rag. Used for abscesses, boils, carbuncles, colds, coughs, pneumonia, sore throats, corns, eye infection, and skin abrasions, infections, and burns.

breeze (o' ween) gale, wind storm. Also **stroife o' ween.** See NE **starm.** Note NE **brewer.**

brewer [BROO-uhr] a calm before a storm. Note NE **starm, stroife o' ween, darty.**

brewis [BROOZ] boiled **ard tack** with **scrunchins,** as in *fish and brewis.* WCE, from OE *bríwas* plural of *bríw,* a thick pottage made of meal, pulse, etc.

bridge [BREEJ] veranda, balcony. Earlier gangway connecting fishing stages and a sailing ship's "bridge" deck. NE.

brin bag [BRIHN-bahg] burlap bag to hold bulk garden produce. SEI, Irish *brean* smelly, rancid from Celtic *brén.* Irish.

brishney [BRIHSH-nee] twigs for kindling. SEI, Gaelic *brosna.* *Irish.* Also **faddle, bavin.**

Britaniola, (New -) a short-lived name given to Newfoundland island in early 1600s.

broidesb'ys [BRUEHDZ-baiz] male wedding ushers, attendants. See NE **faddergiver.**

broidesgirls [BRUEHDZ-gehrlz] female attendants to the bride. NE. See NE **faddergiver.**

b'roights [bee-RUEHTS] properly, rightly, justly. Note Leics. *by rights* [boy ROYTS].

brogue [BROHG] as in *Irish **brogue*** accent. SEI. Note Irish *brogue,* an accent, lilt in speaking.

broke broken, damaged. *Me car bes aaveez **broke.***

broody irritable, sullen. Also **crousty, crookeed**. Note Leics *broody*, as a hen on eggs.

buck lye early alkaline solution for washing clothes.

bucko guy, fellow. SEI *buccaloon*, Gaelic *púicirliún* gloomy, morose person.

buddy [BUHD-dee] what's-his-name. Also **chummy**, *buddy*, *wassesname* [WAHS-eez-naym]. Note NE **wassname**.

bugger [BUHG-guhr] figuratively young scoundrel, rascal. Brit.

bull bird common dovekie or little auk, a table food sea bird (*Plautus alle alle*).

Bullet, The- See **Newfie Bullet**.

bull's-eye, -tongue rhodora (*Rhododendron canadense*), a rose-purple flower. WCE (*bulls-eye* denotes three flower species in Devon, Dorset and Somerset).

bultow [BUHL-toh] a line with hooks, a trawl.

bumboat [BUHM-boh?] a small vessel carrying supplies, commodities, cargo or passengers for a ship moored offshore. Brit., from Dutch *boom-* of *boomshuit* small fishing boat, plus "boat." Note **jollyboat**.

bumbye [buhm-BAI] soon, momentarily. *E be 'long bumbye t' see ya.* "He will drop in **soon** to see you." Note NE **da once, drectly**.

bun See **loaf**.

bungalow-apron a cuckoo-flower (*Cardamine pratensis*) in Whitbourne and Brigus: *lady's smock* (the latter from Brit. *lady's smock*).

b'y [BAI] boy; pragmatic marker[12] of discourse or informal direct address to a male: pal, buddy, guy, chum, man, dude, mate, later tending to be non-gender. *Ow bes ya, me b'y?* "How are you, buddy?" May include personal name: *Good f' we, John b'y, dere bes nar breeze on d' go.* "Lucky for us, **John**, that it is not windy." See NE *me* **son, o man, o trout, o cock,** *skipper,* **sir,** *Mr. Man.* Note Wexford Yola *bye* boy.

C

caaed fer/f' [KAWD fehr] unjustified, inappropriate, not needed, as in *not caaed fer. Dat blather is not caaed fer.* WCE. Note Dorset *call*, need.

caas fer [KAWZ fehr] forecasts, predicts (usually weather): *She caas f' rain on d' radio.* "The radio forecast **predicts** rain."

caca [KAW-kaw] excrement (a child's word). WCE. Note OE *cac-hus* latrine, Irish *cac*. Ultimately from very ancient (approximately 3500BC) Proto-Indo-European *kakka* excrement.

calabogus rum, molasses and spruce beer.

can metal beverage container; Note NE **tin**.

can o' drink or *boddle/bo'le* [BAWD-duhl], [BAWʔ-uhl] *o' drink*, a sweetened, carbonated beverage, "pop," "soft" drink. Note NE **hard liquor, tin**.

cant to lean to one side. *D' skiff were **canteed*** [KAHN-teed] *oer on er soide, she was.* "The fisher's boat was **leaned** to one side."

canteen a snack bar in a school, hospital, other institution. Brit. from FR *cantine*.

canvas (floor-) a type of rather stiff, continuous, patterned floor covering available commercially.

caplin [KAYP-luhn] small, edible smelt-like fish (*Mallotus villosos*) which spawn on beaches in late spring. Note plural: *caplin*. From MF *capelan* from Mi'kmaw *kaplanjetik*, capelin.

caplin wedder foggy, wet, cold weather when caplin spawn on the beaches. See **caplin**. Note **grizzly.**

carboo [KAWR-boo] caribou (*Rangifer tarandus*), a tundra herd animal. From Canadian FR *caribou* from Mi'kmaw *qalipu* "snow- shoveller" from *qalipi* "remove snow."

carboo-burry [KAWR-boo BUH-ree] twisted stalk (*Streptopus amplexifolius*) and rose twisted stalk (*S. roseus*), large vermilion berries. Assumed food for caribou. NE.

carboo moss caribou moss, hand-foraged *Cladonia rangiferina* from the **barrens** soaked with baking powder to rid it of toxic acidity, then candied, brined, and dried to a crunchy meal garnish. Assumed food for caribou. NE.

card a joker, a wit, a "character"; *Dat Dooley, e's some **card**, eh b'y!* Note NE **some b'y.**

cardin [KAHRD-uhn] accordingly, in agreement: *E noddeed cardin.* "He **nodded in agreement.**"

cardin to [KAHRD-uhn TOO] allegedly, reportedly, "rumour has it that...": ***Cardin to**, e bes stio fer aa married to nodder ooman!* "**Apparently**, he is already married to another woman!"

Caribou, **SS-** A 2,000 tonne ice-breaking steam ship beginning Newfoundland Railway connections to Canada at North Sydney, NS, in 1928. The only regular Newfoundland passenger ferry sunk by German Nazi U-boat. Torpedoed 67 km inbound under HMCS escort to Port aux Basques at 3:10 AM, 14 October 1942; 137 casualties including 10 children. *HMS Fame* rammed and sank the *U-69* east of Newfoundland 17 February, 1943; no survivors.

carjel, carjo   [KAHR-juhl], [KAHR-joh] an accordion. Also *cargel, cardeen, squeeze-box.*

carner b'y   hooligan, street-corner lout (**bayman** term for a St. John's ruffian). NE.

carpenter   [KAHR-pehn-duhr] common wood-louse or sow-bug (*Oniscus asellus*).

carrychurch   a large lamp. Also **flirrup, laddin lamp**, *stand lamp*, **tellylamp**

case   [KAYS] (prolonged [AY]) a rascal, disruptive fellow. Also **ard case**.

cast   cask, small wooden barrel. Note **drum.**

cellar   a walk-in root cellar to store vegetables or preserves built into earthworks or an embankment and behind a sturdy, stormproof door. WCE, from ME celer from OF from Latin *cellarium* "storeroom."

chafe   [CHAYF] a bother, prolonged vexation. *Dippin d' dill bes a chafe.* "Bailing a bilge is a **bother**"; small sore or wound. Note London Cant *chafe*, "to fret or fume" (worry). Note *chafing*, friction wear in a sailing ship's standing rigging, requiring constant repair by protective *chafing gear*, (usually shaggy, fringed *baggywrinkle* line-wrapping made of strands of castoff rope).

chamberpot   formerly a covered pail for nighttime calls of nature. WCE, from FR *pot de chambre.*

charm   a confusion of noise or voices, a racket. *Dey bes makin dat much charm, oi can't sleep.* WCE. Note Dorset *charm*, noise; confusion of voices or birds. From OE *cyrm* noise, blended voices.

chaw   [CHAW] chew (i.e. food); a wad of chewing tobacco. From OE *ceowan* bite, chew, gnaw.

chaw an gutch   [CHAW-uhn-GLUHCH] originally a restricted meal of bread and tea as in the "Depression grace," *F' dis bit o' chaw an glutch, we tanks dee Lard so vurry much.* By jocular extension, any meal as in *chaw an glutch toime*, mealtime. From "chew and swallow." See NE **glutch**.

cheeks as in *cod cheeks*, the flesh of the head of a cod fish, an accepted delicacy.

cheque a paper payment for purchase which you tear out from your chequebook. Brit.

chew talkativeness, loquaciousness, chattiness: *Mable aves some chew.* "Mable is very **chatty**." Also *got more chew dan* "is even more **talkative** than": *She got more chew 'n Lauchie's goat.*

chewmouth [CHAW (-mowt)] a chatty person. *A good feller, d' Captain, but steo fer aa e bes a chewmouth!*

chibbles [CHIH-buhlz] chives (*Allium schoenoprasum*). From WCE, Devon *chibbles/ chipples* (thinly sliced spring onions soaked well in slightly diluted malt vinegar with a sprinkling of sugar; scallions) from *chibbal/chib(b)ol* from Fr. *ciboule* scallion from Occitan *cebola*, from Latin *caepulla/cepulla*, diminutive of Latin *caepa/cepa* "onion." Note Leisc. *chibble, chivvle* to crumble, chip.

chimley [CHIHM-lee] chimney. WCE. Dorset *chimley*, chimney.

chin music humming or singing wordless tunes in rhythm, imitating music to accompany dancing; lilting. Also *cheek music, gob music, diddling*. Irish.

chinch [CHIHNCH] to caulk a wooden boat with oakum to prevent leaks; fill the seams of a log house; to stow tightly. Note NE **stog**.

chips "french-fried" potato strips or commercially available dried potato slices in bags.

chips, dressin 'n gravy a popular take-out/take-away dish of "french-fried" potatoes, turkey stuffing and thick brown gravy. NE.

chirpers, chirpen blue flag plant (*Iris versicolor*). From Brit. *cheiper* or *cheepel*, a related species (children achieve a chirping sound by blowing on the thin leaves held between the thumbs). Also **boat, conk**.

chocolate bar [CHAWʔ-lihʔ] candy bar. Brit.

christen a fairy [KRIHS-uhn] referring to very little liquid: *Billy left we wid not enough Screech t' christen a fairy*.

Christmas Seal, MV- a former 32 m 1943 crash rescue boat, *USCB Shearwater* (*P-102*), bought 1947 funded by Christmas Seal sales by Newfoundland Tuberculosis Association as an outport medical screening ship. Sold 1970, chartered to Bedford Institute of Oceanography, exploded and sank 1976 off Halifax, NS, with no loss of life.

chuck [CHUH?], [CHUHK] throw or toss something; discard. WCE, ME *choc* blow to the chin, from FR *choquer* to shock, strike against. Note Dorset and Leics. *chuck*, toss something. Also *foire away*.

chucklehead [CHUHK-uhl-eed] a stupid person. WCE, from Dorset *chucklehead*, a dolt. See **oonshick**, NE **bostoon**, **stun po**.

chummy [CHUHM-mee] person or thing of unknown name. See NE **wassname**.

chummyjigger [CHUHM-mee-jeeg-uhr] a thingamajig. See NE **wassname**, **machine**.

clap, d'– gonorrhea. From ME *clapper* rabbit hole, from OF *clapoir/ clapoire*, slang for genital sore or brothel. Note London Cant *clap*, "a Venereal Taint."

clar (ov) [KLAHR] except for, excepting: *Aa ands was 'counteed* [KOWN-teed] *fer, clar d' skipper. E stayed aboard.* "All the crew were accounted for **excepting** the captain. He remained aboard the ship." Also **outsoide ov**, *cep fer*.

clave [KLAYV] split/chop firewood or kindling. *Y' can clave splits t'day, but not on Sunday.*

clayn [KLAYN] completely, *E got clayn away*; to prepare fish, seabirds, rabbits, other small game for cooking. Note Sussex *clain*. See **panch**.

clever strong, handsome (man); fine (weather).

click nar clue no common sense: *E a'n't got (nar) click nar clue.* "He has **no common sense**."

clit [KLIHT] tangle, knot as in hair. WCE. Note Dorset *clitpoll*, having curled or tangled hair.

clitty knotted, tangled, snarled, as hair. WCE, from Dorset *clitty*, stringy, tangled, sticky.

clew op [KLOO-ohp] finish a task. From originally to draw up a sail for reefing. NE.

clobber an untidy state, litter, a mess. SEI, from Irish *clábar* disorderly. Irish.

close [KLOHS] sweltering, oppressive, sultry weather. Note Leics. *close*. Note **mauzy.**

clum [KLUHM] to hold tight, clutch; a tight embrace. WCE, from Dorset *clum*, clutch roughly.

clumper [KLAHM-pehr] a small, floating ice sheet; also *clamper*. WCE, from Dorset *clumper*, lump, piece. See NE **copy**, **ballycatter**.

coady / cotie [KOH-dee] a sauce made from molasses, butter, flour, water and salt. NE. Also **yankee budder**/*bu'er*.

coast boat one of several coastal passenger and freight steamships of the Reid Newfoundland Company (1897-1923), Newfoundland government (1923-49), and the Canadian National Railway (1949-86). At least five earlier coast boat steamships were pressed into brief official service as sealing ships. Note *coaster*, a coastal cargo schooner.

cobby (ouse) [KAW-bee] child's playhouse. WCE. Note *cubby-hole*, child's snug place. Note Leics. *cubby-house* rabbit hutch or coop.

cod [KAWD] once very common table food fish species, *Gadus morhua*. See NE **fish, peel**.

cod (liver) aal [KAWD LEE-vuhr AWL], [–AIL] oil rendered from cod livers previously for medicinal use, curing leather, and illumination. Originally obtained by months-long rendering of cods' livers collected in a barrel usually left on the head of a wharf.

cod loine [KAWD luehn] stiff, strong 18-thread line to which cod hooks or jiggers are fastened.

cod tongues [KAWD tuhngz] a dish based on the tongues of the cod fish dipped in seasoned flour and fried.

coffer [KOHF-ehr] a lie, fib. From "cough" (of guilt or to distract attention).

co junk [KOH JUHNK] be knocked or fall unconscious, "out cold"; faint: *She it er eed an feel down co junk.* "She struck her head and was knocked **unconscious**." See NE **conked out**. Note NE *junk*.

come [KUHM] past tense of *come*, as in *Oi come op yesday, an ya was out fer a run.* "I **came** up yesterday, but you were out for a stroll."

come agin [kohm ah-GIHN] to affect adversely, ruin, catch up with, overtake: *Mary's blather come agin she.* "Mary's foolish talk **caught up with** her."

come-aa-yer [kuhm-AW-yihr] any traditional Newfoundland song or lyric. From the initial line of a traditional lyric: *"Come aa y' good people/oi'll sing ye a song..."*

come board o' react forcefully to a comment or criticism. *Dey come roight board o' we f' teoin* [TEH-oh-een] *d' trut* [TROOʔ]. "They **were angry with** us for telling the truth." NE. Note **go board (ov), loine** (s.o.) **av.**

comefomaway [KOHM-fuhm-uh-WAY] someone not from Newfoundland. Note NE **opalong**.

comin on at the expected beginning or onset of, on the imminent approach of, as in *Comin on d' fiddeent o' da mont we gets Bessie's weddeen t' go to.* "**On the** fifteenth we can attend Bessie's wedding." Note NE **drectly, da once**.

comin on now at this time of year, presently. *Comin on now we bes settin taties out een d' garden.* "It's soon time to set potatoes out in the garden." Note NE **drectly, da once**.

compass directions See "compass directions" in the **Standard English** section on page 131.

concert an amateur or children's stage performance held during Christmastime.

concert as in *as good as a concert*, a reference to an amusing escapade or misadventure. From NE concert, an amateur or children's stage performance held during Christmastime.

condemn judged useless and discarded. *D' car was condemned affer she was drove too ard een d' Targa.*[19]

conk [KAWNK] large, spiral conch shell used as a boat's fog horn or to announce a bait-fish boat's arrival; big tree knot; blue flag plant (*Iris versicolor*). WCE from OF *conque* from Latin *concha* [KOHNK-uh] from Greek κόγχη (*kónkhe*) mussel. See **chirpers**.

conked out [kawnkt OOT] fainted, has become unconscious, passed out. From Brit. *conk* "punch in the nose" from earlier *conk* "nose." See NE *co junk*. Note early Australian *conk* hit someone.

conner [KAWN-nehr] blue perch, a small fish (*Tautogolabrus adspersus*) common around wharves; tricky person as in *sly as a conner*. WCE. Note Dorset *conner*, a groundfish.

contrary uncooperative; in a disagreeable or irritable mood. *Some contrary, dat Maggie is!* See NE **cranky, crousty, crookeed, broody**.

co, cood [KOH], [KOHD] (prolonged [OH]) cold, frosty; common cold, "virus," mild infectious respiratory disease: *Playse God oi don' catch* [KEHCH] *yer co!*

coopy (down) [KOOP-ee] crouch, squat down. See **quot**.

copy to jump from one floating *tally pan* (small ice sheet) to another before it sinks under you. See NE **clamper, ballycatter**.

cot [KAWT], [KAWʔ] baby's crib. Brit.

couche See **go t' couche**.

country [KUHNʔ-ree] hinterlands, backcountry inland from coast: *Es tilt bees een d' country*. See NE **eensoide, een d' country**.

covechus [KUHV-uh-chihz] covetous, greedy, envious. WCE. From OF *coveitos*. Note Leics. *covechus*.

covel [KUH-vuhl] a covered water barrel. See **puncheon**.

coxenhens [KAWKS-uhn-EENZ] a type of shellfish (*Mya arenaria*).

crabs, d'– crab louse (*Pthirus pubis*), parasitic insect of human hair. Note London Cant, *crab-lice*, "Vermin breeding in…hairy parts…"

crack an insult, desparaging remark, as in *Was dat a crack bout moy car?* "Did you **insult** my car?" From *the craic* "news, gossip, fun, entertainment, enjoyable chatting." Irish/Hiberno-English from *craic*. Scots from *crack*. English from *crak* ME "loud or blustering talk." Note Old High German *chrahhōn* to resound.

cracked [KRAHKT] unreasonable; mentally disturbed. WCE. Note ME *crack* a bold, unruly boy. See **mental**.

cracky [KRAHK-ee] any small dog, especially one that barks a lot, as in *saucy as a cracky*. Also *crackie*. WCE, small person or thing. Note ME *crack* a bold, unruly boy.

cranky [KRAYNK-ee] ill-tempered, cantankerous; also said of a boat that is difficult to manage. SEI. Note NE **crousty, crookeed, contrary**.

crannick weathered or dead root, stump or tree fit for kindling. Also *cronnick*, *cran*. WCE, from Dorset *crannick*, bramble root. Note Cornish Celtic *crann*, tree.

craw upper chest, bosom of a shirt. See **kronk**.

crossackle [KRAWS-ahk-uhl] to frustrate to anger by contrary argument. Note NE **vex, ballyrag**.

cross-andeed [kraws-AHN-deed] managing chores alone.

crows See **pishogue**.

crubeen pickled pig's hock (rear ankle joint). SEI, from Gaelic *crúibín*. Irish.

crump [KRUHMP] a body position, usually uncomfortable. *E got een a bad **crump** unner da ouse.* "He put himself into a **cramped position** in the under-house crawl space." WCE. Note Dorset *crump up*, bend up in a huddle for warmth. Note London Cant *crump-back't* "crooked or hunch-backt," Gaelic *crompa* gnarled tree trunk.

crookeed [KROOK-eed] cantankerous, touchy, easily annoyed. WCE, from ME *crok* from Old Norse *krāka* hook. See NE **crousty, contrary**. Note Wexford Yola *curkite* snappish, contrary. Note Australian *crooked* [KROOKT] *on* annoyed or angry with.

crousty [KROWS-tee] cantankerous, easily annoyed, touchy. WCE, from Dorset *crousty*, ill-humoured. See NE **crookeed, contrary**.

cryin jag a fit of weeping, as in *Aunt Suze bes on a **cryin jag** whenaer Uncle John goes out on da wadder een a breeze.*

crystal tea See **Indian tea.**

cud/cud'n [KOOD], [KOOD-uhn] could/could not. See NE **wud/wud'n**.

cud a' [KOOD uh] contraction for "could have."

cuddle hug. Brit. from ME *cudliche* affectionate.

cuddy [KUHD-dee] cabin; a covered forward or after space in a boat.

cuffs fingerless protective gloves for splitting fish. WCE. Note late ME *cuffe* mitten, glove. Also *haulons* [AWL-awnz], *nippers*.

curvey, kirby [KEHR-vee], [KEHR-bee] a sealer's quilt; a thick blanket. NE.

D

da [DAH] dad, father, grandfather. Also *granfer*. SEI. Irish.

da (d'), dem [DUH], [DEHM] the, as in *Ammer **d'** nail een full. Now, and oi **dem** new nails een da' gert can.* "Hammer **the** nail in completely. Now, pass me **the** new nails in that big can." May have demonstrative meaning: *d' mar, da once, Tom come ome da weyk* "Tom came home this past week." Note NE **dem** *days*, previous days.

daddle [DAHD-uhl] a hind paw of a seal. WCE, "hand." See NE **fipper**.

daddylonglegs crane fly (family *Tipulidae*). *Luh, a **daddylonglegs**. Rain d'mar!* "See the **crane fly**—rain tomorrow!"

dally [DAH-lee] sudden lull of wind; change of wind direction.

da loike [duh LUEHK] such a thing (a phrase of indignant denial): *Oi naer done **da loike**!* "I did not do **such a thing**!"

damper [DAHM-pehr] one of the round covers or lids on a kitchen wood or coal stove, raised by a **lifter**. WCE, from late ME *damp* suffocate, deaden. Note Dutch *dampkap* flue valve, range hood. ***Damper** leaved ov d' stove, company soon be een d' cove.*

damper dog a flapjack or pancake fried on a stove top; also **bangbelly**, **frozie**, *damper boy, damper devil, grace cake*. Note Australian *damper*, flapjack.

dan, 'n [DAHN], [UHN] than, as in *Dose starms, dey bes bigger 'n dey was een dem days.* "Today's storms are bigger **than** they were in days past." Note Sussex *dan*.

da once [duh WUHN?S] soon, momentarily: *Goin home da once?* "Are you going home soon?" *Now da once* "very soon." WCE. Note ME *for þe nones* "indeed," "now" from ME *for þan anes* "for the once," for a particular occasion or purpose. Central. Also **drectly**. Note Somerset *to once* "very soon." Note NE *da yeur*, **bumbye**, **comin on**.

dark cake strong heavy chewing tobacco. Note **plug**.

dart a quick brief visit, as in *take a **dart** down da wharf* "make a **quick visit** to the wharf."

darty (weather) [DAHR?-ee] stormy with high precipitation: *Me son, t'is mad rough an **darty** out t'noight!* "Man, it's **stormy** out tonight!" See NE **tick**. Note NE **starm, breeze**.

darty [DAHR?-ee] off colour, suggestive, lewd, vulgar. *Don' ya be tellin dem **darty** staries!*

Da's it, b'y. [dahs (H)IHT bai] "It happens" (a fatalistic expression). Literally "That is it, buddy." NE

dat, da' [DAH?], [DAHT], [DAH] pronoun that, as in ***Da's d'** skiff wha sunk een d' tickle.* May replace **wha** or **who** as in *She's d' maid **dat** loss er kitten.* WCE. Note Sussex *dat*, that.

dat [DAH?], [DAHT] (before an adjective or adverb) so, to such extent, *D' lops was **dat** bad we andy bout ove op.* "The sea was **so** choppy we nearly capsized."

dat is [DAH? (H)EEZ] pragmatic marker[12] of emphasis: "for sure." *D' fog bes tick enough t' cut wid a knoife* [NUEHF], ***dat is**.*

daw woman's informal direct address to either sex. *Ow is ya t'day, me **daw**?* Note SE "doll." Central. See **babby, ducky, luv**, and Note Brit *luv, honey, sweetie, my dear*. Note NE **girl, maid**.

daybed a traditional, asymmetrical chaise-longue couch, usually open at the foot and often found in the kitchen. WCE.

day on weather conditions (good or bad) for outside activities: *Wha' a day on cloz!* "It is a very favourable **day for** drying clothes (outside on a clothesline)."

d' bumps a birthday tradition: friends lift and lower the young celebrant by the hands and feet, touching the floor for each year. Brit. and Irish custom. See NE **grace faace**.

dear, me- [DEER] informal direct address to an older woman, as in *me **dear***, or as a patronising endearment referring to a senior: *da o **dear***.

dee, 'ee [DEE], [EE] may be heard for *ya* or *you* on the northeast coast. *Me car bes broke 'r oi ud give '**ee** a run op d' road.* "My car is never working or I would give **you** a left." From ME *thee*. See pronoun list under **Small Words** on page 25.

deed in a deep sleep as in *__deed__ t' da world* [WEHRL]; dead, deceased. Note Wexford Yola *deed* dead.

dem [DEHM] them, plural of **e, she, en** (and **hit**, where used). Note Sussex *dem*, them. See NE **em, dey**. See **Small Words** on page 25.

dem may be heard to serve as a variant stressed plural of **da**, the: *Dis longer yere, e id'n straayt, an **dem** starrigans cross d' pond, dey bes not fit f' d' foire.* Note WCE Sussex...*three-score stout men stan roun it, of **dem** stout men of Israel* (SS 3.7) "...sixty brave men stand around it, of the brave men of Israel." WCE. See NE **da.**

dem previously, before now, heretofore, back then, in the past. *__Dem__ days co' come een schooner an was winched ont' da wharf t' lug ome yersauf.* "**Back then** coal (for home heating fuel) arrived in schooners and was lifted onto the wharf for you to carry home."

den then, at that time. WCE.

dere [DUHR] there, away from the speaker, opposite of **yere**, here. WCE. Note Sussex *dere*, there.

dese [DEEZ] for a duration of, during, while: *E ben deed **dese** ten yeur.* "He has been dead **for** ten years" (no plural *-s* after numerals; see **nummers**). See NE **dem**. Note NE **dose**.

devilment playful mischief; *E drapped a fish down da well, jus f' **devilment**.* Also **badness**

devil's carpet hawkweeds (*Hieradum* spp), invasive weed related to dandelion. Irish (Old Perlican).

devilskin mischievous child; prankster. Also *devil's limb*. See **jackeen**. Note Leics *limb of the devil* wicked rascal.

dey [DAY] they, plural of **e, she, en, hit**, as in *E an she, **dey** is affer gettin married*. See **dem**.

deyr [DIHR] their. Note NE **es, er.**

dicker haggle over, bargain for, negotiate. WCE, from ME *diker* from OF *dacre* ten of (hides).

Dildo [DIHL-doh] the **outport,** Dildo Arm, and Dildo Island in Trinity Bay, eastern Newfoundland island, known for area prehistoric sites. From Spanish of early fishermen *deleitó* [day-LAY-doh] "delighted, pleased" as in *Este lugar me deleitó* [EHS-teh loo-GAHR may day-LAY-doh] "This place pleased me" (not to be confused with Sp. *delito* "crime").

dill, dell [DEHL] boat's low point (bilge) from which to bail water. See NE **dip, piggin, spudgel**.

dinner the mid-day meal, "lunch" *Eef ya aves a gert **dinner**, ya ull want nar supper ataa.* "If you eat a big **lunch,** you will certainly want no dinner." Note NE **supper, scoff, feed**.

dip to bail or scoop up water out of a boat. *E **dips** wadder out d' dill wid a piggin.* See NE **piggin, dill, spudgel**.

dis [DIHS] this. WCE. Note Sussex *dis*, this.

dishclot [DEESH-klaw?] dishrag, cloth to wash dishes. Brit.

dis's it. [DIHS ihz ZIHT] answer to greeting **Wha's y' at?** Literally "This is it," as it is, as you can see.

d' goin ov [duh GOHN uhv] how, when, what happened to, as in *Dey naer knowd **d' goin ov** en.* "They never knew **what happened** to him."

d' mar [duh MAWR] tomorrow. WCE, from ME *to morewe* from OE *to morgenne* from *morgan* morning. Note NE *d' mar marnin* tomorrow morning, *d' mar noight* tomorrow night.

do [DOO] auxiliary verb (no ending) as in *She **do** bake er own breed./**Do** Martin fish av Cape St. Mary's?* See NE **doos**.

dob [DAWB] a bobbing gait or walk: *O Jerry **dobbed** 'long shore, nar care een da world.*

do be [DOO BEE(Z)] am, are, is, has/have been continually, over time; habitual tense. *Gramfer **do be** paintin es dory evy chance e gets. D' Revern **do be** roun yere ontoimes.* "The minister visits here occasionally." Irish. Note NE **bes**.

dodge [DAWJ] stroll, as in ***dodge** op, –down, -oer: Tink maybe oi ull **dodge** op d' road*. "I have decided that I may **stroll along** the street." Also *take a **dodge***. See NE **dodge on, marl**.

dodge (on) to continue as in ***dodge on** op, –down, -oer: Tink maybe oi ull **dodge on** op d' road*. "I've decided I may **continue along** the street." Also *take a **dodge on** op–*.

doies [DEUHZ] as in the NE phrase, *Oi **doies** at dat!* [UEH DUEHZ ah DAHʔ] "I find that **extremely entertaining**," usually presented in a SE orthography as "I dies at that!" From 1500s ME euphemism *to die for* "to experience orgasm" ("I will die bravely like a smug bridegroom," *King Lear*, Act IV, Scene VI). From Viking Norse *deyja*.

dole [DOHL], [DOH] government-assisted living allowance, originally a strictly regulated ration of $2 value per month per destitute adult. WCE, ME *dol*, share from AS *daelen* to share. See **dole arder**. Brit. Note Wesford Yola *dole* a deal, an amount. Note Leics. *dole bread* brought to a wake by relatives. Brit. Note Leics. *dole* bread brought to a wake by relatives.

dole arder a list or "order" of household necessities to be paid for by the **dole**. *Back den, toimes was dat bad we people went on d' dole.*

done [DUHN] past tense of **do**, as in *She **done** d' bess she cud*. "She **did** the best possible."

don't be [DOH-bee] "do/does not," "am/are/is not," as in *E **don't** be op dis way offen*, "He **doesn't** visit here often." NE. SEI.

d'ooman [DOO-muhn] "my wife," "the woman of the house." Note Leics. *the 'oman* my wife. See **o ooman**.

doos [DOOZ] main verb **do**, does, as in *Oi **doos**, ya **doos**, e/she **doos**, we **doos**, yiz **doos**, dey **doos**.* "I **do**, you **do**, he **does**," etc. *Oi **doos** all d' cookin an washin at ome*. See NE **do** (auxiliary verb). WCE.

dory wooden row boat used near shore or from a fishing banker schooner. Also *row dory*.

dose days [DOHZ dayz] today, nowadays. ***Dose days** ya can't fix yer own car ataa widout ya got a computer degree*. Note NE **dem days, dese**.

doter [DAWʔ-uhr] an old seal; a bay seal.

doughboy [DOH-bai] a dumpling (of flour, water and baking powder) in thick pea soup.

douse [DOWS] to hit or slap; to throw water on as in extinguishing a fire. See NE **wop, tump**. Note Leics. *douse* dunk, drench.

dout [DOWT], [DOWʔ] to extinguish, as a candle or fire. WCE. Note Devon, Leics. *dout* extinguish.

draf (o' ween) [DRAHF] slight breeze, brief gust, draft.

drap ov, a- alcoholic drink. Brit. See **spot ov**. Note Leics. a *drop* much drink; heavy rain.

draw bucket a bucket to withdraw salt or fresh water. NE.

dreads [DREEDS] be apprehensive about or anxious for, fear the consequences of. *Oi **dreads** da winner, oi does, shut op een d' snow an oice an d' b'ys out on da wadder.* "I am **fearfully pessimistic** about winter confining us in snow and ice and endangering our fishermen out on the ocean." WCE from OE *adrædan* from *ondraedan* be afraid of from *on-* against + *raedan* advise.

dreshel [DRIHSH-uhl], [DRIHSH-oh] doorstep, threshold. WCE. Note Dorset *drashel*, threshold.

dresser a kitchen cupboard. WCE. From FR *dressoir*.

dreaten [DRIHʔ-uhn] warn; warn not to: *She **dreatened** en t' come ome sousht agin.* "She **warned** him **not to** return home drunk again." WCE, Wiltshire.

dreaten to intend to: *Susan **dreatened to** ang out cloz eed ov d' rain.* "Susan **intended to** hang clothes out to dry before it would rain." WCE, Wiltshire.

drectly [DREHK-lee] soon, momentarily, in a minute: *Oi be down drectly.* Note Cornish *dreckly*. Also **da once**. Note NE **bumbye, comin/comeen on**.

dribbly dripping water in small amounts: *Aur wadder comes from a dribbly brook.*

droak [DROHK, DROHʔ] steep-sided (wooded) gully. WCE (Devon) from OE *drock*, a watercourse. Also *droke, dring*.

drove driven: *D' goats was **drove** out o' d' garden.*

drove driven to distraction: *Ya got oi **drove**!* "You **have driven** me to distraction!" Note Leics. *druv: It's her as has druv 'im tew it.*

drowndeed drowned (suffocated); drenched. See **douse, go souse**.

droy possessed of wry humour or wit: *Me son, dat young Lukey, e's some **droy**!*

drubbin [DRUHB-ihn] protective coating of oil and tallow for boots.

drum   larger wooden 128-lb. (58 kg) cask to pack fish. Note NE **butt**, **cast**. See NE **screw**.

drum fish   See NE **screwed fish**.

drung, drong   [DRUHNG] narrow lane between houses. WCE, Note Dorset *drong, drongway*, a narrow path between hedges or walls. From OE *thrang* a throng, crowd. Note Scots *thrang*, crowded.

duck een   temporarily step inside of; briefly hide in. *E ducked een a shop fom d' rain*. "He **stepped into** a store to avoid the rain." WCE, from OE *ducan* to dive, dip or duck down.

duckish   [DUHK-eesh] twilight, evening. Also *eel o' d' day. Bide t' duckish*. "Stay until **after sun-down**." WCE, from Dorset *duckish, duck,* twilight. Note Irish Gaelic *dorchadas* duskiness.

ducky, (me-)   woman's informal direct address to either gender: *Ow is ya t'day, me ducky?* Avalon. WCE, from OE *min duka* "my lord (duke)," said in respect. Note Yorkshire, UK, greeting *Ay up duck!* Note NE **babby, luv, daw, girl, maid.**

dudeen   [doo-DEEN] type of short tobacco pipe. SEI, Gaelic *dúidín*. Irish.

duff   A heavy, dark pudding of flour and water boiled in a bag and served with molasses to seamen aboard sailing ships. From ME *duff* dough. See **figgy duff**.

dulse   edible and medicinal intertidal seaweed (*Palmaria palmata*). From Irish Gaelic *duileasg*.

dumfly   small light-brown dung fly (*Scatophaga stercoraria*). *Dum-* from its seeming stupor.

dumb tit   baby's pacifier, also *dummy, dummy tit* (Brit.), **nuk**. From WCE from OE *dumb* speechless, mute.

dunnage   [DUHN-ihj] poor-quality wood unsuitable for fine work; bough matting to support fish in a skiff's cargo hold. From Brit. *dunnage*, a shipboard wooden fardage or structure to prevent cargo shifting or damage from bilge-water, from ME *dennage*, from Middle Dutch *denne*, flooring of a ship. Note NE **faddle**.

dunch, dunce   [DUHNCH] numbed, "pins and needles" feeling; unleavened, as in baking: *dunch bread* or *dunch cake*. Also *dunchy*. WCE. Note Dorset *dunch*, a bit deaf; dull.

dwall   [DWAWL] a dozing state, half asleep; *Da o man's een a dwall een front o' d' foire, e is.*

dwoy   [DWUEH] a brief snow flurry or rain shower. WCE.

E

e [EE] stressed pronoun he, him: *Skipper give **e** foive bait sticks an **e** los em.* Also refers to inanimate countable things that are not mobile: *Moin dat glass o' beer, ya don' knock **e** over.* WCE. Note Dorset *'e*, he. Note NE **en**, **'m**, and **she**, **hit**.

earwig [EHR-weeg] a centipede (non-insect arthropod, class *Chilopoda*) having a pair of legs on each of an odd number of many body segments. (True earwig insects, order *Dermaptera*, are not native to Newfoundland island; the black European earwig, *Forficula auricularia*, was imported to the Avalon Peninsula in the 1900s.)

eastard [EEST-uhrd] relative to the east, as wind or weather, easterly. See NE **ees**.

eat aloive [EET uh-LUEHV] being bitten by many small insects at once: *Oi bes **eat aloive** evy summer op on d' barrens.* "I am **excessively pestered** (by black flies, mosquitoes) when I visit the open back country in summer." Feeling itchy all over: *Eef oi sees ar spoider, well den, oi bes **eat aloive**!* "Seeing a spider makes me itchy all over!" NE.

eave (op) [(H)AYV] raise or heave up, lift up, as the corner of a house by ground frost or the sea rolling in on shore; to capsize or roll over, as a vessel. Past: **ove**. Note NE **ove back**.

'ee dialectal *you*. Note WCE Somerset *I tell ee...that ee stur not up...* (SS 8.4). See **dee**.

eed ov [EED ohv] before; in front of. *E got dere **eed ov** d' train.* Also **fore**, **op t'**.

-eed [EED] past ending of certain verbs ending in -**t** or -**d**: *Once we start**eed** fer ome, da wedder got bedder. Uncle Ezra was urt**eed** een da war. Dey land**eed** andy bout duckish.*

eef if, whether. *Pick op a pack o' Mark Tens* [TAHNZ] *fer oi at d' shop, **eef** y' moins to.* "Buy me a pack of *Mark Ten* cigarettes at the store, **if** you don't mind." Also *eef'n*, a contraction of *eef* and *an* "if and" *eef'n y' moins to*, "if you don't mind."

eel the heel (end slice) of a loaf of bread. Note Irish *heel* end or crust of bread, cheese, etc.

eel o' d'day evening twilight time, or "heel of the day." Also **duckish**.

een in, into. *Moose got **een** d' rhubarb garden.*

-een dialectal variant of the *–in* ending of present participial verbs ("-ing" in SE). *Oi bes foin**een** me legs somtin wunnerfo een dis caplin wedder.* "My leg pains are agoniz**ing** in this dank weather."

een a tear   busy; rushing chores. See NE **skirr**.

een d' country   [(H)EEN duh KUHʔ-ree] hinterlands, inland from coast. Also **eensoide**. See NE **country**. Note NE **een d' tant woods**.

een d' tant woods   [TAHNT] in forest of tall, straight trees. See **tant**.

een bunk   [(H)EEN buhnk] sleeping late; ill in bed.

eensoide   [(H)EEN-soyd] in the hinterlands, inland from coast. West, South. See NE **country**. Also **een d' country**.

een tack wid   [een TAHK wihd] in the company of, associated or cooperating with (usually said with negative connotations): *Young Harry bes **een tack wid** a crowd ov angishores.*

ees   [EES] east. See 'compass directions' in **Standard English** section on page 131.

eft   [EHFT], [EHF] to weigh in the hand; weight. WCE, from Dorset *heft*, weight.

eh b'y   [AY bai] rhetorical pragmatic marker[12]: "isn't that so?" *T''day's fishin id'n much t' live* [LEEV] *on, **ey b'y**.* SEI. Central. Also *innit*, **idn** *it*.

eider   [EE-dehr], [AID-dehr] in addition, too, as well, "in the bargain," "to boot," as in *Go jannying at Manuel's ouse an ya ull not get away widout a good stiff one, **eider**.* "If you go mummering at Manuel's house you **are sure to** get a strong drink." Also *eider...er,* either...or. See NE **neider**. Note NE **tilly**.

elf   [EHF] axe handle.

em   [EHM] them. *Give **em** a noggin o' swish f' deyr scoff.* "Give a cask of bulled liquor **to them** for their banquet." WCE. Note Dorset *em*, them. From ME *hem* them from OE *heom* them. Note WCE Somerset *Th' wachmen...I zed to um...* (SS 3.3). Note NE **'m** (pronoun).

emmet   an ant (insect family *Formicidae*). WCE, Dorset *emmet*, from OE.

emp (out)   [EHMʔ] to empty: ***Emp out** d' puncheon f' me, will ya, me son?* WCE. Note Dorset *empt* empty.

en   [UHN] unstressed him, as in *Oi wud a' joled **en** f' stealin fom me rabbit slips.* "I would have throttled **him** for stealing from my rabbit trap line"; it, as in *E ad a foine jigger, but e los **en** overboard, e did.* "He had a good jigger, but then he himself lost **it** overboard." From OE *hine*. Note WCE Somerset *I zaut un, but I nivver voun un* (SS 3.2). See NE **e**.

en   [EHN] him, it. WCE. Note Dorset, Devon *en*, him.

er   or. See **eider**.

er   her, as in *Er lassy tea bes d' bess een d' cove*. See NE **she**.

ern   herring, a bait or table fish (*Clupea harengus*).

er wha'?   [EHR WAW?] eliciting pragmatic marker[12]: "or what else?" *Y' dartin down d' road, er wha'?* "Are you going for a stroll, **or doing something else**?" Note NE **ey b'y**.

es   [EEZ] his. May also be heard for "its": *Can't start me hengine 'cause es plug bes darty*. "I cannot start my (make'n'break) boat engine because **its** spark plug is fouled."

e's   [EEZ] he is. May be heard for "it is": *Me new brown coat? E's me bess one ov aa*. See **e**.

evy   [EH-vee] every; each.

evyting   [EH-vee-teeng] everything, all of it. Note NE **nar'n**.

exercise   School student's class notes, practice or work book. NE. Also **scribbler**. Note **slate**.

F

faace   [FAAYS] (with prolonged [AY]) mouth: *D' li'l nipper stogged es faace wid chips*. "The child filled his **mouth** with french fries"; nerve, effrontery, boldness, audacity: *Sally ad d' faace t' tell oi dat loie*. "Sally had the **nerve** to tell me that lie." Note Wexford Yola *faace* face.

faddle   bundle of firewood; twigs gathered for kindling. WCE. Note Dorset *faddle*, bundle, pack, London Cant *fardel*, "a Bundle." From ME from OF a small *farde*, package, from Spanish *fardo* bundle, pack. From Mozarabic Spanish *fardah*, package. Also **brishney**, **bavin**. Note *dunnage*.

faddergiver   [FAWD-dehr-gee-vehr] bride's father, or other male chosen by her, to ceremonially agree to the union. NE.

fadge   [FAHJ] manage or do chores alone. WCE, from *fadge*, make suitable. Note London Cant *fadge*.

fadom (out)   to understand. Also **twig**. From "fathom," to take a sounding of (check) water depth. WCE from OE *faethmian* embrace, surround

fagged (out)   fatigued, tired, exhausted, as in *aa fagged out* "completely exhausted." *Oi is too fagged out t' sleep*. Brit. from drooping *flag*. Note **beat out**.

faggot [FAY-gut] a bundle of half-dried, salted cod fish; a covering for that bundle. WCE, "tied collection of twigs." From OF *fagot* "bundle of sticks." From Italian *fagotto*. From Ancient Greek *fakelos* bundle (Modern Greek envelope, folder). Note Wexford Yola *fagoghes* "kindling bundled." See **yaffle**.

fair very, extremely: *Jack was* ***fair*** *ravness* (hungry) *when e got av da wadder.* See **some**, **wunnerfo**.

fair (op) straight, *aligned*; (*-op*) to straighten or align: ***Fair op*** *dat board.* Note NE **faired av**.

fairies the personification of the elements and bad luck as obscure, deceptive and magical "little people" to be respected and avoided. WCE, SIE. From a rendering of early West Country faierie fable, and from the *aos sí* [ees-SHEE] or *siabhra* [SHEE-vrah] of Celtic lore of southern Ireland. Avalon.

fairy charms bread in your pocket, clothing worn inside out, silver coins, "cold iron" (sharp weapon), or religious objects to avoid mishap, abduction, or becoming bewitched or waylaid and lost due to fairies. See **fairies**.

fairy ground an obscure, quiet, barren spot or path to avoid for fear of disturbing the fairies. Avalon. See **fairies**.

fairy music hypnotic piping in or near fairy ground that can bewitch the human listener. See **fairies**.

fall Autumn. WCE, from ME *fall* "a falling," from OE *feoll* "fell, decayed, died."

far'chun [FAHRʔ-chuhn] fortune, riches.

fashion ov, got d'- [FAHSH-uhn] has the personal habit or idiosyncrasy of, habitually. *She* ***got d' fashion ov*** *readin een bed* [BAYD]. Note Wexford Yola *fashoon* fashion. Note NE **aavo_fer**.

feed any large meal. Note **scoff**.

feelin ___ sauf sensing one's well-being. *Oi id'n* ***feelin*** *me***sauf** *t'day.* "I **feel** out of sorts today."

feel yer boots! yield to your impulse(s), indulge your urge, please yourself. Said negatively or flippantly, as in *You stio at d' table? Aw, den, b'y,* ***feel yer boots****!* "You still eating? Well, then, help yourself!" Brit., from lower mess-deck sea cook's cry at mealtime (lit. "Eat up 'til you fill your boots"). See NE **give'r**.

feller male person, guy, fellow. WCE. From OE *feolaga* a partner, colleague.

feller to, d'-   the second of a pair of something. *Oi loss **d' feller t'** me bess pair o' cuffs.*

felt tins   thin, tin washers on *felt nails* to fasten **tar felt** onto a roof in preparation for tarring it.

fer, f'   [FUH] for, as in *We'm got brewis **f'** tea.* "We have fish and brewis **for** dinner." *T'is not **fer** oi t' say.* "It's not my decision."

ferks   [FEHRKS] crotch or "forks" of trousers.

ferto   [FUHR-duh] so that, in order to, for the purpose of, as in *Ya needs a ticket **ferto** get aboard* and *She done d' course **ferto** get d' job.*

fetch   a ghostly premonition. Also **tokens**.

fidgety   [FIHJ-uh-dee] restless, hyperactive.

figgy duff   [FEEG-ee DUHF] a bag pudding (or steamed in a mould) of bread crumbs, raisins, molasses, butter, flour etc., cooked in a pot with **jigg's dinner**. Also *figgy puddin*. WCE. Note Dorset *figged-pudden*.

fipper   [FIHP-pehr] a seal's forepaw. See **daddle**.

fipper pie   a meat pie made of seal forepaws. NE.

firs goin av   [FIHRS gohn avv] initially, at the beginning, at first, from the start, originally. ***Firs goin av** she scarched er harm on d' hoven daar.* "**Straightaway** she burned her arm on the oven door."

firs nar las   [FIHRS nuhr lahs] never, at no time, not at all. *D' constable naer showed **firs nar las**.* "The policeman did **not** arrive **at all**."

fish   [FEESH] designates only codfish, *Gadus morhua*, as pronounced by a 1915 Supreme Court of Newfoundland decision, all others referencing specific name, *herring, salmon, mackerel*, etc. Also **cod**. See **peel**, **tomcod**.

fish cake   a patty of salt **cod**, potato, savory, onion, egg and **scrunchins** fried in *pork fat* until brown.

fisherman's basket   the carnivorous, wetlands pitcher plant (*Sarracenia purpurea*). Also *watercup, waterjug, waterlily* and, as a medicinal plant of the Mi'kmaq and other First Nations, *Indian-cup, Indian-jug*, and *Indian-pipe*. Its image appeared on Newfoundland's first bronze penny issue of 1865; officially declared the provincial flower in 1954.

fish merchant   the chief capitalist entrepreneur in larger outports who ruled local economies by control of fish exports and by the use of **truck** and *store credit* to the local fishermen.

fish peas   [FEESH peez] roe (eggs) of female **cod** fish (considered a delicacy). Also **breeches**.

fit-out   outfit, equipment; provide equipment to someone.

flake   wooden platform for drying fish. Note NE on *flake*, occupied in drying cod fish. WCE. Note Dorset *vleake* [VLEH-ahk], flooring support.

flankers   [FLAYNK-ehrz] sparks or hot flakes above a chimney or fire. WCE. Note Dorset *vlankers*.

flask, flasque   [FLAHSK] a popular, pocket-sized, flat, glass or metal bottle of whiskey or brandy. WCE, from ME *flaske* "keg," from OE *flasce* "case," influenced by OF *flaskon* a wicker-covered jug from Late Latin/Frankish *flasko* "wickered bottle." Note London Cant *flasque* "five Pints and half...of any Wine."

flat talk   [FLAH-tawk] a critical reference to an exagerated local, colloquial, or dialectal NE accent or usage. NE. Also *newfy talk*. Note **accent**, **slang**.

flick d' stick   See **tiddly**.

flirrup   [FLUHR-uhp] large lamp. Also **tellylamp**, **laddin lamp**, *stand lamp*, **carrychurch**.

flinders   [FLIHN-derz] small pieces. WCE, from Dorset *flinders*, flying bits of something smashed.

floor canvas   See **canvas**.

floater   a hired summertime fisherman who lived aboard an English schooner. Note **landsman**, **livyer**.

flowers   [FLAH-wehrz] dangerous rocky shoal. Also **sunkers**, **warshballs**, *warshrocks*. From FR *rochers à fleur d'eau* rocks awash.

flummy   [FLUHM-mee] trappers' bread from unleavened dough toasted over open fire. Also *flummy dum*, **stove cake**. Note NE **dunch(y) bread**.

foine   [FUEHN] very acceptable: *a foine day*; a fine, penalty of money paid for a legal offense.

foine   [FUEHN] be discomforted in a body part: *Oi foines me legs somtin wunnerfo whenaer da ween comes round t' d' nardees.* "My legs **pain** terribly whenever bad weather approaches from the northeast." Note NE **struck een, smert**.

foire   [FUEHR] throw. *Knock av foirin rocks at d' cat!*

foire away   discard. Also *chuck*.

fiorin av d' gun originally a salute of musketry fired successively by each man in turn along a line and back. Also *feu de joie* (FR "fire of joy"). Once used by local residents to greet visiting dignitaries, for newly married couples leaving the church, and at midnight to herald in the New Year.

foive (fi') [FUEHV] five: *Ey, o man, len oi fi' dollars t' payday, aaroight?* Note Leics. *foive* five, *foi-pun-ote* a five-pound note.

folly [FAWL-lee] follow. *Pish follied oi ome aa da way.* "Pish (dog) **followed** me home." WCE. Note Dorset *volly*, follow.

fom [FUHM] from, indicating direction or origin. *Me cabin bes tree moile fom d' pond.*

footins [FOO?-uhnz] footprints as in *rabbit footins*.

fore [FOHR] before. Also **eed ov, op t'**, *afore*.

for'd [FAHRD] bow (forward) end of boat or vehicle.

foreparts the crotch or genital area. Note sailing ship term *forepart*, the bowsprit area of a ship.

fortnight [FAHRT-nueht] two weeks. Brit., from ME *fourteniht* and OE *foewertyne niht* 14 nights.

found [FOWN] provided for, equipped: *Dem men bes paid a unnerd twenny dollars a day an found*. "The men are paid a hundred and twenty dollars per day with meals **provided**." Note NE **sot op**. Note Leics. *His master foinds 'im in butes an' all.*

fousty [FOW-stee] stale-smelling, mouldy, spoiled. WCE, from Dorset *fousty*, stale, damp, stuffy. Note Brit *fusty*, Scots *foosty* mouldy, musty. See **smatchy, gone av.**

frankum hardened resin of black spruce *(Picea mariana)* chewed as a type of gum. From *franckumsence* (frankincense) from OF *franc encens* free or pure incense.

frapse [FRAYPSS] to dress up, go formal.

friend-girl a girl's female friend.

frig, -gin [FREEG, FREEG-geen] slang, mildly offensive intensifying expletive or modifier: *Frig, oi loss me friggin purse!* "**Dammit**, I have mislayed my purse!" Brit., originally obscene reference to masturbation.

frore [FROHR] frost; covered with icy spray. *Me faace was frore een d' starm.* WCE, from OE *frore* frost, ice, icicle. Note Dorset *a-vrore*, frozen, Brit. *frore* frozen (poetic, archaic). See NE **ballycatter**.

froze frozen; very cold. WCE, from OE *freosan*.

frozie [FROH-zee] fried dough, flapjack, pancake. Also NE **bangbelly, damper dog, touton,** *grace cake.*

fudge [FUHJ] manage chores alone without help.

full tilt (een) [FOO TEHLT] at reckless speed (usually colliding with something): *First toime a' da wheel, an 'e went* **full tilt een** *a loight po! Full* from OE *ful* thorough, intense, excessive; *tilt f* from early ME *tylte* jousting (as in mounted knights with lances) from OE *tealt* "totter or lean unsteadily." See NE **tilt**. Note Leics. *full-tilt* utmost speed.

funk [FUHNK] a stink. Note London Cant *funk* "Tobacco Smoak; also a strong Smell or Stink." From FR *funkière* smoke.

f'y' playse [FYAH PLAYZ] *eef ya playse,* please.

G

Gaff Topsails One of several highland rocky **tolts** in central Newfoundland. From the triangular topmost fore-and-aft sailing ship sail above a *gaff* or spar. See **Topsails, tolt**.

galin [GAY-lihn] to be hyperactive, scamper about, as in *Cats bes aaweez* **galin** *fore a starm.* "**Hyperactive** cats forecast a gale." WCE. Note Devon *galley*, Dorset *gally*, frighten, scare.

gamogin [gaw-MAHG-uhn] intenionally deceive someone for personal advantage. *E bes* **gawmogin** *jus t' stay ome fom skoo.* "He **pretends** illness to avoid attending school." See **gamogue**.

gamogue [gahm-AWG] a silly trick. SIE, from Gaelic *gamóg* clown, oaf, imbecile. See **gommy.**

gandy [GAHN-dee] a pancake of bread dough fried in pork fat all topped with **coady**. Note NE **frozie, bangbelly, touton,** *grace cake.*

gannet [GAHN-niht] as in *You* **gannet!** referring to someone who gulps food or to a hyperactive child. From the behaviour of the large northern gannet, *Morus bassanus*, a deep-diving seabird. Brit.

gape [GAYP] to gasp for breath; to yawn.

garden kitchen garden, a small summertime plot for rhubarb, fruit or vegetables for kitchen use; yard.

garden party [GAHR-uhn PAHR-dee] annual summertime church parish event of games, eating and fund-raising, now evolved into community celebrations or "*Day(s)*," such as the St. John's Regatta. NE.

gardless anyway, in any case, nevertheless.

garnsey, gansey [GAHRN-zee], [GAHN-zee] a woolen roll-neck sweater. From Guernsey, British Channel Isles off France. Note NE **jumper**.

Garnteed! [gahrn-TEED] affirmative expression: certain; surely, for sure. See **sure (an)**.

gaze [GAYZ] a rock-pile blind from which one hunts game birds. Note ME *gaze* long look.

G'day [guh-DAY] Good day.

G'deevn [guh-DEEV-uhn] Good evening, Good afternoon, Good night.

gelt [GEHLT] gold-coloured metallic paint. Note Dorset *gilt*, golden-coloured.

gert [GEHR?] great, huge, big, *E buildeed a **gert** big ouse.* "He built a **huge** house." WCE. Note Dorset *girt*, great, big, Devon, *...a gurt bunch o' myrrh...* (SS 2.14), and Sussex, *...terrubul as an army wud gurt flegs.* (SS 6.4)

get long wid coexist with, maintain friendly terms.

get faired av get a haircut or trim. *Jonas **got faired av** f' d' toime t'noight.* Note NE **fair op**.

get (a-)hold ov contact as in *E a'n't **got a-hold ov** er yet.* "He hasn't **contacted** her yet."

get-t'gedder [GEHT-tuh-geh-duhr] a house party. Also *breaker-down*. See NE **toime**.

giddy [GIHD-dee] dizzy; foolish. *Woine makes oi roight **giddy**!* SEI. Note Irish *giddy* giggly, lighthearted. Note Leics. *giddy*, the reeling about of sheep from *the gedd* brain parasite.

gig [GEEG] sign of life; a soft sound. *O Pish bes some good dog, naer a **gig** out ov en.* SEI, from Gaelic *giog.* Irish.

gilderoy [GIHL-duh-roy] vain, conceited, or arrogant person. SEI, from Irish Gaelic surname *Mac Giolla Rí* "son of the king's servant." Irish.

gilguys [GIHL-guehz] trinkets; showy attire. From sailing ship term for a temporary guy rope.

gillycup buttercup (*Ranunculus* spp.), a small, yellow, toxic field flower. Also *gilleap*. WCE. Note Dorset and Devon *gilcup* or *giltycup*. From *gilt*, golden-coloured (see NE **gelt).**

girl   woman's direct address to woman friend, *Yes, **girl**, oi be oer bumbye.* See **maid**. Note NE **babby, daw, ducky, luv**, and Brit *luv, honey, sweetie, my dear.*

give er, give'r   [GEE-vehr] exert an effort: *Take dis mallet an **give er!*** "Take this mallet and **hit it hard!**"

glander   [GLAHN-dehr] coughed-up phlegm. *O Tom awked op a **glander**. Got d' flu, e did, an andy bout doied.* Note London Cant *glanders*, mucus "at (Horses) Noses..." From *glanders*, a horse disease from OF *glandres* swollen glands.

glance (av)   [GLAHNS awv] bounce (off), as in *Da idle devilskins **glances** es baa **av** o' d' loffen evy chance e gets.* "The rascal **bounces** his ball **off** the ceiling at every opportunity." WCE, from late ME weaponry *glancen* a glancing blow, from OF *glacier* to make slippery.

glass   [GLAHS] aneroid barometer. *D' glass is down. Starm comin!* "The barometer indicates that a low pressure weather front is approaching." After British Admiral Robert "FitzRoy's storm glass" of the mid 1800s, a sealed glass tube of specific ingredients in water; resulting crystal patterns within were used to forecast weather.

glassen   [GLAHS-uhn] made of glass, as a teapot. ME "of glass" from OE *glaes* glass, amber. Note ME *brasen* (OE *braesen* of brass), SE *wooden, woolen,* "of wood, of wool."

glean   [GLEEN] smirk; show a smug, self-satisfied grin. WCE, from Dorset *glean*, sneer. Note Irish Gaelic *gean* a smile.

glitter   [GLIHD-dehr] any ice-glazed surface after freezing rain. WCE, any frosted surface.

glutch   [GLUHCH] to swallow, especially with difficulty. WCE, from Dorset *glutch*, gulp.

G'marn   [guh-MAWRN] Good morning.

go   tolerate, accept, be brave about, do; eat: *Oi can't **go** her brewis.* "I **dislike to eat** her fish-and-brewis."

go av   [GOH awv] spoil, as of food. Brit. See NE **fousty, smatchy**. *Da yeur's moose meat bes **gone av**;* **-to**, a change of weather or wind direction, *She ull **go av** t' saudard and rain b' marn.* "The wind will **become** southerly and it will **turn to** rain by morning."

gob   [GAWB] the mouth (derisive). WCE, from OF *gobe* "mouthful" influenced by Irish *gob* "mouth." Note London Cant *gob*, "the Mouth." Australian *gob* mouth. See NE **faace**.

go board (ov)   [GOH BOHRD] chastise, reprimand. *D' revern went board Jake f' makin swish.* "The minister **criticized** Jake for making bulled liquor." Note *board* (besiege) a ship. Note NE **tongue-bangin**, **loine** (s.o.) **av, come board.**

gob ov, a–   [GAWB uhv] a bit of, some, an unspecified amount of something, especially a fish catch. See **gob**.

go dog fer   to be a helper for someone. NE.

go fer a run   take a short drive, go "cruising." Note NE **dodge, dart**.

go good fer   financially co-sign for, or legally or personally support someone else: *Johnny wud'n ave got es car eef es fadder di'n go good fer en at d' bank.* "Johnny would not have got his car if his father had not **co-signed a bank loan** for him."

go good wid   complements, adds to, enhances or completes. *Dat toie goes good wid yer suit.*

goin on...   [GOHN AWN] during, for approximately, as in *Skipper a'n't ad nar chew o' baccy goin on tree weyks.* "The old gentleman had no chewing tobacco **during nearly** three weeks."

goin (on) fer...   [GOHN fuhr] approaching or nearly (hour), as in *She's goin fer a'pass two* (o'clock). "It's nearly two-thirty." Also **aamos, noigh (on), andy bout.**

goins-on   [GOH-ihnz-awn] fuss, wrangle, complicated argument, snarl or muddle. *Well, wha' a goins-on down on da wharf when d' coast boat come een.* WCE, from Dorset *gwains on*, behaviour, happenings. Note NE **kick about.**

go long wid   [GOH LAWNG wihd] agree with, accept: *Free beer? Oi ull go long wid dat!*

gommy, gommil   [GAW-mee], [GAW-muhl] gaping fool. Also *gom* [GAWM]. SEI, Gaelic *gamal* stupid looking fellow. Irish. Note Wexford Yola *gom* fool, idiot; Scots *gommy* simple-looking, idiot; Leics. *gomeril, gawney* fool, simpleton. Note Dorset *gummy*, clumsy, thick. See **gamogue**.

gone away to   lost body weight, become thin: *Clem is gone away t' nodding fom ard work.* Note **rake.**

gone fer, (fair–)   longing for: *We'm fair gone f' some brewis.* "We **long for** fish-and-brewis."

gone out, (aa–)   out of style, discontinued, old-fashioned; *Dat koin o' cloz bes aa gone out now.* "That style of clothing has become old-fashioned."

goowiddy   variously applied to sheep laurel, red oiser dogwood, rhodora and other similar often toxic, low, flowering shrubs of the bog or barrens. Also *gould withy, gouldwoody, goowoody, goudy/goudie, goodwithy, goldwithy, gowithy, goldleaf* and *lambkill*. From the blooms's golden pollen and from WCE (Devon) *withy, widdy*, a flexible willow stem. Note NE **Injun tea**.

go av   spoil, as of food. Brit. See NE **fousty, smatchy**. *Da yeur's moose meat's **gone av**.; – **to**, a change of weather or wind direction, *She ull **go av** t' saudard and rain b' marn.* "The wind **will become** southerly and it **will turn** to rain by morning."

go on   [GOH awn] rely or depend on, agree with, usually used negatively: *Ya can't **go on** da wedder forecast.*

go souse   [GOH SOWSH] to go plunging into water; also *go souso* [SOWSH-oh]. Note Leics. *sosh* dunk, drench. Note NE **douse**.

got a jag on   See NE **jag**.

go t' couche   [GOH tuh KOOSH] to go to bed for the night. From FR *coucher* "to go to bed." Also *alley-couche* [AHL-ee KOOSH], *couch-couch* [KOOSH-koosh], **turn een**. Note London Cant *couchée*, an evening reception that "attended the King at his going to Bed."

go t' work an   make preparations and do something. *Mus' **go t' work an** fix me roof.* "I have to **get things ready and** repair my roof." See NE **mus go an**.

gowdy   [GOW-dee] awkward.

grace   [GRAYS] herring oil, rendered salt pork fat used in frying **bangbelly**; margarine; gravy. WCE. See **sulick**.

grace faace   [GRAYS FAAYS] birthday custom, a well-wish greasing of the nose with butter so to lubricate the celebrant's entry into a new year and avoid bad luck. See NE **d' bumps, grace**.

greens   boiled leaves of cabbage, turnip or dandelion. Also *turnip tops*.

grizzly wedder   damp, foggy weather. Note **caplin wedder**.

grog   a small alcoholic drink. From "Old Grog," Admiral Edward Vernon, (1684-1754), and his habitual grogram cloak, who in 1740 issued his seamen only diluted rum. Brit. Also *toddy*, **twig**. Note Australian *grog* alcohol.

groggy   *sleepy*.

gross   [GROHS] disgusting, ugly, awful. WCE, from Dorset *gross*.

grounds   a fisherman's squid or cod fishing area. Also **banks**. Note **shoal**.

growler   a dangerous iceberg likely to capsize (and potentially wreck any nearby vessel). Note **pillar, pinnacle**.

grub   food, foodstuffs; a meal. Note WCE Devon *grubbish* hungry. Note NE **prog**.

gruel   [GROOL] oatmeal porridge. Also **mush**.

gruffy   a toadfish or sculpin (*Myoxocephalus scorpius*). Also *scopie* [SKOH-pee], *scopim* [SKOHʔ-uhm], (*whip*) *gubby*.

grumpus   [GRUHM-puhss] a whale; from *grampus*, killer whale from ME *graspeys*, from OF *graspois* salted whale meat.

guess cake   five-penny auction cake won by the bidder who can guess the object baked inside. NE.

guff   insolence. From imitative. Also **sauce**.

gulche   [GUHLCH] originally jocular for pothole in a roadway. "…unless something is speedily done, in the way of filling up the 'gulches' traffic will be at a standstill" (*St. John's Evening Telegram*, February 19, 1880). From American English *gulch* deep ravine, from *gulsh* sink down (land), from ME *gulchen* gush out, drink greedily. Replaced by "pothole" under 1940s Canadian and American Military presence influence. Note NE *glutch*.

gunny   to size up something, take the measure of.

gunshot   a rough measure of a short distance, about fifty yards (46 m).

gurry   fish offal; unprocessed seal oil. See **slub**.

gurry kid   Wooden container secured or built on deck of a banker to hold gurry. Also *gurry pot*.

gut-foundered   very hungry. Note London Cant *gut-foundred*, "exceedingly Hungry." Also **ravness**.

gut out   make empty (a room): *Oi mus' gut out Marie's room fore oi paints en.* "I will have to **empty** Marie's room before I paint it."

Guy Fawkes Night   See **Bonfire Night**.

Gwan! (b'y!)   Is that so! No! (expression of disbelief). Also *Gway (wid ya)! Gway (b'y)!* Note Somerset *g'woam* going home, Dorset *gwain*, going.

H

Note: As in the West Country UK dialects, Newfoundland English initial [H] is unstable and, in connected speech, may be silent. Alternatively [H] or [Y] may be heard before words beginning with a stressed vowel, depending on speaker and dialect area. Familiar Standard English items defined below are those most likely seen in print with an initial "h."

handbag [AHN bahg] lady's purse or bag. Brit.

hand lines [AHN-luehnz] manual fishing lines having cod hooks attached. Also *sudlines*. See NE **jigger**.

hangishore See NE **angishore**.

hapse See **apse**.

hard liquor distilled alcoholic beverage (rum, whiskey).

hard tack See **ard tack**.

harp [AWRP] type of seal, *Phoca groenlandica*. From its harp-shaped markings.

hawl [HAWL] awl, a leather hole punch tool.

heads, eeds [EEDZ] heads or knitted ends of a lobster trap.

hengine [HEEN-juhn] a fuelled internal combustion power device; train locomotive. See **make'n'break**.

hot toddy [awt TAW-dee] a drink of whiskey, hot water, and sugar. Brit. from *taddy*, Hindi for a hot, spiced concoction with fermented palmyra juice, from Sanskrit *tala–s*.

hoven [HOH-vihn] oven.

human wind gauge **Wreckhouse**-born Lauchie [LAW-kee] MacDougall, a weather-sensitive trapper-farmer of Scots descent. Officially advised safe train and truck passage through extreme **Wreckhouse** winds by telephone, 1939–1965. His wife, Emily, continued to 1972 until replaced by wind sensors and, later, electronic signage.[20]

hit, it See **it**.

hurts [UHR?S] blueberry (*Vaccinium angustifolium*). Also *ground hurts* also used for tundra bilberry (*V. uliginosum*) and the small lowbush hurts (*V. boreale*). Hurt first used in *A Report of the Voyage and and Successe ... by Sir Humphrey Gilbert* by M. Edward Haie, 1583. From Brit. *whort/wort* "plant," from OE *wyrt* "root, herb." Note WCE *hurts* (similar blueberry *V. myrtillus*).

I

id'n [IHD-uhn] am/is/are not: *Oi **id'n**, ya **id'n**, e/she **id'n**, we **id'n**, yiz **id'n**, dey **id'n*** as in *Oi **id'n** jannying dis Christmas.* "I **am not** mummering during this Christmas season." WCE and SEI. See **'tid'n**, **'twud**, **'twud'n**.

idle [HUED-uhl] mischievous, naughty.

ignevity [eegh-nuh-VAI-dee] a very hard, durable wood used to make belaying pins, dory rollers and other sailing ship gear. From *lignum-vitae*, a Caribbean and S. American trade ironwood.

ignorant [HEEG-nihr-ehn?] rude, ill-mannered, inconsiderate. Note Irish *ignorant* rude.

Indian cup [EEN-juhn kohp] See **fisherman's basket**.

Injun tea [EEN-juhn TAY] Indian or **Labrador tea**, a clear, somewhat narcotic and toxic tea-like beverage brewed from evergreen boglands and tundra species *Rhododendron groenlandicum* and *R. tomentosum*. The sticky bloom is a small, low, white cluster. Also **crystal tea**. NE. Medieval Europeans brewed both plants to make a herbal beer before hops use. Note NE **goowiddy**.

inshore [(H)EEN-shohr] operated near shore, as in small-boat family coastal fishery, as opposed to large-vessel *offshore* commercial ocean fishery.

io [EE-oh] hill, knoll, promontory, incline.

is [(H)EEZ] present tense verb form of to be (SE *am, are, is*), as in *oi **is**, ya **is**, e/she **is**, we **is**, yiz **is**, dey **is*** and contractions *oi's*, *y'is*, *e's*, etc. Note NE **bes**, **'m**.

ist [(H)AIST] raise, lift, hoist. *T'is dat warm e ad t' **ist** a winder.* "It is so warm that he had to **raise** a window."

it, hit [IHT], [HIHT] *It* persists from ME *hit* under the influence of Irish and SE to refer impersonally to neutral things that cannot be counted: substances, events, situations, and abstractions. It is represented by set phrases, **t'is** "it is," **t'was** "it was" **t'id'n** "it is not" etc. Traditional NE otherwise shows two genders: see **e** and **she**.

itchy palms See **pishogue**.

J

jackeen a mischievous boy, young rascal. Also *devils pelt*. See NE **devilskin**.

jackatar Newfoundlander of mixed French and aboriginal Mi'kmaw descent. From dialectal Brit *Jack Tar*, sailor (from *tar*, sailor, from wooden sailing ship practise of tar waterproofing). Also *jacky tar*. Pejorative term.

jag [JAYG] as in the phrase *got a jag on*, walking unsteadily from drink.

jake to stay out all night.

janders [JAWN-dehrz] as in *yellow janders*, jaundice. WCE, from Dorset *janders*, jaundice.

janny [JAHN-ee] a mummer. OE *johnny*, fellow. Also *jenny, teak*. NE. See NE **jannying**.

janny-talk high-pitched disguised vocalization using in-drawn (ingressive) breathing, beginning with the usual request *Ar mummer lowed een?* "Any mummers allowed to come inside?"

jannying [JAHN-ee-uhn] visiting friends and neighbours using **janny-talk** in Halloween-like disguise from Christmas Day to **Teak Day**. *Mummering*. NE. See **mummer**. Note: not to be confused with the *belsnickeling* tradition of central Nova Scotia (New Ross area) or of Pennsylvania or the Virginias, USA.

jeez [JEEZ] intensifying adjective; accursed, damnable. *Loss me jeez moose down een da alders!* NE. Note **bluddy**.

jeezler a disorderly fellow, hooligan, ruffian. See NE **case, ard case, ral**.

jigger [JEEG-uhr] one or more unbaited and lead-weighted hooks suspended from a **hand line** to catch **cod** or squid by snagging them in quick, upwards jerking or "jigging" motions.

jigg's dinner [JEEGZ] a Sunday evening meal of pickled salt ("corned") beef or riblets with boiled potatoes, carrots, cabbage, turnip, and homemade **pease pudding**. From the preferred meal of Jiggs, an Irish-Catholic character in the long-running (1913-2000) American comic strip by George McManus, *Bringing Up Father*. Also *salt beef an cabbage* or *boiled dinner*. See **dinner**.

jine [JAIN] engage in sexual intercourse. WCE. From ME *join*, from OF *joindre* "join, connect, unite, engage in sexual intercourse." West.

Jingo! (b'–) [JIHNG-goh] euphemistic expletive "by God!" Note NE **b'juice, begob**! Note Leics. *by Jingo*, Australian *Jingoes*! "Wow!"

jinker [JEENK-uhr] one who beings bad luck. WCE, from ME *jyng* an incantation, ultimately from Latin and Greek *iynx,* a wryneck (*Jynx torquilla*) a Eurasian woodpicker used in witchcraft and divination.

jockey-club one-flowered wintergreen (*Moneses uniflora*), a temperate forest flowering herb.

jogging slowed sailing. *D' Skipper jogged wid d' sails sot t' wait on d' dorymen out on da wadder.* "The Captain **tacked into the wind with the sails arranged to await** the ocean dorymen jigging for cod."

jollyboat [JAWL-lee bohʔ] a small vessel convenient for rough work or minor tasks. WCE from ME *jolywat* a ship's small boat. Note **bumboat.**

jole [JOHL] to grab or clutch the throat of, to choke or strangle: *Oi wud a' joled en f' stealin' fom me rabbit slips.* "I would have **strangled** him for stealing from my rabbit trap line." WCE, from ME *cholle* "under-jaw" from OE *ceole* "throat," influenced by ME *chawl* "jaw" from OE *ceafl* "jaw."

jug pitcher, jar. WCE, from *jugge.*

juice [JOOS] electricity; ignition spark in boat or car engine. NE.

juice!, (b'-) [JOOS] exclamation. Brit "by deuce!" ("by Zeus!"), euphemistic form of "by God!" Note NE **begob, jingo.**

July Drive The July 1 offensive of the First World War opening the first battle of the Somme in 1916, remembered as the "big push" of the British Army when the Newfoundland Regiment suffered great casualties at Beaumont Hamel. Long thereafter many Newfoundland fishermen would take the afternoon off, festoon their boats with flags and take their wives and families out for a memorial picnic.[25]

jumper sweater. Note NE **garnsey**. WCE, from *jump* short coat, from FR *jupe* skirt, from Arabic *jubbah* loose outer garment. Note NE **garnsey.**

junk [JUHNK] a short log for a wood stove. WCE. Note Dorset *chunk*, piece of wood; Leics. *chunk* tree stump.

junk, co– See NE **co junk.**

jus a' soon [JEHS uh SOON] would rather, prefer instead: *Oi jus a' soon not go t' work t' day.*

jut [JUHT] to hit the elbow of another. WCE, from Dorset *jut*, nudge someone.

K

keen [KAYN] cold, crisp, clear: *T'was a keen day f' teelin rabbit slips.* WCE. Note Wexford Yola *keen* sharp.

keener clever or witty person. Note Irish *keener,* professional funeral lamenter, from Irish Gaelic *caoineadh* to wail for the dead.

keep a-olt ov [KAYP uh-HOH? uhv] retain; hold for: *Oi ull keep a-olt ov dis money fer ya, aaroight?*

keep-e-goins [KAYP-uh-gohnz] small firewood gathered to supplement one's winter supply. Also *keep-a-goins, kippy-goins.* NE. Note: NE **bavin, brishney, faddle**.

keepin ouse in the position of **ousekeeper**.

keg, kag [KAYG] small wooden cask used as a fishnet or cod trap buoy.

kick about, a- consternation, disturbed reaction: *Dey roised a wunnerfo **kick bout** Matty's moonshine.* "They were **very alarmed about** Matty's moonshine." Note NE **goins-on.**

killick [KIHL-ihk] small anchor-stone enclosed in a wooden frame, as in *Douse d' killick.* "Drop **anchor**"; also *kellick, killock, kellegh.* Note Dorset *killick stwone,* fisherman's anchor, Irish *killech* killick, and Scots *killick,* anchor fluke.

kinkarn [KEENK-ahrn] "Adam's apple," windpipe, throat. WCE, from Dorset *keakharn,* windpipe. Note NE **craw, weasand**.

kipper a smoked herring. WCE, from ME *kippered* (cured by cleaning, salting and spicing), from OE *cypera* "male salmon" influenced by ME *kip* a male breeding salmon's hooked lower jaw.

kippin [KIHP-pihn] short, small slender stick. SEI, from Gaelic *cipín* small kindling; a trifling thing. Irish.

kiss d' cod part of the **screech-in** ceremony of an "Honourary Newfy" first-time visitor to Newfoundland.

klick the stiffening at the back of a shoe.

knap [NAHP] a small rounded isolated hill, hummock. WCE, from Dorset *knap,* hillock, from OE *cnaep,* knob. Note Wexford Yola *knapp* knob, bunch, thick button. Note NE **tote,** *tolt.*

kneebens [NEE-behnz] genuflection or kneeling in religious reverence. From "knee bends" term of certain evangelical churches. NE, Central.

knit [NIHT] gave birth to, as in *Who knit ya?* "Who is your mother/are your parents?"

knobs [(PIHP-mihn) nawbz] a type of humbug or bull's eye hard-boiled, white, mint candy with raspberry-flavoured red stripes, once readily available in British Commonwealth countries. Also *nobs*.

knock av ·[NAWK AWV] quit, finish, end as in *We knocks av work a' foive.* "We **quit work** at five PM"; *Knock av!* "Stop annoying me! Quit it! Stop that!" Note London Cant *knock-off*, to abandon one's position or lifestyle.

knocked [NAWKT] accomplished it, reached success, on easy street, as in the phrase *got'er knocked. Won d' lotto, eh? Got'er knocked now, b'y, got'er knocked f' shore.*

komatik [KOH-maw-tehk] sleigh, sled on runners. From Labrador Inuttut/Inuktitut *qamutik*.

konk [KAWNK] to blow the nose loudly.

knowed [NOHD] knew, past tense of to know: *Oi knowed t'was gonna rain!* NE.

known [NOHN] exceptionally perceptive, aware, knowing; well trained. Said of unusually attentive and familiar animals. *Me o dog, Skipper, was some known. E knowed whaaer oi was tinkin.* "My old dog, Skipper, was very **perceptive**. He knew what I was thinking." WCE, from ME *beknown* aware of.

knows__not__eider [NOHZ...AI-dehr / EE-dehr] to be confident that, ironically stated. *Oi knows e not fom opalong eider, way e talks!* "I **am sure that** he is from mainland Canada by the way he speaks."

kronk [KRAWNK] pridefully or carelessly leaving one's throat open to the cold wind, doing without a scarf. *Don' y' be goin out een d' co wid yer troat aa kronk.* Note Leics. *crank* sick, ailing, German, Dutch *krank* [KRAWNK] sick.

L

Labrador, d'- [DUH lahr-bah-DOHR] the usual designation for the mainland portion of the province. Land granted there to explorer João Fernandes by Henry VII at about 1500 was shown on later maps as *Terra Laboratoris*, "land of the *lavrador*," (Portuguese for "landholder"). Also the Harrington Harbour area on the Basse-Côte-Nord shore, Quebec.

Labrador, on d'- commercial summer fishing along the coast of Labrador and off Harrington Harbour along the Basse-Côte-Nord shore of Quebec.

Labrador sloice [lahr-bah-DOHR SLUEHS] an extra-thick slice of bread.

laddin lamp a large ("Aladdin's") lamp. Also **tellylamp**, **flirrup**, *stand lamp*, **carrychurch**.

Lady, me- [mee LAY-dee] after the Western Charter of 1634 the required address to the Rear Admiral, a non-naval claimant to general seasonal governing privileges by being second or third British captain in a harbour or fishing room. See NE **me Lard, room**. NE. Note NE fish merchant.

laid op [layd OHP] temporarily ailing, injured or otherwise restricted to inaction or confined. *Ontoimes ee bes laid op on d' daybed from es rheumatiz.* "On occasion he is **indisposed** and laying on the sofa due to his arthritis."

lake [LAYK] leak in a boot, boat, bucket or auto tire. Note NE **pond**.

lanch [LAHNCH] lance or cut the skin with a lancet to release infected matter as from a boil. WCE from OF *lancette*, a small lance or spear. Note Leics. *launch*.

landsman [LAHNZ-mehn] initially a fisherman based on shore; one of a seasonal "winter crew" left to tend shore properties; 1800–1900s land-based seal hunter. Note NE *livyer, floater*.

lanwash [LAHN-wawsh], [LAHN-wahrsh] beach, shoreline. Also *lamwash, lanwatch, lamwatch*.

lap to fold over or under: *Lap dat clot unner yer buns.* "**Fold** that cloth under your loaves of bread." Note Leics. *lap* wrap.

larburd [LAHR-buhrd] the left, wharf, port or loading side of ship showing red navigation light. WCE, from ME *laddeborde* (*ladde*, cargo), opposite the *steorbord* side (to avoid damage the side-rudder was never docked against the wharf.) Note NE **starburd**.

Lard, me- [mee LAHRD] after the Western Charter of 1634 the required address to the "lord (of the harbour)" or Fishing Admiral, a non-naval claimant to general seasonal governing privileges by being first British captain in a harbour or fishing room, duties (policing, magistrate, performing marriages) often determined by whimsy or vested interest. NE. See NE **me lady, room**. Note NE **fish merchant**.

Lard liftin/lifteen! euphemistic expression of annoyance or frustration. *Lard liftin, dem floiys bes tick round yere dis toime o' noight!* Note reference to the Ascension, Acts 1:9, "...He [the Lord] was lifted up while they were looking on, and a cloud received Him out of their sight."

larn [LAHRN] to cause to learn something; teach. *Granfer larned Joey ow t' mend es nets.* WCE, from ME *leren* teach, learn, from OE *laeran* teach, influenced by OE *leornian* learn.

lashins [LAH-shuhnz] plenty, a great amount: *lashins o' caplin.* Note WCE *laceing, lacer* huge. Note NE **loike flies, maggoty, tick.**

lass goin av [LAHS gohn avv] at the end of a sequence of events, finally. ***Lass goin av****, affer tree days, e painteed d' pantry whoite.* Note **firs goin av, goin on**.

lassy tea [LAHS-see TAY] tea sweetened with molasses.

lassy loaf LAHS-see LOHF] a bread slice with molasses spread. As in *a bit ov **lassy loaf***. A bread slice spread with molasses, then butter on top, often eaten by children who first gnaw away the bread to savour the large, sticky, sweet wafer remaining. Also *lassy bread*. See **loaf**.

Lauchie MacDougall   See **human wind gauge**.

Lauchie's goat [LAWK-eez GOHT] as in *more chew dan ('n)–,* excessively talkative: *Politicians got more chew 'n **Lauchie's goat**.* "Politicians are **extremely long-winded**."

lay ois on   to recognize, to see: *Oi naer **laid ois on** en op t' dis.* "I've never **seen** him (or it) before."

laysin [LAY-suhn] corporal punishment. WCE, from naval disciplinary *lashing* as with a whip. Note London Cant *lacing* "Beating, Drubbing." Also **trimmin**.

len [LIHN] to loan, lend: *T'is airsome t'noight. **Len** oi yer gansey.*

let-op   an ending, halt, finish: *Rain, rain, an nar **let-op** in soight.*

let ___ sauf go   behave personally negligent from loss of self esteem or respect. *She **let ersauf go** affer d' priest loined she ov on d' road.* "She became **slipshod** after the priest reprimanded her in public."

lessons   day school pupils' homework or study task; specific Bible excerpts. *Da skoo master gived Johnny es lessons t' larn b' d' mar.* WCE, from OF *leçon* from Latin *lectio* a reading.

lifter [LEHF-tuhr] a short iron handle to lift a stove **damper** to insert wood, coal or discard flammable trash bits.

limb (out) [LIHM] to cut off tree branches; to threaten physical violence: *Back av, oi loike t' **limb** ya!* "Go back to the stern, (or) I may **trounce** you." Note Leics. *limb* tear limb from limb.

lippy   impertinent, disrespectful, **saucy, brazen**.

livyer [LIHV-yehr] coastal settler (from *live yere* "live here"), planter. First applied to Labrador Métis, later to those European colonists who remained year-long in fishing settlements. Note NE **bayman, planter, landsman, floater**.

loaf "soft" bread (as opposed to "hard" bread or **ard tack**). Also *bun*, **bannock**.

lob, lawb of little value, worthless; garbage, refuse. Brit. from *loblolly* thick gruel. Also **scroff**. Note London Cant *loblolly*, "any ill-cookt Mess."

lob sauce [LAWB SAWS] thick soup. Note Scouse (Liverpool) dialect *lobscouse* stew, from northern German dish *Labskaus*.

lodge settle, stick, land, situate. *E got a fish bone **lodged** een es weasand.*

loffen [LAWF-fuhn] ceiling. WCE, from ME *lofte* air, sky, attic. Note NE **planchen, planken**.

logans [LOH-gahnz] rubber boots with leather pull tops. A generic term from *Logan*, a U.S. trademark name.

loggy [LOHG-gee] tired and drowsy. WCE. Note Dorset *loggy*, to lag, loiter.

loike, da- See NE **da loike**.

Loike ducks! [LUEHK DUHKS] Not likely! No way! (a child's phrase of denial or refusal).

loike flies [LUEHK FLUEHZ] plentifully, in great number: *Dem jannies was out dis Christmas **loike flies***. Note **lashins, maggoty**.

loike to [LUEHK tuh] will probably, may possibly, could. *Dem hair shocks on dem o skidoos **loike t'** blow when you bes way een d' country, eh b'y.* "The air shocks on old snowmobiles **could** explode when you're far into the woods, I'm sure you agree."

loike ya wud [LUEHK yuh WUHD] as is expected, customary, as: *Oi seen she comin an, **loike ya wud**, oi said ullo.*

loime [LUEHM] to apply **slack** to a fence or other exterior surface. See **slack, slatch**. Also *white-wash*.

loine (s.o.) ov [LUEHN ... AWV] seriously reprimand someone: *Aunt Maggy **loined** oi ov f' walkin on er wet floor.* Also NE **come board o', go board (ov)**; note **tongue-bangin**.

lolly [LAW-lee] floating ice too soft to walk on. WCE *loblolly*, gruel, soup.

longers [LUHN-gehrz] tall thin tree trunks used as fence rails or pickets. NE. Note NE **strouters, wattle**.

longer fence [LUHN-gehr] high fence of **longers**.

longsoide [lohng-SUEHD] near, close to, alongside. Note Cornish English *'longzide*. See NE **ome to, andy to.**

loo the loon (*Gavia immer*), a large table food bird of lakes and inshore seas.

look-een, get a– [LUHK-een] chance, opportunity. *B'y, eef ya comes late, y'ull* **get** *nar* **look-een!**

look-out prospect, outlook. *She's a bad **look-out** f' d' cod.* "The **prospect** for the cod fishery is unpromising." Note Leics. *look out.*

loom haze or mist over morning water.

lops, lop on [LAWPS] small breaking seas in high wind. *A foine lop on da wadder, Skipper, er wha'?* "Rough **seas**, Captain?"

low [LOW] to suppose, reckon. *Oi **lows** e made a far'chun.* Note SE *allow* for "comply," "agree to."

low moindeed [LOH MUEHN-deed] mentally challenged; deranged, insane. Note NE **mental**.

luard, lew [LOO-uhrd], [LOO] leeward, downwind side of ship, etc., sheltered from bad weather. *D' skiff was takin shelter een d' luard o' da island.* See **lun(d)**. WCE, from Dorset *lew*, lee, shelter from wind, from OE *hleow*, shelter, warmth. Note NE **winard, luff**.

luff [LUHF] windward side, sailing into the wind. From OF *lof* or Old Dutch *loef*. Also **winard**. Note NE **luard, lun(d), lundy**.

lug carry or drag a burden along with difficulty. *E **lugged** d' dory op d' bawn aa by eesauf.*

Luh! "Look there!"; look at. ***Luh!** A moose! An we wid nar gun!* WCE from OE *La!* emotive exclamation influenced by ME *Lo!* Look!. Note SS 2.11 in Devon, *Vur, lo, tha winter es past...*, and in Dorset, *Vor, lo, the winter es awver...*

Luh-luh-luh! Expression of surprise or excited amazement at an on-going action. ***Luh-luh-luh**, d' caplin bleachin av d' lanwash!* "**Just look at** those caplin jumping just off the shore!"

lun(d), lundy [LUHN(D)], [LUHN-dee] downwind side, sheltered from wind and bad weather: *Get een d' **lun** 'r y'ull get drowndeed wid d' rain.* "Move to **shelter from the wind** or you will get wet from the rain"; abate, as of wind. *D' starm **lunned** b' marnin.* Note NE **luff, winard**.

luv informal direct address to either sex: *Ow's ya t'day, me **luv**?* See NE **babby, daw, ducky**. Note NE **girl, maid**.

M

'm contracted form of **em** from ME *him*, "him/it," as in *Give'm es cap back, b'y*. "Return his cap **to him**, man."

'm dialectal form of verb "am, are, is, have, has"; see **be**. *We'm ad a noice scoff.* "We **have** had an enjoyable meal." Note *Oi'm* [UEHNG] "I am," South. Note WCE, East Devon *we'm comin'* "we are coming." Dorset *What do ee call you'm doing?* "What do you think you are doing?"

machine general word for an implement, instrument, device, tool. Note NE **chummyjigger**, **wassname**.

mad excessively, a lot, madly: *E was **mad** hungry at d' table.* See **some**, **wunnerfo**.

mad rough stormy with driving rain or snow. See **darty**.

maggoty (wid) [MAYG-guh-dee] plenty of. NE. See **lashins**, **loike flies**. *Andy t' Christmas d' Mall bes **maggoty** wid people.*

maid a girl, daughter, young unmarried woman; informal address to a woman: *Ow bes ya, me **maid**?* See **girl**. Note **babby, daw, ducky, luv**.

maiden vane the Milky Way Galaxy seen edge-on from Earth as a band of stars across the sky.

Mainlander a non-Newfoundland Canadian. See NE **opalong**. Note **comefomaway**.

make a go ov earn a living by, successfully engage in an occupation by doing. *Jake **made a go** o' selling lobster pots t' Mainland tourists.*

make out pretending, pretending to (do or be); *E was jus' **makin out** e was hurteed.* "He was **pretending** to be injured."

make fish to dry and salt cod fish to preserve it.

make'n'break a popular, early type of manual flywheel-start, one-cylinder inboard, small-boat, 4-hp internal combustion engine which replaced sail (or rowing) thus changing the Newfoundland inshore fishermen's routine and lifestyle. So named from the use of its heavy, momentum flywheel to help enable ("make") and disable ("break") the ignition cycle to control power and speed.

make notice ov observe: *Ned **made notice** o' d' sky at duckish.* "Ned **noted** the sky at sunset."

make strange behave as a stranger: *Welcome, an' don't **make strange** een dis ouse!*

mamateek [MAHM-ah-teek] conical birchbark wigwam or tipi of the Indigenous **Beothuk**. From Beothuk *mammateek / mammatik* dwelling.

mang [MAHNG] as in *mang op* or *mang t'gedder*, mix together, assemble or build carelessly: *She manged op d' grub on account we'm so ravness.* "She **threw together** a meal because we are very hungry." Note WCE, *Ii mang un.* "He kneads it (bread)." Note Leics. *mang* a jumble, mixture.

manse residence of non-RC clergy. WCE, from ME *mansion house*. From Late Latin *mansus* dwelling. Note Scots *manse*.

mantel(piece) [MAHNʔ-uhl-pees] a sometimes decorative shelf above a fireplace to display novelty or souvenir items. From OE *mentel* and OF *mantel*, each from L *mantellum* "cloak."

manus a serious crew demand or outright mutiny aboard ship. From Mickey McManus, an Irish mutineer. SEI.

mar See NE **d'mar**.

mark out to draw, sketch, paint, create a likeness by hand. See NE **sketch**, **snap**.

marl saunter, stroll casually, meander. WCE

marn, marnin [MAWRN] morning, *een d'marn* "in the morning, on tomorrow morning." Note WCE Somerset *marnin*.

martle [MAHRʔ-uhl] person, individual, mortal, as in *poor martle* "unfortunate person." South.

mathers See **blueberry hurts**. WCE, from Dorset *mathers*, chamomile, an unrelated species.

mauzy [MAW-zee] misty warm weather (from *muzzy*, hazy); also *muggy*. Note Leics. *mozy* muggy weather, warm and damp.

May bush blasty spruce or fir saplings limbed to near the top and attached to fences or gates and decorated with ribbons or strips of coloured cloth, a Roman Catholic tradition to celebrate springtime on the first day of May, adopted from an ancient pagan Celtic tradition of Beltane. Irish, Avalon.

May snow springtime snow that falls in May, alleged to banish freckles and be a cure for sore eyes and stye (oil gland infection).

me me; my: *Oi got me o car painteed* [PAYN-teed] *tawniers an now she looks loike a hearse.* "I had **my** old car painted very black and now it resembles a hearse." See NE **moy**.

mental [MIHʔ-uhl] mentally disturbed, deranged; stupid. *You'm mental, b'y!* "You're crazy, guy!" Also *go mental* become deranged. Note NE *low moindeed*. WCE, mental, crazy. Note Geordie (UK) *mental* [MIHʔ-uhl]. See NE **cracked**.

Mental, d' - historic Hospital for Mental and Nervous Diseases, St. John's, 1854–1972, today's Waterford Hospital complex. *Enn dem days, people was put een **d' Mental** f' shock tratement on deyr nerves.*

mesauf [mee-SOWF] myself. See reflexive pronouns under **Small Words** on page 25.

Methodist bread See NE **auler's bread**.

midsummer men roseroot, arctic root (*Rhodiola rosea*), a cold-climate, spinach-like plant, variously medicinal, historically an aphrodisiac and girls' true love test (by leaf position). Also *Aaron's rod*, from its tall straight stem. Also habitat-similar *scurvy grass (Cochlearia officinalis)*, in error.

Mi'kmaq [MEEG-mawh] (singular and adjective *Mi'kmaw* [MEEG-maw]) First Nations descendants of the Eastern Woodlands aboriginal Algonquian *L'nu'k* (sg. *L'nu*); inhabitants of Newfoundland island concurrent with, and subsequent to, the **Beothuk** era. From *mi'kmaq* "the friends, allies" from earlier L'nu greeting *ni'kmaq* "my kin." Also (formerly) *Micmac*. Note Algonguian Anishinnaabe (Ojibwe) *Miijimaag* "the Allies" for "Mi'kmaq."

mish [MIHSH] marsh, bog, wetlands. WCE. South. Also *bog meadow*. Note Dorset *meesh*, moss.

misfarchun [mihs-FARCH-uhn] a mishap, accident, as in *a bad misfarchun*. Note Leics *misfortune* an illegitimate child.

misky misty (weather), as in *misky rain*, "light rain."

moin, -s [MUEHN] remember, recall *Oi moins dem good o days*; tend well, care for: *Moin dat choil, now, e don' ave a misfarchun.* "**Tend to** that child to prevent his becoming injured"; take care, be careful: *Moin wher ya puts yer gert feet, b'y!* WCE, from Dorset, *mind*, remind, keep in mind, consider. Note NE **naer moin**.

moight (ave) [MUEHT], [MUEHʔ] may do; could have done. *She **moight** rain.* "It **may** rain." *E **moight ave** sove op fer a car b' now.* "He **could have** saved to buy a car (but didn't)."

monts [MONʔS] months: *Januarymont [JAHN-ree-muhn], Februarymont [FEV-ree-muhn], Marchmont [MAHRCH-muhn], Aprilmont [AYB-ruhl-muhn], Maymont [MAY-muhn], Junemont [JOON-muhn], Julymont [jool-OY-muhn], Augustmont [AW-guhs-muhn], Septembermont [seh-TEHM-buhr-muhn], Octobermont* *[awk-TOH-buhr-muhn]*, Novembermont *[nuh-VEHM-buhr-muhn]*, Decembermont *[dee-SEHM-buhr-muhn]*. Note NE **twowvemont**.

moreish [MOHR-eesh] tempting, producing a desire for more (said of food). *Alice, yer apple poie bes* **moreish***!* WCE. Note Dorset *mworish*, wishing for more. Note Leics. *moorish* ready for more: *Ollus a moorish un, is aour Ned.*

more toime den 'nough [mohr tuehm dehn NUHF] unecessary expediture of time on an unworthy effort. *E puts een* **more toime den enough** *on dat o car ov es.* "He spends **too much time** on his old car." NE.

moretoimes [MOHR TUEHMS] on other occasions: *Sometoimes e fished av Harrington,* **moretoimes** *down een d' bay.* Also *moretoimes dan not* more likely. See **ontoimes.**

mother-in-law door the once popular provision of an otherwise unused external house door specifically for emergency escape only, thus uniquely lacking actual entrance access. So-called in jocular derision of mothers-in-law. A "suicide" door.

moy stressed form of NE *me*, my. *She's* **moy** *car, not yers.* Note WCE Somerset *...moi love, moi vair wuon...* (SS 2.9).

moyn [MUEHN] mine (possessive pronoun). Note WCE Somerset *moi belovad be moine, an' I be hiz.* (SS 2.16).

mudjurine [MUHD-jehr-een] a young herring.

mummer a Christmastime visitor costumed in disguise, a **janny**, *jenny*. Subject to a 20 shillings fine and 7 days in jail in 1861. Note Dorset *mummer*, Christmas visitors bedecked with ribbons and tinsel who reenact King George battling a Turkish knight. Note Irish *mummer*, a person in disguise. See NE **jannying**.

mundle [MUHN-duhl] wooden soup ladle. Note Leics. *mundle* wood utensil to wash potatoes

muggy [MUHG-gee] sultry, damp weather. WCE, from Dorset *muggy*, misty weather.

mug-op a snack with a **mug o' tay**. Note **bile-op**. NE.

mug o' tay a drink of tea (commonly in a mug). See **tay, switchel**.

mush [MUHSH] porridge; also **gruel**. Brit. *mash.*

mus [MUHS] should, had better, must: *Oi* **mus** *write dat down fore oi forgets en.* "I **had better** make that a memo or I will forget it."

mus go (an) [MUHS GOH] give attention to, take leave and do. *Oi* **mus go an** *wadder me flowers.* "I **have to go** water my house plants **now**." See NE **go t' work an**.

myrrh bladder [MEHR blahd-dehr] congealed turpentine resin on fir or spruce trees applied to wounds to hasten healing. From OE *myrre*, from Latin *myrrha*, from Greek *myrrha*, from Akkadian *murru* bitter. Also *murre*.

N

naer [NAH-ehr] never: *Skipper naer bes ome long enough t' see es faace*; not, didn't, as in *Dey naer comed yere da weyk loike dey was s'posed to*. "They **didn't** arrive this week as arranged."

naer aer [NAH-ehr EHR] not at any time. An emphatic negative redundancy: *She naer aer missed Church ar Sunday*. "She has **definitely never** missed any Sunday at Church."

naer blowed t' woke up at: *Nex' marnin we naer blowed t' noigh on nine o'clock*. "We **woke up at** nearly 9:00." Note **blow on, blowed.**

naer moin [NAH-ehr MUEHN] not to mention, even excluding. *E a'n't got woolies een es purse, naer moin dollars*. "He has no lint in his wallet, **not to mention** dollar bills."

naer used to had not done. *E naer used to fish av d' Labrador op to da yeur*. "He **had not** fished off Labrador until this year."

naise [NAIZ] noise. WCE, from Dorset *naise*, noise, uproar, a scolding.

nar [NAHR] no, not one: *Dere bes nar soign o' rain t' day*. WCE. Note Dorset *nar*, never. Note Wiltshire *You be ael foir, my love: thur's nar a spot in 'ee*. (SS 4.7).

nard, nardard [NAWRD], [NAWR-dehrd] relative to the north (wind, weather), northerly.

nardees [nawrd-EES] northeast. See **compass directions** in the **Standard English** section on page 131.

nardeester [nawrd-EES-tehr] nor'easter, northeaster, a severe North Atlantic storm with precipitation and intense, onshore northeast winds.

nar'n [NAHR-uhn] none, neither one. Note WCE Wiltshire *...ael on 'em got twins, an' nar'n on 'em's barren* (SS 6.6) "...every one beareth twins, and there is not one barren among them." Also *nar one*. See **ar'n**.

narry [NAHR-ee] narrow; to make narrow. *E's some narry yere*. "It's very **narrow** here." Note WCE, *Iiz sum naeruh iuh*. "It's very narrow here."

nature   sexual drive; *Sally's* **nature** *bes wha' got she married av so young.*

neck   a narrow harbour entrance; a strip of forest extending into a meadow, **barrens**, or **mish**. Note NE **tickle**.

neider   [NEE-dehr], [NAI-dehr] in addition, too, as well, "in the bargain," "to boot" in a negative context: *E's a sly one, an don' tink e's not crookeed,* **neider**. "He's deceitful and don't think that he's not dishonest, **too**"; neither one, none of them. See NE **eider**.

Newf   see **Newfoundland** (dog).

Newfie Bullet   colloquial reference to the longest narrow gauge rail train service in North America, 1898–1988, running 1,458 kilometres (906 miles) between ferry terminus at Port aux Basques and capital St. John's in twenty-three hours.

Newfiejohn   Dominion capital "St. John's" to Second World War convoy sailors.

Newfie jokes   humourous and often acerbic antidotes, often based on word-play, caricaturing Newfoundland or Newfoundlanders, sometimes in publication by 'Newfies' themselves. Note **black joke**.

Newfy, Newfie   a Newfoundland islander. Previously a potentially pejorative **Mainlander** term. From a jocular reference by garrisoned Second World War servicemen.[21]

Newfy toast   various toasts used in a **screech-in**. Popular example: *"Long may yer big jib draw"* (*jib* a type of sail, *draw* catch the wind).

Newfoundland   [noo-fuhn-LAHN] the oldest British-colonized region of North America; a native water rescue working dog bred for gentleness, size, strength, endurance and loyalty from the **St. John's Water Dog** and Portuguese mastiffs.

Newfoundland pony   a registered (1980), protected breed of small sturdy work horses original to the island derived over 400 years from ponies brought by English, Irish and Scottish settlers.

Newfoundland wolf   The "Beothuk Wolf," a large, white, island subspecies (*Canis lupus beothucus*) of the grey wolf. Colonial government £5 bounties of 1839 resulted in its official extinction by 1930. Subsequent alleged sightings are likely the related and similar Labrador Wolf, one of a dozen later arrivals that include the moose, coyote, mink, chipmunk, snowshoe hare and two mouse species. See **native species**.

Nfld, Nflder   earlier abbreviations for "Newfoundland" and "Newfoundlander". "Newfoundland and Labrador" became official in 2001 and was briefly designated by "NF" in accordance with postal requirements for two-letter abbreviations until changed to "NL" to recognize Labrador.

nipper   a mosquito. NE, from Brit. nip, sharp bite. Note Dorset *nippy*, very hungry.

nipper   a child. WCE, from Dorset *nipper*, a boy hired for work. From OE *cnapa*, boy. Note **wadder nipper**.

nish   [NIHSH] soft, delicate, easily injured. WCE. Note Dorset *nesh*, tender, and Leics. *nesh* tender; dainty; coy, reluctant. From OE *hnaesc* feeble, weak.

noddy   [NAWD-dee] a **bayman** (mildly derisive). Note London Cant *noddy*, "a Fool."

noggin   [NAWG-gihn] small wooden cask or tub; a small enamelled metal mug or cup. Note Leics. *noggin* small drinking mug; small shot of liquor. Note Irish *noggin* wooden mug; a drink measure. Note London Cant *noggin*, "a Quarter of a Pint" of brandy. Note NE **bannikin**.

noice   [NUEHS] acceptable size, as in *T'was a **noice** crowd at d' church*. Also **bess koin.**

noice b'y   [nuehs BAI] (ironically) good fellow, good man. *Nate got sousht agin. **Noice b'y**!* WCE, *noice* ultimately from Latin *nescius* ignorant, unaware, incapable, foolish, stupid.

noice fix   [nuehs FIHKS] unfortunate predicament: *You'm een a **noice fix** wid nar painter f' d' punt.*

noigh (on)   [NUEH AWN] approximately, nearly, as in *Skipper a'n't ad nar chew o' baccy **noigh on** a mont'.* "The old gentleman had had no chewing tobacco **for nearly** a month." Also **andy bout**, **goin on**. Note Leics., *nigh–hand* "likely."

no odds   as in ***no odds**, all d' same* it does not matter, is unimportant. ***No odds** t' me eef she rains er snows.* Also **aa loike**. Note Leics. *odds* difference, opposite, reverse.

norwes   [nawr-WEHS] northwest. See **compass directions** in the **Standard English** section on page 131.

not a bad bit noice   attractive, a positive reaction to something as in *Dat skiff's **not a bad bit noice**.* "That skiff is **quite attractive**." North.

not af bad   [nawd ahf BAHD] an approving reaction to something as in *You looks **not af bad** een dat dress, maid!* "That dress **becomes you well**, girl!" See **not a bad bit noice**.

not easy [nawt AY-zee] perceptive, capable, successful. *Roy got a promotion!* ***Not easy****, eh, b'y!*

not fit! Exclamation of disgust or exasperation about an extremely disreputable situation or person. *Dat streel! She's* ***not fit!***

not fussy ('bout) not fond (of), dislike: *Oi'm* ***not fussy*** *'bout goin out een a breeze o' ween.*

nuk [NOOK] a baby's pacifier. A generic term from the "NUK" pacifier of the German company MAPA GmbH, now NUK USA LLC, a subsidiary of Jarden Corp., USA. (Gerber's "NUK" brand name is used under license.). Also **dumb tit**, *dummy tit*, *dummy.*

nummers [NUHM-mehrz] numbers. Countable measures of time, distance and amount may drop plural **-s** after **da** or a number. *Da yeur oi ben drivin a taxi f' tirdeen yeur.* "This year I've been driving a taxi for thirteen year**s**." Cardinals and numerals are:

one [WAWN]	firs [FIHRS]
two [TOO]	secun [SIHK-uhn]
tree [TREE]	tird [TIHRD]
far [FAHR]	fard [FAHRD]
foive (fi') [FUEHV], [FAI]	fid [FIHT]
six [SEEGZ]	sixt [SIHGZD]
sebn [SEHB-uhn]	sebnt [SIHB-uhnt]
eight [AYʔ], [AYT]	eight [AYʔ], [AYT]
noine [NUEHN]	noint [NUEHNT]
tan [TAHN]	tent [TEHNT]
lebn [LEHB-uhn]	lebent [LEHB-uhnt]
twowv [TWOWV]	twowf [TWOWF]
tirdeen [TIHRʔ-deen]	tirdeent [tihr-DEENT]
fardeen [FAHR-deen]	fardeent [fahr-DEENT]
fiddeen [FIHD-deen]	fiddeent [fihd-DEENT]
sixdeen [SIHGZ-deen]	sixdeent [sihgz-DEENT]
sebndeen [SEBN-uhn-deen]	sebndeent [sih-buhn-DEENT]
eighteen [AYʔ-teen]	eighdeent [ayʔ-TEENT]
nointeen [NUEHNʔ-teen]	nointeent [nuehn-TEENT]
twenny [TWUHN-nee]	twenniet [TWUHN-nee-eht]
terdy [TEHRD-ee]	terdiet [TEHR-dee-eht]
fardy [FAHRD-ee]	fardiet [FAHRD-dee-eht]
fiddy [FIHD-dee]	fiddiet [FIHD-dee-eht]
sixdy [SIHGZ-dee]	sixdiet [SIHGZ-dee-eht]
sebny [SIHB-uhn-ee]	sebniet [SIHB-uhn-ee-eht]
eighdy [AY-dee]	eighdiet [AY-dee-eht]

noiny [NUEHN-ee]　　　　**noiniet** [NUEHN-ee-eht]
unnerd [HUHN-nehrd]　　　**unnert** [HUHN-nehrt]
tousand [TOWZ-ehnd]　　　**tousant** [TOWZ-ehnt]

Note Dorset dialect *one, two, dree, vower, vive, zix, zeven, aïght.*
Note Leics. *wan* 1, *foive* 5, *fift* 5th, *seb'm* 7, *sebn't* 7th, *noin* 9, *noint* 9th, *tent* 10th, *lev'n/lev'm* 11, *leb'nt* 11th, *twelft* 12th, *oonderd* 100, Dorset *zebn* 7.

nunnyfudgen [NUHN-ee-FUHJ-uhn] uncommited, indifferent or capricious person of idle, selfish comforts. Also *nunnyfudger*. Note **angishore**, *slack arse*. From 1500s Brit *nullifidian* having no religion, from Late Latin *nullifidius* from *nullus* none, plus *fides* faith.

O

o [OH] old. Comparison: *o, oler, olest.*

o' [UH] unstressed **ov** of, from. Note SE *o'clock* "of the clock."

O Christmas Day December 25 as celebrated in the British Empire according to the older calendar devised by Julius Caesar's astronomers in 42 BC. The Julian Calendar contained an accumulating annual error only corrected by the newer, more accurate calendar of Pope Gregory XIII in 1582. By 1752, when finally adopted by Great Britain, the Gregorian Calendar required a twelve-day adjustment to match the true position of Earth in its orbit around the sun. December 25 would now occur twelve days earlier than its occurrence on the old Julian Calendar. However, traditionalists retained the Julian "Old" Christmas Day, then January 5, as the end of "Twelve Days of Christmas," a custom still maintained despite the subsequent loss of two more days since the 1700s due to the ever-accumulating Julian Calendar error.

odd occasional, random, casual: *Da **odd** visitor draps by now an den*. Also **scattered**.

odder [UHD-dehr] other. Also *d'**odder** one* the other one. Note NE *nodder* another.

oar eggs sea urchins (*Strongylocentrolus drobachiensis*); also *(h) ozzie eggs, orz eggs, whore's eggs*.

o cock direct address to a male friend: *Ow bes ya, me **o cock**?* Also **b'y, o man, o trout**, *skipper*, *(o)* **son**.

oer [OHR] over, above; about, concerning; overly, particularly, very: *Dey bain't **oer** playsed wid d' new proice.* Note Leics. *ovver* regarding.

offen [AW-fihn], [AW-vihn] often, occasionally.

o hag [oh AYG] Old Hag, waking nightmare or sleep paralysis syndrome. Also *d' hag* or *hag rid* (ridden). WCE from OE *haegtesse* "witch".

Oh, me nerves! Expression of annoyance or frustration. Note **drove**.

oi [AI], [UEH], [OY] I, me: *Oi plays d' carjel, but not noigh as much.* "I play the accordion, but not nearly as often." Note [AWL] may be heard for *oi ul* 'I'll," and [UEHNG] for *Oi'm* "I am," South. Note WCE East Devon *Ai be zworthy but geude-leukin'...* (SS 1.5), and Somerset *... a' stand'th behind our wall.* (SS 2.9).

Oi doies at dat! See **doies**.

Oi'd say! [OYD SAY] "That's for sure!" *Tom bes d' bess boat-builder een d' bay. – **Oi'd say**!* Emphatic agreement phrase. Also *Oi ud say!*

oice candle [HUEHS kahʔ-uhl] icicle. Also *conkerbill*. WCE, from Dorset *ice-candle*, icicle.

olt, (a-) hold, as in *Grab **a-olt** o' dis!* Note Leics. *holt*: *Ketch 'olt!* See **keep a-olt ov**.

omadhaun [OH-mah-dahn] fool; simpleton. SEI. Irish. Also **bostoon**, **chucklehead**, **stun po**.

o man [oh MAHN] genial male greeting; informal or affectionate direct address or reference to one's father or husband: *Woise words fom da **O Man** bes aaveez welcome.* "Good advice from **Father** is always welcome."

ome to [OHM] very near to: *Granfer's shop bes roight **ome to** es ouse.* "Grandfather's work shop is very **close to** his house." Note **longsoide, andy**.

on da wadder [awn daw WAWD-dehr] off-shore, on the ocean, shipboard. Also *on da wa'er* [WAWʔ-ehr].

on d' go [awn duh GOH] happening now, currently trending, as in, *Wha's **on d' go** w' d' b'ys down een d' club d' noight?* "What activity will the guys **be involved** in down at the pub tonight?"; occupied, busy doing something: *Uncle Joe bes aveez **on d' go**, naer stops.* "Joseph **continues to be occupied** without end." NE.

one time [WUHN TUEM] previously, on an occasion. *Oi moins **one time** when oi was on d' Grand Banks...*"I remember **on one occasion** when I was fishing on the Grand Banks..."

one ting an nodder "All things considered..." as in *Tween* **one ting an nodder**, *she's ben a bad yeur fer we fellers.* "**All things considered**, we have had an unprofitable year."

ontoimes [AWN TUEMZ] sometimes, occasionally: *Ontoimes d' toide comes oer da wharf.*

on two moins [awn too MOYNZ] undecided, unsure.

oonshick a stupid fellow; Christmas mummer. SEI, from Irish *óinseach*. Also **bostoon, chucklehead, stun po, omadhaun**.

onny [OHN-neh] only; just. Note Sussex *...she's da onny one of her mother* (SS 6.9).

op [OHP] up, upwards.

opalong [OHP-uh-lawng] further along the coast; by extension mainland Canada, specifically Ontario. Note **comefomaway**. NE.

opalonger [OHP-uh-lawng-uhr] someone from **opalong**, not native to Newfoundland. Also **comefomaway**. NE.

opm, o'm [OH?-uhm] open. *O'm d' tin, we aves some bayns.* "**Open** the can and we'll have beans."

opsot [ohp-SAWT] upset, anxious, disturbed. Note **vexed, opstrapless**.

opstrapless upset, distressed; disrupted. Lnwd of SE folk etymology from SE *obstreperous*. See **vexed, opsot, real put out**.

op t' [OHP tuh] before, until. *Wunnerfo warm* [WAHRM] *op t' dis weyk.* Note **fore, eed ov**.

op t' now [OHP tuh NOW] already, by or before now, previously, by this time. Also **aaready**.

ood, ooden [OOD], [OOD-uhn] wood, wooden. Note WCE Somerset *King Zolomin meäde hiszel a charyet o' th' 'ood o' Lebanin* (SS 5.9).

ood arse wood-horse, sawhorse, sawbuck.

o ooman [oh OOM-uhn] informal or affectionate reference or direct address to mother or wife: *Da o ooman wid eighty-fi' yeurs an stio fer aa a'n't got a whoite air on er eed.* "**My wife** at eighty-five still has no white hair." WCE. Note Somerset *ooman* woman. See **d'ooman**.

Orangemen [ARNJ-mehn] organized supporters of King William of Orange in the overthrow of Irish Catholicism, 1690. Note *The Orange Order, Orange Hall, Orangemen's Day* (July 12th), *Orangemen's Parade, Orangemen's Time* (dinner and dance). SIE.

o trout   direct address to a male friend: *Ow bes ya, me **o trout**?* Also **b'y**, **o man**, **o cock**, *skipper*, o **son**.

ouse, ouses   [OWS], [OWSEHZ] house, houses.

ousecleanin toime   [OWS-klayn-ihn] Traditional spring cleaning. ***Ousecleanin toime** evyting bes aa op een slings.*

ousekeeper   [OWS-kay-puhr] a live-in domestic; a common law wife.

out-migration   the historical migration to mainland Canada of many Newfoundlanders to find employment. See NE **opalong**.

outport   coastal village. See NE **bayman**.

outsoide ov   [owt-SUEHD ohv] excepting, not including. Also **clar ov**, *cep fer*.

ov   [OHV] of, from. WCE. Note Dorset *ov*, of. Note Wexford Yola *ov* of.

ove   [(H)OHV] past of **eave**.

ove back   hindered, delayed, held back, as in *Wedder **ove** we **back** fom settin pots.* "Bad weather **delayed** us from setting lobster traps."

oyster leaf   [(H)OY-stehr leef] a hand-foraged wild-growing leafy herb, *Mertensia maritima*, having an oyster taste, used to garnish seafood or a salad.

P

painter   [PAYN-ehr], [PAYʔ-ehr] a rope for mooring a boat. WCE, OE *pantere* a noose, snare. Note London Cant *painter*, a mooring rope. Note Irish *painteir*, Gaelic *painntear* a net, gin, snare.

pan   small, separate slab of ice. See NE **copy**.

Pancake Day   Shrove Tuesday (from the *shriving* or purging of sins), the last chance to use up forbidden foods before Lent. Objects baked within pancakes (penny, button, nail) predicted wealth, tailor/dressmaker, carpenter, etc. Brit. Also *Pancake Night*.

panch, planch   [PAHNCH], [PLAHNCH] to butcher large game. WCE. Note Dorset *paunch* a cow's forth stomach, from ME *paunche*, from OF *panche*, Latin *pantex* "belly." Note Shakespeare *paunch*, to "disembowel." Note NE **clayn**.

pank   [PAYNK] pant, breath heavily. WCE. Note Dorset, Devon *pank* to pant. Note **wadder panks**.

pantry [PAHN?-ree] traditionally a separate, often small scullery with door also serving for tableware washing and storage. Note London Cant *pantry* "Buttery" (food/liquors storeroom).

pardon? (beg -) [PAHRD-uhn] "What did you say?"

park buns [PAHR? BUHNZ] small bread roll of pork, flour, baking powder, salt, and mixed spices.

partridge [PAHR?-reej] willow or rock ptarmigan (*Lagopus* spp.), native subarctic grouse (the grey "partridge" *Perdix perdix* is Eurasian).

partridgeberry lingonberry or cowberry (*Vacdnium vitis–idaea*), a specific Newfoundland barrens berry, presumably a food source for "partridge" (ptarmigan). This berry has other names elsewhere and shares its name with other species elsewhere.

pawn __ av on deceptively transfer an unpleasant chore or undesirable item to another. *E troide t' **pawn** dat ard job **av on** we*. "He tried to **pass** that difficult chore **off on** us." WCE, ME from OF *pant* something acquired as security; booty.

pease pudding [peez PUH?-uhn/PUHD-deen] or *pease porridge*, a baked vegetable meal of split yellow or Carlin peas, water, salt and spices, often cooked with bacon or a ham joint. WCE, from OE *pease*, from Latin *pisum*, pea. Seamen's *dogsbody*.

peck tiny piece; smallest amount of. *We'm got nar **peck** o' snow da win'er*. SEI, Gaelic *pioc* small bit. Irish.

peckish somewhat hungry, a tiny bit hungry; beginning to be hungry. Brit. Note NE **gut-foundered**, **ravness**. Note Leics. *peckish* hungry; having a good appetite.

peel immature or small codfish. Also *fishpeel*, **tomcod**.

peeze small leak; to leak a little. WCE, from Dorset *peaze*, ooze out, as water. Also *weep*. Note NE **lake**.

pelt to skin a seal; also **sculp**.

penguin, pinwing originally the great auk (*Pinguinus impennis*), now extinct. WCE, from Cornish Celtic *pen gwyn* white head (as applied to the great auk in white winter plumage). Later misapplied to the *Spheniscidae* (today's "penguin") bird family. NE.

people [PEE-poh] one's own family or community; *Brydie bes longin t' go back to er **people***. Also in the phrase *we people*, for NE *we*, SE *us*.

perch a measure of 19.183 feet, or 5.847 metres (lineal); 368.0 square feet, 40.89 square yards, or 155.33 square metres (square or "superficie" measurement). From FR *perche*.

Peter Easton (1570-1619) Atlantic Ocean's richest pirate based at Harbour Grace, Ferryland, and Aquaforte. Retired as Marquis of Savoy on Côte d'Azur.

piddly See **tiddly**.

piggin a 10-lb (4.5 kg.) tub or other container for bailing a boat. From Irish *pigeadh,* an earthen jar. See NE **dill, dip, spudgel.**

pillar [PEHL-luhr] pinnacle iceberg. Note **pinnacle, growler.**

pinchers [PIHN-chuhrz] pincers, pliers. WCE from OF *pinceour.* Note Leics. *pinchers.*

pinnacle [PIHN-nah-guhl] tall slabs or peaks of ice projected upright in an ice-floe. Note **pillar, growler.**

pint [PAINT], [PAIN?] headland, outer end of a small peninsula. *Nar fish ov d' **pint** dis marn, oi lows.* "(There are) no cod (to be caught) off the **headland** (early) this morning, in my opinion."

pip [PIHP] tongue pimple or blister due to a virus or bacteria known as *primary herpetic gingivostomatitis,* a herpes simplex 1 (HSV-1) infection. Brit., from ME *pipen* seed.

piper specifically a tea kettle. Also *keddle.* Brit. Note NE **slut**.

pipkin earthenware cook pot. WCE, North Devon.

pipsi cod or trout preserved without salt by drying completely in the open air. From Inuttut/ Inuktitut *pipsik* dried fish. North, Labrador.

pish [PEESH] common name for a small dog. Brit., exclamation of contempt. See **cracky**.

pishogue [FIHSH-awg] tall tale. *Tokens? Fetches? Da's aa **pishogues**, b'y.* From Irish Gaelic *piseog* [pih-SHOHG] hex, spell, or superstition such as counting magpies (or crows in Newfoundland) to tell the future: "*One f' sorrow, two f' jye* (joy), *tree fer a weddin, far fer a b'y, foiv f' silver, six f' goe* (gold), *sebn fer a secret naer t' be toed* (told)," or having itchy palms: "*left palm 'new money soon,' roight palm 'meet a stranger,'*" others.

piss-a-bed common, edible dandelion (*Taraxacum officinale*). WCE, from Dorset *pissabed,* a potential diuretic, from OE *pissabed,* vulgar for dandelion.

pissarse one who blunders into the way or activity of others; also *pissass.*

pisspoor thing or action exceedingly unacceptable: *Young Addy done a **pisspoor** job fixin me roof. Oi ull be affer needin a bucket drectly.* "Young Addy did a **useless** repair of my roof. I will need a bucket (for leaks) soon."

pitch   tar heated to a temporarily thin liquid to weatherproof a boat or felted roof.

pitch   to land as a bird or aircraft. *Oi jus come to **pitch** yere f' a bit.* "I dropped in briefly."

pitnagen   common swamp aster (*Aster puniceus*). Brewed as a tea, burned for reviving or a ceremonial smudge. Its white roots dried with potato peels make an Indian tobacco substitute. Also *tea-flower*. Note Labrador Innu-Aimun *pituananu* they smoke, or *pituaunakan* place for ashes. NE.

planchen   [PLAHK-kehn], [PLAHʔ-ehn] the floor; a ship's deck. From FR *planche,* floor board, from OF *planke* board, plank, from Late Latin *planca* board.

plank down   [PLAYNK DOWN] pay in a deliberate manner. *Isaac **planked down** twenny dollars fer es supper.*

planken   See **planchen**.

plank'er down   [PLAYNK-ehr] celebrate by dancing energetically; an energetic dance.

planter   settler, pioneer, colonizer. Also (western) *adventurer.* Note Irish *planter* settler. Note NE **livyer, bayman**.

plim   [PLIHM] to swell out of shape, as wood by absorbing water. WCE, from Dorset *plim*, swell. Note Leics. *plim*, swell.

plug   dory drainage hole stopper; a flat, rectangular, chocolate bar-sized chewing tobacco. *Yere, me son, get oi a **plug** o' Beaver down to Uncle John Walter's store.* See **wad**.

plug tobacco   chewing tobacco (as compared to loose pipe tobacco). See **plug**.

pluteed   [PLOO-teed] drunk, intoxicated. Also **sousht, af-cut**. From American English *polluted* drunk.

po, pole   [POH] back of head. *E slurpt an struck es **po**.*

pod auger   [PAWD AW-gehr] the more difficult past without modern conveniences as in *back een d' pod **auger** days*. Brit., from *pod auger,* a manual drilling tool.

poisoned (wid)   disgusted (with someone or something). *Sis was **poisoned** wid 'm f' kickin er cracky.* "Sis was **disgusted with** him for kicking her little dog."

Pom moy so!   [PAWM MUEH SOH] "Really!" "No kidding!" "Is that so!" An expression of surprise or wonder. Literally "upon my soul."

pond lake, pond, any small body of fresh water. NE.

pook mound of hay, hay stack. WCE.

poor sympathetic or respectful reference to a deceased person. *Poor Aunt Mable bes gone dese twenny yeur.* NE.

pram baby carriage, baby buggy. Brit.

prate box [PRAYʔ bawks] chatterbox; busybody. From *prate*, tedious or foolish chatter. NE.

pratie [PRAY-dee], PRAYʔ-ee] potato. SEI, Gaelic *préata*. Irish. See **tatie**.

proud pleased. *She's roight proud t' see en.*

preddy very, as in, *Comfort Cove bes a preddy good place to live.* Note Dorset *pirty*, great. Also *peddy, puddy*. See **some, wunnerfo**.

prise [PRIZE] a lever; to lever open. WCE.

proper t'ing! phrase of agreement. Note Somerset Proper job! Great work, good job done. See **Roight on!** NE.

prog [PRAWG] food; trappers' winter food. WCE, food got by begging. Note Irish *prog* food provisions; steal. Note London Cant *prog*, "Meat." Note **grub**.

prog bag trapper's sack for **prog**. Also *grub bag*.

puddick [PUHD-dihk] a bird of prey. Note Shakespeare *(Henry VI.* III.ii.191; *Cymbeline* I.ii.71; *Troilus and Cressida* V.i.58), *puttock* kite (*Milvus milvus*), greedy scavenger. By extension glutton, then stomach. *When we was onny nippers aur puddicks got lots o' cod liver aal, sir.*

pudding [PUHʔ-uhn/PUHD-deen] blood pudding (meal filler in a sausage skin); Christmas or plum pudding (steamed dome-shaped cake of nuts and fruit); type of thick butterscotch or chocolate dessert. Brit.

puff pig common harbour porpoise (*Phocaena phocaena*) or northern pilot whale (*Globicephala melaena*). NE. Also *puffin pig*.

pug dense moist mud or clay. Note Brit. *pug*, a bargeman of the late 1500s.

pumbly uneven or loose rocky ground making walking difficult. WCE. See NE **bawn**.

pumbly-footeed [–FOOT-eed] unsteady, wobbly in walking. WCE. Note Dorset *pummel-vooted*, club footed.

pump [POHMP] to urinate, *to have a pump*. Also *to make water*. Note Middle Dutch North Sea sailors' *pompe*, pipe, a water conduit.

pump   [POHMP] cajole one's private matters. Note London Cant *pump*, "to wheedle Secrets."

pump ouse   [POHMP ows] men's lavatory or urinal. NE.

puncheon   [PUHNCH-uhn] large wooden barrel of at least 72-gallon (327 L.). From FR *poinçon*. See NE **covel, puncheon tub**. Note NE **cast, butt**.

puncheon tub   barrel cut in half for fishermen's use.

punt   [PUHN?] small in-shore undecked fishing boat. See NE **rodney, dory, skiff**.

purchase   secure footing, traction, grip: *E got good **purchase** on dem clumpers an stayed droy.*

purse   wallet. WCE, from ME *purs/burs* from LL *bursa* leather hide. Note Welsh *pwrs* woman's purse; a scrotum.

put   a boatload of fish.

put d' boots to   to physically attack or assault someone. Irish.

put...een moin ov   remind: *Wha' ya said jus' **put** oi **een moin ov** Fadder Jones.* "Your remark **reminded** me **of** something Father Jones said." Note **moin.**

put't past, wud'n-   See **(w)ud'n put't past**.

Q

queer (h)and   a joker, a wit, an amusing "character," one having unusual behaviour; *Dat Dooley, e's some **queer hand**!* Note NE **card, some b'y.**

quick loike   quickly. *E. ducked een d' shop real **quick loike**.* "He **quickly** stepped into the store."

quid   [KWIHD] a wad of chewing tobacco; the cud. WCE. Note Dorset *quid*, a cud, from ME *cudde* from OE *cwidu*.

quintal   [KAH?-uhl] Brit. 112-pound (51 kg) weight measurement for cod fish. From OF for "hundredweight" from Latin *quintale* from Arabic *quintar* from Late Greek *kentenarion* from Latin *centenarius* "containing a hundred."

quot   [KWAWT] sit on one's heels, crouch. WCE, from *squat* sit on heels, from OF *esquatir* lay flat. Note Dorset *quot* wider than low. See **coopy**. Note **squat**.

R

'r wha'? [uhr WAW?] a rhetorical question tag at the end of a sentence, as in *Ya comin wid me, 'r wha'?* "Will you accompany me, **or won't you?**"

rabbit snowshoe hare (*Lepus americanus*).

rabbit garden small area set up to snare snowshoe hares.

racket, (skin -) a snowshoe. From FR *raquette*, snowshoe, from MF *rachette* tennis racquet from Spanish *raqueta* from Arabic راحات (*rāḥat*) palm (of hand).

rags, on d'- an indelicate, explicit reference to menstruation. A reference to cloth absorbents prior to commercially available feminine hygiene products.

railway, d' the uniquely narrow-gauge railroad track system in Newfoundland, 1898 to 1988.

rake a very thin person, as in *skinny as a rake*.

ral [RAHL] a troublemaker, disorderly fellow. From *ral*, a rioter of the harsh "winter of the rals" of 1817 when provisions were plundered from merchants' stores. Avalon. See **case**, **ard case**, **jeezler**. Note MF *railler to* tease, joke or scoff.

rames [RAYMZ] skeleton, bare bones. WCE, from Dorset *reames* [REH-ahmz], skeleton.

ravel [RAH-vuhl] a short stray length of fine clothing fabric thread. Brit. "broken thread."

ravness ravenously hungry. Also **gut-foundered**.

rawny thin and boney (person or animal).

real put out peeved, upset, annoyed. *Da o ooman was **real put out** oer me boddle o' Screech.* Note **vexed, opsot**.

red Injun a member of the **Beothuk**, extinct (1829) Newfoundland island Aboriginal people, from their cosmetic or functional use of red ochre. NE.

reeve sailing term meaning to pass something through a hole or opening, as of a rope. Note Brit. *reef* to take in or roll up a sail.

rench [REHNCH] rinse, wash lightly. WCE from OF *reincier* to wash. Note Leics. *rench*.

Resettlement Provincial government economic Resettlement Programs 1954-75 which relocated 30,000 residents from 300 outports to larger towns.

retarded   [ree-TAWR-deed] a preposterous, absurd, asinine, or foolish situation. *She bes workin dere aa noight dis mont? Da's preddy retarded!* "She is working all nights there this month? That's **highly preposterous!**" Note **mental, low minded.**

rig out   [REEG-owt] clothing ensemble; arrangement of sails, masts, etc. on a ship. NE.

rind   [RUEHN] bark stripped from the tree; to strip bark from a tree. WCE, from OE *rinde*.

ring op   call or phone someone. Brit.

rinso   a generic term for laundry soap. From *Rinso*, a 1908 UK to 1970s US brand name.

roary-oied   very angry, roaring wide-eyed; also *roary-oied mad.*

roar   [ROHR] a noisy, riotous commotion. *Dere bes some wunnerfo roar down at d' parsonage 'bout white-warsheen d' church,* "There is **pandemonium** at the minister's residence concerning the painting of the church with slack." From 1600s Brit. roar to loudly intimidate others for the purpose of gain, ("We'll roar the rusty fellow out of his tobacco," *A Fair Quarrell* Act IV, Scene ii, Middleton, 1617). See NE **bawl, blear.**

roast leggie   a **cod** fish too small to be filleted so is roasted as is.

Rock, the-   Newfoundland island (**opalong** term).

rock een er killick   pregnant. See NE **killick.**

rodney   a small rowboat, dinghy. See NE **punt.**

roight   [RUEHT] right, correct, proper. *Was you aer roight, b'y* "You were definitely **right,** buddy"; exceedingly, excessively. *Me Da was roight proud t' see oi graduate.* See **some, wunnerfo.** Note WCE, Bristol *Oroit, me old lover?* (a familiar greeting).

roight round   completely encircling. *We goes jannyin roight round da arbour evy Christmas.*

roight on!   [ruehd AWN] expression of enthusiastic agreement made popular by Snook, a local TV comic character of the 1980s. See **proper t'ing!** Note Leics. *roight on* immediately, at once; positively.

rollers   small, grooved, wooden wheels on the side of a dory over which trawl lines are pulled aboard.

rompse   [RAWMPSS] wrestle, rough play. SEI, Irish Gaelic *ramsach* play-fight. Irish.

room   the premises of a fish merchant or allotments of a planter or fisherman with any structures relating to the cod fishery. NE. Note NE **livyer, lard, lady**.

Rose Castle, SS-   one of four large iron ore carrier ships sunk by Second World War U-boats at the Wabana DOSCO iron ore mine on Bell Island. *Rose Castle* and *PLM 27*, torpedoed by *U-518* on its first patrol on November 2, 1942, killed sixty-nine people. *U-518* was sunk on its tenth patrol April 24, 1945, off the Azores by two USS destroyer escorts; no survivors. The *Rose Castle* still lies intact in 35 metres (115 feet) of water.

rote   [ROH?] distant roar of the ocean before a storm. Note Old Norse *rauta* roar.

rounders   an ancient type of ball game considered the origin of baseball. Brit., from *rounder* a posted guard (who makes his rounds).

row   [ROW] loud angry argument, quarrel, commotion. Also **tear op, set to.**

Royal Readers   a series of eight British comprehensive Royal School Series texts from primer to final matriculation, 1870s into the 1900s.

rubber   eraser. *Geh Debbie yer **rubber** t' rub out er wrong answer.*

run   a stroll or leisurely drive. See **go fer a run**. Note NE **dodge, dart**.

rushy   as in the phrase ***dragged trou a rushy***, having a haggard or exhausted appearance. *Get some sleep, b'y. Ya looks loike y' ben **dragged trou a rushy**.* From *rushy* dense brambles or thick rushes, from Anglo-FR *russher* drive back or down, from OF *ruser* "repel, fend off." Note Wexford Yola *rusheen* rushes.

S

-s   invariable verb ending for present tense verbs: *Oi goes, ya goes, e goes, dey goes*, etc.

s'aa   [SAW] merely, simply, just, only: *Oi knows d' place see'n oi blongs dere, **s'aa**.* "I know the place **simply** because I am from there." *Ya wants t' tarment d' poor b'y, **s'aa**.* "You **only** want to aggravate the unfortunate boy."

sabos   [SAW-bohz] humourous reference to shoes or boots. *Mus get me big **sabos** on f' d' snow.* From FR *sabot* clog shoe.

sack ship   a non-fishing, English or foreign cargo ship carrying supplies and fishermen to Newfoundland, dried cod to France, Portugal and Spain, and wine (*sack*) to Britain. Brit.

sally suckers   sheep sorrel (*Rumex acetosella*), open area herb, detoxifying, antibacterial, and edible cooked or raw, found June to October in inferior soils (roadsides, etc.). Also *sweetie* or *sweet leaf*, ironically for its sourish taste, or *Sally cives* from Brit. *sallet* (salad), and from ME *cives* (chives) from OF *cive*.

Salvation Army   A branch of the well-known international quasi-military charitable organization having status of a Newfoundland Christian denomination; managed separate province-wide religious school districts to 1997 and the major urban Grace Hospital at St. John's to 2000.

salt 'n' pepper cap   a traditional Newfoundland visored soft hat typically knitted randomly black-speckled on grey often with a penny knitted into a small knob on top.

sauce   impertinence. Note Leics. *sauce* abuse, and Shakespeare *sauce* to rebuke (*As You Like It*, III v.69). Also **guff**.

saucy   [SAW-see] impertinent, belligerent; also **lippy**, **brazen**. Note *saucy* in London Cant and Shakespeare (28 incidences) impudent, defiant, bold. Note Irish *sauncy* lively, tipsy (of a girl).

saud   [SOWD] south. Note **saudees** [sowd-EES] southeast, and **sauwes** [sow-WEHS] southwest. See 'compass directions' in the **Standard English** section on page 131.

says   [SAYZ] speak, utter, vocalize; pass an opinion. *Oi **says** Elvis bes stio aloive.* See **spakes.**

says (one's) moin   pass a personal opinion. *Oi **says** me **moin** widout da o ooman andy.* "I **give my opinion** unless my wife is nearby." See **spakes.**

scatter ov   as in a sprinkling of snow, flour or other particulate.

scattered   occasional, random: *We gets a **scattered** nipper a' duckish.* Also **odd**.

schooner   fore-and-aft sail-rigged (and occasionally powered) decked wooden vessel of 150 tons up to 700 tons with two or more masts with shorter foremast, first built at Gloucester, Massachusetts, 1713, favoured for speed and fewer crew. From Scots *scoon* "skim or skip along the water," affected by Dutch *sch–*.

scoff   [SKAWFF] a big meal (typically at a house party); informal banquet, **toime, get-t'gedder**. Brit. from *scoff* to eat quickly, from OE *sceorfan* gnaw, bite. Note S. African *scoff* gobble, US *scarf down* gobble. Note **feed**.

scoff 'n' scuff   banquet and dance social event. NE.

scopie, scopim [SKOH-pee], [SKOHʔ-uhm] toadfish or sculpin (*Myoxocephalus scorpius*). Also, *gruffy*, (*whip*) *gubby*.

scrammed numb with cold (as one's hands). WCE, from Dorset *shrammed*, hunching the body from intense cold. Note Dorset *scram*, awkward, clumsy.

scrawb tear with the fingernails or claws. SEI, Gaelic *scrábaim* scratch, scrape, as the skin. Note Irish *scrab* scratch. Also *scrob*, *scrope*.

screech any cheap, high alcohol, Newfoundland beverage; moonshine; **S–** a trade name.

screech-in initiation of a first-time visitor as an honourary Newfoundlander who must wear a sou'wester, kiss a cod, give a Newfy toast, and swallow **screech** (or **Screech** rum); other tasks vary according to circumstance. NE.

screw to press dried cod-fish tightly into wooden *drums* (casks) under mechanical pressure for preservation during export. NE. See **drum.**

screwed fish dried cod-fish **screw***ed* into 128-lb. (58 kg) wooden *drums* (casks). Also **drum fish**. NE.

screwing room area in a merchant's premises to press cod-fish into casks for export. Also *screw store*. NE.

scribbler school student's class notes, practice or work book. NE. Also **exercise**. Note **slate**.

scroff [SKRAWF] a useless thing or person. WCE. Note Dorset *scroff*, small, dead wood leavings. Also **lob, lawb**. Note **dunnage**.

scroop to squeak; a squeak, creaking sound. WCE, from Dorset *scroop*, a low, scraping sound. Also **whizzle**.

scroopy squeaky, rattling, as of an old automobile. WCE, from Dorset *scroopy*, scraping, rasping.

scrumptious [SKRUHM-shehs] delicious, tasty. NE.

scrunchins [SKRUHN-shehnz] crispy-fried cured pork diced fine (ingredient in **fish cake**s, **brewis**, other). WCE, *scrunchings*, broken meat, Dorset *scrunch*, to crunch, as of a dog with a bone.

scuff a dance event, formerly held in a house. WCE, from Dorset *scuff*, shoving one's foot along the floor, from Old Norse *skufa* shove, push aside.

scull school of fish as in *caplin scull*. Note **caplin**.

sculp   to skin a seal; also *pelt*. FR *sculpter* carve.

scun   steer a vessel; careful searching scan. SEI. Irish.

scunned   sown together roughly or quickly, as a fishing net; move a thing easily. *Jack scunned d' boat een on d' bawn roight quick loike.* SEI. Irish.

scunned back   pulled back tightly, as long hair. Irish.

scut   [SKUHT] a mean, stingy person; a tightwad. Note Dorset *scute*, reward, pay.

scutty   [SKUHD-dee] mean, undependable. WCE. Note Yorkshire *scutty* scruffy.

seems t' see   can imagine, can picture (said ironically). *Oi seems t' see her gettin married t' Tom.* "I **think it unlikely** she will marry Tom."

see'n (dat/as)   [SEE-ehn] considering that, because, due to: *E let oi een see'n as oi knowed es fadder.* "He admitted me **because** I knew his father." Also *on account ov, bein (as).* See **beens.**

service, een-   [een SAWR-vuhss] indentured as servant to a household in return for board and **found,** a holdover from the adolescent apprenticeship and servitude practice of post-plague England. Note **servin girl.**

servin girl   [SEHR-vuhn gehrl] a female domestic worker of any age, usually live-in. *Young girls what leaves skoo early bes servin girls.* Note **een service.**

set to   a loud angry argument, quarrel, scene, brawl. Also **row, tear op.**

shag   [SHAYG] common black cormorant sea bird (*Phalacrocoracidae* spp)

shag   exclamation of disappointment. *Shag! Oi los me bess pipe overboard!* Also *Shag dat!* Interrupt or prevent an advantageous or desirable opportunity or activity: *Dis wedder ull shag aur plans f' d' day.* From Brit. *shag* copulate, from ME shake, waggle.

shaver   [SHAY-vehr] a young boy. Brit. Note Leics. *shaver* a keen bargainer; huckster.

she   she, her, as in *Aunt Dot? Oi give she a toimepiece fer er birt' day.* Also "it" on occasion: *Aer ben on d' Lady Luck? She's a foine ship, she is.* **She** usually refers to mobile things (vehicles and vessels), guns, abstractions and capricious situations (weather, conditions, predicaments), and cats. Other countable things and dogs are considered male. See **e, (h)it.**

shed   small, detached workshop, usually firewood-heated, often used for local socializing and to eat a traditional scoff, play traditional music and sometimes dance; a traditional communal party hut. Note **store, shop**.

Sheila's Brush   a final wintry blizzard of around 18th of March, named after St. Sheila of Ireland, an associate (of uncertain relationship) of St. Patrick. Irish.

shell bird   red-breasted merganser duck *(Mergus serrator serrator)*, a table food sea bird; any sea bird game fowl. (*Shell* as in "shot gun shell"). Note NE **birdin**.

shepherd's coffin   yellow rattle, cockscomb (*Rhinanthus crista-galli / minor*), a maritime or alpine, semi-parasitic, yellow-flowered herb. Its ripe seeds rattle in their capsule. NE

shift   [SHEEF] move something. *Dey **shifteed** d' gert big rock av d' road.*

shift oer   [sheef OHR] move to one side (to make room).

shoal   [SHOHL] shallow depth, as in ***shoal** wadder.*

shockin good   excellent, as in *Er fish cakes bes some **shockin good**.* Irish.

shop   a place of business; a work shop. Brit., from OF *eschoppe* booth, stall. Note **shed**, **store**.

shop door   the unbuttoned fly of one's trousers.

shore   [SHOHR] land bordering the ocean; a post to support a house, wharf or stage. Note NE **strouters**.

shuff (av)   [SHUHF] to push aside; **shuff av** [AWV] to push away from, as a boat from the wharf.

shute   a chute of wooden boards to shoot firewood or pulpwood over a hill. Note Dorset *shoot*, a steep hill, a steep road.

silver thaw   [SIHL-vuhr TAW] a coating of clear ice by freezing rain. Note NE **ballycatter**.

singlet   a men's sleeveless, shoulder-strapped, white cotton undershirt. Brit. Note Australian *singlet* vest.

sir, sar   [SUHR], [SAHR] pragmatic marker[12] of a convincing or seriously considered statement or conclusion. *Well, **sir**, oi wud say dis govment ull ave a ard job t' get een agin.* "I **seriously** think that the incumbents will have difficulty being reelected."

sish   [SEESH] a thin layer of new sea ice. NE, imitative.

sish over   to form thin pond or harbour ice.

sithers   [SIHDH-ehrz] scissors. WCE, from a folk "over-correction." Note Leics. *scithers*. See NE **snips**.

skank   [SK AHNK] slovenly lewd, promiscuous, and generally disreputable female. Origin undetermined. Slang lnwd. Note northern England from Norse *skank* limping, lame; Jamaica creol dancing to reggae music by raising legs up high; 1920s American Black English slang for "nasty, ugly, low-life slut" from *skag* lewd girl. See **streel**.

skeet   an unconventional, anti-social or loudly uncouth person of sometimes low repute. Pejorative slang term. From WCE to spit from between the teeth from OE *scitel/scytel* dung from *scítan* to excrete, from Old Norse *skýt-*, stem of *skjóta* to shoot out, throw. Note *skeet* Linc. diarrhoea of animals; Scots *skite* to spray or spit; Manx Gaelic *skeet* a skulking person; ogle, gawk into others' windows. Note **angishore, nunnyfudgen, slack arse**. Related to SE *scoot, shoot*.

sketch (av)   [SKEHCH] to photograph. ***Sketch av*** [AWV] *we tree wid yer new digital camera, eh?* See NE **snap**. Also **mark out**.

skiff   [SKEEF] small one- or two-masted sailing vessel of less than twenty tons; small powered in-shore fisher's boat sometimes with a deck house . See NE **trap skiff, smack**.

skirr   [SKIHR] to hurry. WCE move hastily. Also **een a tear**.

skoo   school. *Li'l Jacky toddles av t' **skoo** evy marn, rain 'r shoine.*

slatch   [SLAHCH] to make **slack**. WCE, from Dorset *slatch*, to make slack. See **slack, loime.**

slack   [SLAHK] lazy; lime and water solution previously used as an exterior paint.

slack av   [slahk-AWV] to alleviate, ease up, relent. *D' rain **slacked av** affer d' sun come op*; become lazy.

slackarse   a procrastinator. Also *slackass, slacker.*

slang   an indiscriminate and disparaging reference to local NE dialect usage. Lnwd, SE *slang* very informal speech, patois, argot, cant, jargon. Also *Newfy talk*. Note **accent, flat talk**.

slate   school student's erasable practice tablet or pad. Also **chaulk slate**. Note NE **scribbler, exercise**.

slauso   [SLOWS-oh] fallen completely into, down, backwards. *Gabe went **slauso**, een d' ditch!*

sleep   [SLAYP] dried rheum deposited in the corners of one's eyes after sleeping.

slieveen [slee-VEEN] a deceitful person, crook. SEI, Gaelic *slighbhín,* sly trickster, rascal. Irish. Note Wexford Yola *sleeveen* deceitful.

slinge [SLIHNJ] avoid work. Brit. loiter. Note **slack av**.

slings, een- in disorder, disarray: *Sadie made bread an leaved d' kitchen een slings*.

slip slipway; wire hoop snare secured across a rabbit pathway, ideally in a **rabbit garden**. See **teel**.

slob [SLAWB] new or soft salt water ice unable to be walked upon. See NE **sish**.

sloide [SLEUHD] a winter activity in which one slides down a snowy hill seated on a sled or toboggan. *D' b'ys went fer a **sloide** down Big Tote*. NE.

sloo move aside. See **veer av, shift oer**. Brit. *slew* turn, swing. from *slued* drunk, from nautical Dutch. Note SE *slew-footed*.

slub [SLUHB] gelatinous slime on fish or gear.

slurp [SLUHRP] to fall to the ground or floor; to slip and fall. *Annie is affer **slurpin** on da oice* [HUEHS].

slut, (ol'-) [SLUHT] flat-bottomed camp kettle. *Put d' **slut** on f' tea.* Also *piper*.

sly conner [SLAI KAWN-nehr] a secretive, tricky person; a small fish (see **conner**).

smack small one-masted decked vessel to carry fish or lobsters to market. See NE **skiff**.

smatchy [SMAH-chee] early stage of food spoilage. WCE. Note Dorset *smatch* a taste. See NE **fousty, gone av**.

smell-boddle [SMEEL-baw?-uhl] leafy white orchid or bog candle *(Platanthera dilatata)*. Also *bog-lily*. NE.

smert [SMEHRT] to smart, pain, sting. WCE, from late OE *smeart* causing a sharp pain. Note **foine**.

s'more t'was pragmatic marker[12] response indicating agreement. *Oi tinks t'is affer rainin. **S'more t'was**, b'y.* "You are **likely correct**."

smut soot; dirt on one's face. WCE from ME *smutten* to defile. Note London Cant *smutty*, "Bawdy."

snacker to shiver with cold. Also *biver, bibber*.

snap a photograph; to photograph (a person, thing). Also **sketch.** Imitative, influenced by *snap* "quick bite."

snapper boat   boat equipped to fish using long lines, a *long-liner*; a small open boat towed behind for lifeboat or other use. West, South. NE.

snarbuckle   hard knot; burnt or charred remnant of food.

snips   a scissors, shears. From Brit. *snippers*.

snock   [SNAWK] a low snapping noise. WCE, from Dorset *snock*, a short, quick knock.

snotty var   old fir tree showing dried sap or resin on its bark. See **var**. WCE.

soak   overcharge, swindle; deceive for profit: *E got **soaked** bad on dat deal.* Brit.

soaker, o−   [oh SOHK-ehr] a large (thus old) fish; a worldly person. Note London Cant, *old soker*, drunkard.

soign   [SUEHN], [ZUEHN] a small bit or portion; little evidence. *Not a **soign** o' wedder*; trail sign of animal presence, as in *rabbit−, moose−*.

some   favourable, *T'is **some** day on cloz!* "It is a very **favourable** day for drying laundry outside"; very, exceedingly, excessively: *Da ween bes **some** shockin co.* "The wind is always **very, very** cold." See **wunnerfo**.

some b'y   adverse judgement, damning with faint praise. *Teddy got took op agin. **Some b'y!*** Note **wha' is ya loike**.

someting nodder   [SUHM-tihng NUHD-duhr] an indefinite or unclear thing or opportunity: *Dem carner b'ys, dey aaveez bes een **someting nodder**.*

some good   [SUHM GOOD] Expression of satisfaction or enjoyment, "very satisfying", as in *Some shockin' good!* or *Some good, tell yer mudder!* Or, as a modifier, *Some good buns you bakt dere, missus!* "Those bread rolls that you baked, madam, are **very delicious**." NE.

son, me−   direct address to male friend: *Ow bes ya, **me son**?* Also **o man, o trout, o cock**, *skipper*, **sir**, *Mr. Man*.

sook   an immature, fawning, wimpy, over-emotional person, especially a child; crybaby: *Some **sook**, you is!* Also *sooky baby*. N. England and Scotland, a calf reared by hand, a "suck-calf" [SOOK−]. Note "sook" Australian, New Zealand slang for crybaby; a call to summon cows or sheep.

sooky   [SOOK-ee], [SOO?-ee] immature, fawning, wimpy, over-emotional, peevish: *Dat Eddy, e's some **sooky** baby!* WCE from Dorset *sucky* dull, bad. Note Australian, New Zealand slang "sooky" for shy, timid, sulky, whining, cowardly, sentimental.

sorry soight   [SAHR-ree SUEHT] a regrettable situation, as in Shakespeare's *Macbeth* of 1605, Act 2, Sc. 2: *This is a sorry sight* ; untidy, in disarray.

so soigns   [SOH SUEHNZ]] in that case; therefore, thus, so. *Billy come ome sousht agin so soigns es wife locked en outdoors.* Irish (Conception Bay).

sot   [SAWT] past of *set* and *sit. D' table was sot f' tree o' we, an den we aa sot down.*

sot op   [sawt-OHP) provided for. *She bes aa sot up affer da o feller passed.* "She is **well provided for** after the old man died." Note **found**.

sousht   [SOWSHT] drunk, intoxicated, as in *sousht t' d' two oies.* Also **af-cut, pluteed**.

sou'wester   a banker fisherman's traditional waterproof hat with wide slanting brim longer in back than in front to shed rain or sea spray. Also *linkum*. Brit. nautical usage.

sove op   [SOHV] past tense of save; *Suze sove op tan dollars fer a new handbag.*

spakes   [SPAYKS] utter words, talk. *Dey spakes loike opalongers affer dey bes away da yere.* "They **talk** like Canadians after being off the island all this year." See **says.**

sparble   [SPAHR-buhl] a short nail or tack; studs, cleat or hob nail in boots preventing slipping on ice. WCE, from Dorset *sparbill*, shoe tack, from *sparrows bill*, a cobbler's tack.

spell (take a-)   a short rest from work. *"How do you spell 'swile'?"* – *"We don't spell 'em. We mostly hauls 'em."*[22] Note NE **spurt, toime av.**

speller   day school text of common word spellings.

spile   [SPAIL] a peg or plug for a draining hole in a cask. Northern Brit. for "splinter" from Middle Dutch "splinter, skewer, spindle."

spitey   [SPUEHʔ-ee] revengeful, disagreeable, contrary. *Dat Meg bes a spitey li'l streel.*

spit jack   (hairy) rove beetle (*Creophilus maxillosus*), a fly predator attracted to decaying matter and out-houses. Displays abdominal tip irritant or curls up when threatened. NE.

split   to clean fish for eating or salting and drying.

splits   [SPLIHTS] kindling, small firewood. *Peter took a spell fom cleavin splits.* "Peter rested from making **kindling**." NE. Note: NE **bavin, brishney, faddle, keep-a-goins**.

split d' rocks   as in *'S'marn d' sun is splittin d' rocks*. "This morning it is **very hot**."

spot ov, a-   [SPAW7 uhv] some a little amount of. Brit. *Take a spell an ave a spot o' tea!* Note NE **a drap ov.**

spratt   a large rosefish, ocean or red perch *(Sebastes norvegicus)* from the North Atlantic, one of 130 species of rockfish having venom glands in its dorsal, anal, and pelvic spines.

sprong   pitch fork of fisherman and farmer.

spruce beer   a beverage of fermented needles of the spruce tree. Also **calabogus**.

spudgel, spudjo   [SPUHJ-uhl] wooden bailing bucket for a row boat. WCE, from Dorset *spudgel*, a small shovel for baling water. See **piggin**.

spunge   [SPUHNJ] to frequently borrow. Note London Cant *spunge*, "to drink at others' cost." Also *spunge av* (someone).

spurt   a brief period, as in *A spurt o' wunnerfo bad wedder we ben affer avin*. "We've had a **short duration** of inclement weather." WCE.

spy glass   [SPOY-glahs] glass-bottomed viewer to see fish under water. Also *spy-bucket, fish glass*.

Spy Wednesday   [SPOY WEHNZ-dee] Holy Wednesday before Good Friday. From spies set on Jesus to justify his arrest. Irish.

squabby   soft as jelly. Note Swedish dialect *skvabb* flabby fat.

squashberry   highbush cranberry (*Viburnum trilobum*), a cranberry-like edible with maple-like leaves. Also *thrashburry, thrasherwood berry, white-wood (berry)*, the latter from similar Brit. *whitten-tree*. Name denotes similar *V. edule* across N. America.

squat   [SKWAWT] to pinch (a finger); crush flat (tin can). WCE, from Dorset *squot*, to flatten by a blow, from ME *squatten* crush, from OF *esquatir*. Note **quot**.

squish, squishy   not upright, vertical, nor plumb; crooked, not aligned; sound of water inside boots. NE

St. John's Dog   *St. John's Water Dog* or the *Lesser Newfoundland*, an original, now extinct breed with black with white tuxedo markings, ancestor to the Newfoundland and to all today's retrievers worldwide.

stage (eed)   a fisherman's wharf, flake, sheds, etc. for drying fish. From ME "raised exhibition floor" from OF *estage*, stage of a building.

stalligan   small armful of fire wood, a turn. See **starrigan**.

starburd   [STAHR-buhrd] right, starboard or "steering board side" of ship with green navigation light. From OE *steorbord*, "steer-board" (from Viking *styri borth*) or side-rudder on the right side (for the usual right-handed ruddermen). Note **larburd**.

starrigan   thin, dry tree for firewood. SEI, Gaelic *stearagán* or *stairricín*, dead stump; an obstacle. Irish. Also **stalligan**.

starm   storm, *breeze o' ween*. See **breeze**. Note Leics. *starm* a fall of snow on the ground. . Note Wexford Yola *starm* storm.

starters, f'-   to begin with: *D' magistrate give en a tirty-dollar foine jus f' starters*. "The magistrate **began by** imposing a thirty dollar fine on him."

steady   [STEHD-dee] space of still water on a river, as in placename *Steady Brook* on the Humber River. NE.

stepeens   [stehp-EENZ] ladys' underpants, panties, "step-ins." NE. Central.

stigger   a full load, a "staggering" load.

stio fer aa   [STEE-oh fuhr aw] nevertheless, in any case, anyway; even so, yet. *Buildeed essauf a wunnerfo gert ouse op on da io, an* **stio fer aa** *naer got nar ooman*. "(He) built a very big home on the hill, but never attracted a wife, **anyway**."

stog   [STAWG] to stow tightly; to overeat; to overfill one's mouth. WCE. Note Dorset *a-stogged*, caught in mud; Leics. *stodge* cram or stuff full.

stoppage   stutter. *Da choild got a* **stoppage** *een es speech*. "That child **stutters**." SEI, from Irish *stoppage*.

store   a storage shed. Brit. Note **shop**, **shed**.

store-bought   commercially made and purchased, not homemade.

stove cake   See NE **flummy** or **bangbelly**.

strayt   [STRAAY?] straight; strait; street. Central. Note Wexford Yola *streyght* strait.

streel   an unkempt or slovenly woman. SEI, Gaelic *straoill* a ragged bedraggled person; sloven, slattern. Note Irish *streel* untidy mess.

stresset   [STRIHS-iht] desolate, bleak: *Oi moins dem Resettlement outports was* **stresset** *affer 1975*. Also *strusset*. Note SE *distressed*.

stroife o' ween   [STRUEHF uh WEEN] gale, wind storm. Note **starm**, **breeze**, **brewer**, **darty**, *breeze o' ween*.

strouters [STROW-derz] fishing stage support posts. WCE. Note **shores, longers**.

struck een to feel sudden discomfort in. *Somtin **struck een** es leg.* "He **has a sudden pain** in his leg." Note NE **smert, foine**.

struck on attracted to, impressed by: *Jack bes real **struck on** Sally from Chance Cove.*

stuck fer seriously lacking: *Davie come home an now e's **stuck fer** a job.* Also **ard op (fer)**.

stun stupid, clueless: *O Ned bes as **stun** as me arse.* WCE, from OF *estoner* to stun.

stun po stupid, clueless person, being tall (as a "pole") without an adult's life experience. WCE, from Dorset *stunpoll*, a blockhead; an old dead tree.

sudard [SUHD-ehrd] relative to the south, as wind or weather, southerly.

suent / suant [SOO-ent] graceful, smooth (as of a ship's lines). WCE, from Dorset *suent*, smooth and even. Note Devon *suent*, spread evenly; uniform, smooth, even.

sufferin comfort a tolerated discomfort. South.

sugawn [SHOO-gawn] a rope of twisted hay, used to make home-made chair seats. SEI, from Irish Gaelic *súgán*, rope; a sugawn chair.

sulick [SOO-lihk] gravy. SEI, from Gaelic *súghlach*, juice. Irish. See **grace**.

summer moes freckles (said to be accentuated by the summer sun). Also *sun moles*. WCE. Note Dorset *zummermwolds* freckles on the face.

sunbonnet headgear of women drying fish on a **flake** or **bawn**.

sunkers dangerous submerged rocks or shoal. NE. Also **flowers, warshballs**, *warshrocks*.

supper the evening meal, "dinner." *D'ooman aves **supper** ready f' we evy day at six.* "My wife has **dinner** ready for us daily at six." Also **tea**. Note **dinner, scoff**.

sure (an) [SHOHR] for sure, surely. ***Sure an** she bes d' bess cook on d' shore.* SEI. Irish. See **garnteed**.

swarv [SWAHRV] to move about annoyingly and unnecessarily. Also **trapse**.

swatch weak spot in sea ice; shoot seals among ice flows.

swig [SWEEG] to drink (an alcoholic beverage) from the bottle. Brit. Note **grog**.

switchel [SWIHCH-uhl], [–oh] unsweetened tea. WCE. From *swizzle,* an intoxicating drink at sea.

swish rum leached or "bulled" with hot water from used wooden rum barrels.

swoile [SWUEHL] a North Atlantic seal (any of the family *Phocidae*). WCE. From dialectal insertion of *w* glide into ME *soile* "seal".

swoile gun [SWUEHL GUHN] originally, a muzzle-loaded, smooth bore, matchlock long gun, recoil-fired from the shoulder using lead balls and loose powder to shoot seals, similar to muskets of early trappers and hunters. Facetiously nicknamed "*li'l darlints.*"[22]

swoilin [SWOEHL-uhn] seal hunting on sheets of southward-drifting arctic ice.

T

tabanask a trapper's toboggan, a long, flat-bottomed sled. From aboriginal Innu-Aimun (Montagnais) *utapanashkw.*

table budder [TAY-buhl BUHʔ-ehr], [-BUHD-dehr] dairy butter (as opposed to Margarine, a fortified, colour-added, butter substitute). Also *good budder.*

tacker [TAHK-uhr] tacking, waxed hemp thread for sewing boots.

tail (out) See **teel**.

tail stretch a boat's **painter** from its mooring; **tail on** grip tightly and pull a rope. See **painter**.

take affer [TAYK ahf-fehr] act like, or be as predictable as an older relative. *Young Jim **takes** roight **affer** es fadder.* "Young Jim **acts just like** his father." WCE, from Dorset *teake* [TEH-ahk] *after* look or behave like another. Note **turn affer**.

take away fom detract from, lessen the importance or clarity of. *Terry id'n one t' **take away fom** yer weddin b' showin op late.* "Terry isn't the sort to **ruin** your wedding by attending late."

take er easy [TAYK-ehr AYZ-ee] to pace oneself, relax. *Oi ull **take er easy** affer oi poils op enough foirewood.*

take d' good (roight) out ov to cause to feel dispirited or ill. *Loosin es skiff **took d' good** roight **out ov** Skipper Joe.*

take op [tayk-OHP] buy on credit; barter. Note **truck**.

talk a manner of speaking; a regional variety of speech, as in *Newfy talk*. Note Wexford Yola *talke* language, speech.

talkin flat a somewhat negative appraisal of colloquial or regional diction. *Yes b'y, oi seems t' see dem fom oer dere comin long w' we people, garnteed! —Haha! You bes **talkin** some **flat!*** "...Haha! You are speaking very **colloquially**." NE. Also *newfy talk*. See f**lat talk**. Note **accent, slang**.

talqual [TAHL-kwahl] good with the bad; all fish bought at a flat rate. From Latin *talis qualis*, as they come, with no sorting for quality.

tanks thanks. Also *tank you* thank you.

tanners, tannels claws, as a cat's claws or hawk's talons.

tant [TAHNT] tall and slender (tree, woods, ships' mast). Note London Cant *tant*, tall mast or man.

tarment [TAHR-mehnt] an annoyance, a tormenting person or thing. WCE, from OF *torment* pain, anguish, from Latin *tormentum* instrument of torture.

tar felt a thick, tarred paper product supplied in rolls and painted with pitch to weatherproof a roof. Also **black jack.** Note **felt tins**.

tar mop mop brush, often of discarded cloth, used to apply pitch to a boat or felted roof. NE.

tatie [TAY-dee] potato. See **pratie**. SEI.

tatie/tater salad a side dish of mashed boiled potatoes with mayonnaise or salad dressing, boiled eggs, and beets or mustard.

tattletale a child who betrays the confidence of another, a gossip. Also *tattle-tongue*.

tawniers [TAWN-yerz] intense and vivid black. Note SE *tawny* swarthy, dark coloured.

tawt thwart, a seat set athwart (across) the sides of a rowboat. WCE. Note Dorset *thaut, thwart*, bench of a boat, *athwart*, across. See **adurt**.

tay [TAY] tea; evening meal, dinner. Also **supper**.

Teak Day January 6th or "Old (pre-1752) Christmas Day," the twelfth or last day of the Christmas season. SEI from Irish *tadhg*, Irishman. Irish. See **O Christmas Day**.

tearce, tierce [TEHRS] British liquid measure, 159 litres, 35 imperial gallons, 42 (US) wine gallons, a half-puncheon, coincidently equal to one modern petrol/oil barrel; the barrel of that measure. From FR *tierce*, third of a *pipe*, from Latin *tertia* third. See **puncheon**.

tear op   [TEHR-ohp] an angry argument, disagreement, quarrel. Also **row, set to.**

teel   set out rabbit **slips** or set fur trapper's traps. Also **tail**. See **slips, rabbit garden, rabbit**.

teeveen   a patch on one's boot. SEI, Gaelic *taoibhín* boot or shoe patch. Irish.

tellylamp   a large lamp; also **flirrup**, **laddin lamp**, *stand lamp*, **carrychurch**.

tick   [TIHK] intense, dense. *She's **tick** o' snow.* "It is snowing heavily"; close, friendly. Note Irish *thick* close.

ticklas   [TECK-lays] black-legged kittiwake (*Rissa tridactyla*), a cliff-nesting, table food gull species, also found in UK and Europe. From their alleged diversionary tactic of pecking other birds's tail feathers to swipe their food. Also *tickleace* [TEHK-lays]

tickle   [TIHK-uhl] narrow, inshore passage, sometimes dangerously turbulent due to tidal action; an **outport** accessed by narrow entrance. WCE, from ME *tikelen* from OE *tinclian* to stir up, agitate.

'tid'n   it is not. WCE. Note Dorset *tidd'n*. See NE **id'n**.

tiddly   simple children's game: a short *tiddly stick* is placed across two stones to be flicked away and replaced by a longer *puss stick*. An opponent catches the *tiddly stick*, or throws it to strike the *puss stick* to put the player *out*. Also **piddly**, **flick d' stick**. WCE, from "tiddlywinks" game.

tilly   [TIHL-lee] extra, bonus or added quantity free. SEI, Irish Gaelic *tuilleadh* extra amount given free. Irish.

tilt   a sturdy trapper's or woodman's shack; initially a settlers' inland winter home. WCE, from OE *tealt* unsteady. See **bough whiffen**.

tin   can, as in *a **tin** ov peas*. Note **can**.

Tipp's Eve   December 23, early end of Advent allowing pre-Christmas sampling of home-made alcoholic beverages. From fictitious Irish St. Tibb influenced by "Tibb," Elizabethan trollop stage character.

tipsy   nearly drunk. Note London Cant *tipsy*, "a'most Drunk." From ME *tip* topple, knock down.

t'is   [TIHZ] it is. See **t'was, id'n**.

titivate   to greatly adorn, embellish. Note **gilguys**. Brit., from *tidy* plus Latin-like ending.

to, t' [TUH] (unstressed) to (direction or destination); [TOO] to a location, as in *Wher's me at gone to?* "Where is my hat?" WCE. Note Dorset *to*, as in *Where do ye bide to?*

toddies See NE **piss-a-bed**.

toe small pieces of cotton batting once used as medical bandaging pads.

toide __ oer [TUEHD...OHR] temporarily assist, support or provide for, lend or advance money to: *Me fadder toideed oi oer t' payday.*

toime [TUEHM] a party, celebration. Also *breaker-down*, **get-t'gedder**.

toime back as in *Eef oi ad me toime back...* "If I could redo my **past actions**..."

toime av time off work, a vacation, holiday. *Granfer naer seen ar toime av een es loife.* "Grandpa never had a **vacation** in his life."

toimepiece [TUEHM-pees] clock, watch.

tole, toll [TOHL], [TOH] to entice with bait.

tokens ghost, ghostly premonition. From OE *tacen* sign, symbol, evidence. Note London Cant *tokens*, gifts; "the Plague." Also **fetch**.

tom/tommy cod a small or immature codfish, **peel**.

Tom Pop d' Devil jocular reference to mischievous person: *Es a real Tom Pop d' Devil, dat one!* See NE **jackeen**, **devilskins**, **idle**. WCE, Brit. from *tom-pop* a "chain" or heavy smoker.

tongue-bangin [TUHNG-bahng-uhn] reprimand, scolding, chastisement. *Me fader give oi some tongue-bangin f' bein out late.* Note **come board o'**, **go board** (ov), **loine** (s.o.) ov. NE.

took op [TOOK OHP] served, as in a plateful of food. *We's got fish. Want some took op?* "We have cod fish. Do you want a **plateful**?"; obtain on credit, see **take op**

took op fer detained for questioning, arrested for: *Tom was took op fer lobster-catchin out o' season*; supported (someone) in an argument: *E took op f' Joany stio fer aa she was wrong.* "He **supported** Joany even though she was wrong."

top ov __ lungs shout at full volume: *D' gommy bleared at d' top ov es lungs.*

tops See NE **greens**.

Topsails, The- [TAWP-suhlz] several high **tolts** in central Newfoundland island highlands, altitude 1554 ft (474 m), known for high winds, deep snows, train delays. Each tolt is named after a sailing ship top sail. See **tolt, Gaff Topsail**.

tote, tolt [TOHT], [TOH?] an isolated high rocky knoll remaining after lower terrain glacial erosion; an inselberg or monadnock. *Granfer trapped foxes een on Green Garden* **Tote** *f' yeurs.* WCE. Note Dorset place names (e.g.: *Tyneham Tout*), from *tout, toot*, a look-out or hill to spy from. Note **knap**.

touton [TOWT-uhn], [TOW?-uhn] bread made the previous day allowed to rise once, then hastily stove top-baked in round pans; a pork cake bun (diced pork, water, baking powder, molasses); fried dough, a flapjack or pancake. NE. Also **bangbelly, damper dog, frozie, gandy**, *grace cake*.

townie a resident of a larger town, specifically St. John's. Note urban UK *townie*, slang for any unkempt, loud, uncultured street youth.

towpins [TOH-pihn] pairs of wooden pegs inserted into the gunwale of a rowboat as a fulcrum for oars in rowing. WCE, from OE *tholl*, peg, from Old Norse *thollr*.

trap cod-fishing net; lobster pot; furrier's trap. Note **trap skiff**.

trap skiff [TRAHP SKEEF] a **skiff** fitted for **cod** trap fishing or lobster harvesting.

trapes [TRAYPSS] walk idly without purpose, necessity or care; **swarv**. WCE, from OF *trepass/trespasse* travels across. Note Dorset *trapes*, of a woman boldly tramping about; Leics. *trapse* [TREEPS] walk in a slovenly manner; London Cant *trapes* an unkempt woman.

tread-po, / -pole wooden staff or pole used with others to temporarily bridge a stream. NE.

tree [TREE] three. See NE **nummers**.

trig op [TREEG] set something up temporarily or poorly. *E* **trigged op** *a scaffold t' paint es ouse.* WCE. Note Dorset *trig*, prop or hold up.

troifle [TRUEH-fuhl] popular cold dessert of cream, sponge cake, fruit and custard. Brit.

troid out fer [truehd OW? fehr] applied to qualify for, or interviewed for an employment position or training. *Peter* **troid out fer** *'eavy 'quipment op'rator affer trade skoo.* Note **went een fer**.

trou [TROO] through, from side to side; straight.

trimmin corporal punishment. Note Dorset *trimmen*, great, ample, as in *A trimmen crop*. Also **laysin**.

truck previous fish merchant practice of payment for fish by merchandise; barter. WCE from OF (North) *troquer* to barter.

trunk 'ole   a hole in a *stage* floor for drawing up sea water; also *truck 'ole, trink 'ole.*

trunnel   a shipbuilding dowel or peg of hard wood allowed to **plim** and so fasten timbers tightly together. WCE from *treenail.*

tuckamores   [TUHK-uh-mohrz], [TUH?-uh-mohrz] trees or bushes growing close to the ground such as white spruce (*Picea glauca*) or black spruce (*P. mariana*). *More* from OE for tree root. NE.

tump   [TOOMP] blow, smack, whack; thud, boom, bang. Note Devon *dump* thump. See NE **douse, wop**. From imitative.

turn   an armful; a piece of wood. See **stalligan**.

turn affer   resemble an older relative. *Young Jim* **turns** *roight* **affer** *es fadder.* "Young Jim very **much resembles** his dad." Note **take affer**.

turncoat   [TUHRN-koht], [TUHRN-koh?] one who deserts his religious denomination for another. Note London Cant *turn-coat*, one who abruptly exchanges his associates or friends for others.

turn een   [tuhrn-EEN] to go to bed. Also **go t' couche**, *alley-couche*. Note *turning in and out*, timesharing a berth by seamen.

turn out   [tuhrn-OWT] to get up (out of bed); to turn to sleep facing the outer edge, away from another sleeper. *'***Turn out***', she said, ' fore ya starts t' snore a' me'.*

turr   [TEHR] common murre (*Uria aalge aalge*), a table food sea bird. NE. From imitative call. Newfoundlanders are the only non-indigenous North Americans with traditional murre-hunting rights, given shortly after Confederation, 1949.[23]

twack   [TWAHK] to examine goods and buy nothing; window shopping. WCE, from ME *thakken* "touch, stroke" from OE *thaccian* "tap, stroke."

t'was   [TWAHZ] it was. *T'was onny a gunshot away.* "It was only fifty yards away." Note **'tid'n**.

twowvemont   [TWOWV-mon?] year. *Ned ben on d' Labrador dis* **twowvemont**. Note Leics. *twelvemont* year.

twig   [TWEEG] a small drink of rum; to understand, **fadom out**. SEI, from Irish and Scots Gaelic *tuig*, understand. Note Leics *twig* understand, observe. Note SE *tweak* understand.

'twull   [TWUHL] it will. See NE **id'n**.

'twud / 'twud'n   [TWUHD-uhn] it was / it was not. See NE **wud, ud, id'n**.

U

ud [UHD] would; *Aunt Tilley **ud** knit a couple ganseys evy winner.* Note WCE Somerset *I 'ood cauze thee ta drink o' spiced woines...* (SS 8.2). Also **wud**. May become **'d** if unstressed after a vowel: *Oi'd say!* See **ull**.

ud a' [UHD uh] would have, intended to. *Jimmy **ud a'** gone t' skoo, no odds eef t'was darty.* "Jimmy **would have** attended school even on a stormy day." Also **wud a'**. See NE **id'n**.

ud'n [UHD-uhn], [OOD-uhn] was not, were not: *Sally **ud'n** home, so we dodged on up d' road.* "She **was not** at home, so we continued up the street." Note WCE, Somerset *I took hold on un, an' 'ood'n let un goo...* (SS 3.4). Also **wud'n**. See NE **id'n**.

ud'n put't pass   See **(w)ud'n put't pass**.

ugly stick   a traditional rhythm instrument to accompany accordion and fiddle music and made of a mop handle set in a rubber boot topped by a cymbal, and having attached bottle tops, felt tins and jingle bells. Thumped on the floor with a drum stick glissando on the tins, bells, etc.

ull [UHL] will, shall. Future tense and intention marker. *Pish **ull** come ome drectly.* "My dog Pish **will** come home soon." Note WCE Sussex *I ull goo up to da palm-tree...* (SS 7. 8). May become **'ll** after vowel: *Oi'll go see wha' e wan's* [euhl goh SEE waw? ee WAN?S]. Note NE Somerset *I 'ool get up now...* (SS 3.2). Note NE **ud.**

unbeknownst [uhn-bee-NOHNST] unknown, unsuspected, unaware: *Unbeknownst t' me, d' maid was aaready married.* WCE. Note Dorset *unbeknown* not known of, Leics *unbeknownst* unknown, secretly.

uncle [UH?-oh] general term of respect to an older man regardless of actual family relationship (first or full name used: *Uncle John* or *Uncle John Walters*).

unner [UHN-nehr] under, underneath. *Tom los es gear **unner** da oice.* "Tom lost his fishing gear **beneath** the ice."

unthaw [awn-TAW] to thaw, as ice to water.

urge   to retch, dry heave. WCE, from Dorset *urge*, retch. Note **awk op.**

urt [UHR?] a wart. WCE, from ME *hurt* wound, injury.

used to [YOOST tuh] completed or repeated in past: *Brad **used to** fish inshore.* "Brad **had** fished near the coast." See **naer used to.**

usen't to [YOOSS-uhnt tuh] negative of used to, didn't used to, didn't habitually: *Bert **usen't t'** be af-cut all d' toime.* "Bert **had not been** frequently drunk." Note **bain't.**

V

vamp [VAHMP] sole of sock or stocking; to walk. WCE. Note Dorset *vamp*, sole of shoe, from ME *vamp* travel, Anglo-FR *vaumpé*, OF *avantpié*. Note London Cant *vamp*, "a Sock." See **dob**.

vandue [VAHN-doo] sale by auction. From Dutch *vendu* from OF *vendue*, sale.

vang [VAYNG] fried salt pork used to flavour a cod fish dish. Also **bang**. Note **scrunchins**.

var [VAWR] wood of the balsam-fir *(Abies balsamea)*. WCE.

veer av move aside to avoid. From MF *virer* to turn. See **sloo, shift oer**.

verver forever, always. See **aaveez**.

vexed frustrate to anger. *Id'n ya vexed wid d' li'l devil's limb f' stealin yer flowers?* From MF *vexer* to harass. Note **crossackle, tarment, bullyrag, real put out**.

W

wad [WAWD] a small portion of chewing tobacco. WCE, from *wadde*. Note ME *wadmal* woolen cloth, Swedish *vadd*, wadding. See **plug**.

wadder [WAWD-dehr], [WAWʔ-ehr] water; the open ocean, sea: *T'is wunnerfo on da **wadder** d' summer.* "It is pleasant on the **ocean** this summer." Also dialectal variant *wa'er*.

wadder, on da– on the ocean, on the sea, at sea, offshore.

wadder arse a stack of filleted, pre-salted, rinsed cod fish left to drain on beach stones or on a flake.

wadder nipper youth employed to carry drinking water to workmen on the job. See **nipper**.

wadder panks [WAWD-dehr pahnks], [WAWʔ-ehr pahnks] excess saliva or drooling from sudden or excessive exertion. WCE. See **pank**.

wants a word (wid) wishes to speak (with), as in *Da o ooman wants a word wid me 'bout comin een late las noight*.

warsh [WAHRSH], [WOHRISH] wash; laundry. *Dem jackeens naer warshed der ands fore d' table.* South. WCE. Note Somerset *worsh*, late ME Somerset *warsyne* washing.

warshballs dangerous submerged rocks. Also *warshrocks*, **sunkers, flowers**. NE.

warsh ouse   processing area of salted fish before drying.

wawkin stick   walking cane. Brit. walking stick.

wassname   [WAHS-naym] thingamajig, what's-its-name; also **chummyjigger**, **machine**; person of unknown name, also **buddy**, *wassesname*, *wassesfaace* (masc.), *wassername*, *wasserfaace* (fem.).

wattle   [WAWʔ-uhl] small slim fir tree. Note **longers starrigans**. WCE, from OE *watols* roof thatching.

way   so that, in order that, making possible, as in E *barred d' door way we wud'n get een*. "He locked the door **so that** we would not enter." NE.

WD-40   a generic term for any mechanical spray lubricant. The unpatented product name of WD-40 Company, San Diego.

we   we, us. *D' breeze drove we av da wadder.* "The storm forced **us** to return from the sea." Note WCE Wiltshire *What's yer beloved mwore than another beloved, that ye do zo charge we?* (SS 5.9).

weasand   [WEE-zuhn] windpipe, throat. WCE. Note Dorset *wizzen*, windpipe, from OE *waesend* gullet, from Old Norse *hvaesa* to wheeze. See **kinkarn**, **craw**.

wedder   [WIHD-duhr] bad weather. See **breeze**, **starm**, **brewer**, **stroife o' ween**.

weigh-de-buckedy   play at children's see-saw. *Back een dem days we **weighed d' buckedy** when we was onny small.* SEI, from Gaelic *bacaideach* undulating. Irish. Weigh from OE *wegan* to lift, to weigh (note seaman's *weigh anchor*).

"we'll rant and we'll roar"   a line of the chorus of a popular ten-verse Newfoundland song originally composed in 1875 as "The Ryans and The Pittmans," and based on four verses of "Spanish Ladies," a traditional English capstan shanty.[24] See NE **roar**.

we'm   See **'m**. Note WCE, Note East Devon *Yeu 'm vurry geudeleukin* (SS 4.1).

wensy, da-   [WEN-zee] extremely, as in *bile da **wensy**,* "boil madly," and *go da wensy*, "move very quickly"; *gone da wensy*, gone free, gone wild. WCE. From "gone to windward."

went on   continued on ("–our way"): *Sally wud'n home, so we **went on**.*

went een fer   received career training. *Aunt Vy's son **went een fer** a priest.* "–**took instruction for** the priest-hood." Also **went een t' be**. Note **troid out fer**.

we people   we, us. *Dey aves a dif'rent talk een Snail Cove dan **we people** yere.* See **people**.

wes [WEHS] west. See 'compass directions' in the **Standard English** section on page 131.

westard [WEHS-tuhrd] relative to the west, as wind or weather, westerly.

Western Ocean the northwest Atlantic between Britain and Newfoundland's fishing banks. Brit.

weyk [WAYK] week.

wha/wha' [WAW], [WAWʔ] "What did you say?"

wha/wha' [WAW], [WAWʔ] What, as in *Oi yeard wha ya said*. May be heard for **dat** (that) as in *E onny shot d' carboo wha was slow*.

whaaer [WAW-ehr],[WAWʔ-ehr] whatever.

wha'...fer [wawʔ fehr] why, as in *Wha's she comin yere fer?* "**Why** is she coming here?"

wha'fer [wawʔ -FEHR] Why? *She's comin yere. Wha'fer?* "She's coming here. **Why?**"

wha' is ya loike [WAWʔ EEZ yuh LOYK] a reference to a distinctive, peculiar, or unusual individual, a "character"; an expression of amused surprise at another's antics: *Ah, Sarah, wha' is ya loike, ataa.* "Oh, Sarah, **you are a character**, in any case." Note **some b'y**.

wha' odds! [WAWʔ-awdz] It does/did not matter. *Aaat, wha' odds!* "**What th' heck!**" Also **Aa d' same**, **Aa loike**, **No odds**. Note Leics. *odds* difference.

wha's "What is/are-" as in *Wha's Skipper Bob so roary-oied mad 'bout?*

wha's y' at? [was-yuh-AHT] A Newfy greeting "What are you doing?" (Ans: *Dis's it* [DIHS ihz ZIHT].) Note Wexford, Belfast (Ir.) *Wadderye at? —Nahtin!*

who [OO] relative pronoun often replaced by **dat**: *She's da one dat bought a new car.*

whoaer [oo-EHR] whoever.

whose [OOZ] whose, as in *Whose car is she?* Whose may be heard to replace inanimate *dat* as in *She's da one whose toires is flat.*

when; whenaer [WEEN] when; [ween-EHR] whenever.

wher; wheraer [WUHR] where; [wuhr-EHR] wherever.

whistle diver common goldeneye (*Bucephala clangula*), a migratory sea duck. From their rapid wing beat sound and underwater foraging. NE.

whiting [WAIT-ing] tree with bark removed.

whizzle   [WIHZ-uhl] to squeak; a creaking sound, squeak. See **scroop**.

who owns you?   "Who are your parents (and what are their names)?" as said to a child.

wid   with, among, including. Also **long wid**.

widout   [WIHD-owt], [WIHD-ouʔ] unless. *E ull get nar job widout e haves dem papers.* "He will get no employment **unless** he has certification."

winard   [WIHN-uhrd] windward, unprotected side of ship, etc. Also **luff**. Note **luard, lund**.

winner   winter. Also **win'er** [WIHNʔ-ehr].

witlow   [WIT-loh] infected fingernail (a dory fisherman's hazard). WCE. From ME *whitflaw* from Dutch *vijt* abscess + "flaw." See **ampered.**

witch/wych hazel   [WIHCH HAY-zoh] birch tree wood (*Betula* spp.), yielding fragrant wintergreen (*methyl salicylate*) and hardwood for shipbuilding, flooring, cabinetry, firewood. *Witch* from ME *wiche* from OE *wice*, "bendable."

wop   [WAWP] wasp. WCE, a false singular of Dorset *wops,* from OE *waeps,* from Old Saxon *waspa.* Note Leics. *waps,* Northhumberland *whamp.*

wop   [WAWP] a slap of the hand. WCE. Note Dorset *whop,* a heavy blow from a swung arm, Devon *woppit* to box the ears of. See **tump, douse.**

wood   See **ood**.

work out   solve, determine, figure out. Brit.

Wreckhouse   A glacial morainic area between the southern Long Range Mountains and the ocean on the Cabot Strait coast north of Port aux Basques noted for extreme wind conditions and occasionally endangering previous train service and present vehicular traffic. A 186 km/h wind gust record was set 26 March, 2014 (Environment Canada). See **human wind gauge**.

wrinkle   common edible periwinkle sea snail, *Littorina littorea.* WCE.

wud, wud a', wud'n   [WUHD], [WUHD uh], [WUHD-uhn] variants of **ud, ud a', ud'n** would, would've, wouldn't. Note WCE Cornish, *I wud laid tha, and bring tha 'to my mother's house, who wud taich me* (SS 8.2), and Sussex,...*ef a man wud give all he's got in his house for love...* (SS 8.7). See **'twud, 'twud'n.**

(w)ud'n put't pas   would not consider one incapable of, as in *Oi wud'n put't pas Abe t' steal me punt.* "I **would not consider** Abe **incapable of** stealing my rowboat."

wunnerfo   [WUHN-nihr-foh] awesome, to be wondered at, as in *wunnerfo bad starm*, *wunnerfo good scoff.* Other intensifying words: **some**, **roight**, **preddy**, **fair**, **mad**, **aavo**, *terrbul*, **shockin**, *pure*, *ugly*, *cruel*. Note Leics. *woonderful* very, remarkable, superbly.

X

xac same   [ZAHK SAYM] precisely the same, identical. *Me bruder bought d' xac same car as moyn.*

Y

ya   [YUH], [YAW] singular unstressed you as in *'T'is too hot t' biver*, *ya silly gommy!* May be contracted to *y'*. Also dialectal **dee**, **'ee**. See pronoun list under **Small Words**, introduction.

yaffle, yaffoe   armful of dried fish. WCE from provincial *jag* small load. See **faggot**.

yankee budder   sauce made of molasses. Also **coady/cotie**.

yap   a dog's bark (imitative); angry or insolent retort; also **back answer**. From Icelandic/ Old Norse *gjalpa*. Note SE *yelp*. Note Leics. *yap* to yelp snappishly.

yarkin   net mooring lines to a head rope

yarry   early-rising; alert, energetic; athletic. WCE from OE *gearo* ready, prepared.

yawny   pale, pallid. *She bes wunnerfo yawny affer er flu.*

ye   [YEE] alternate stressed plural "you." Irish. Central, Avalon. See pronoun list under **Small Words**, introduction.

yeah   [YEH] affirmative "yes," unique in sometimes being made in casual conversation with an inhalation rather than normal exhalation (see "Gaelic Gasp," **Preface**).

year, yeard   [YUHR], [YUHRD] hear, heard. *D' cat yeard d' mouse.* Note Somerset...*let me yeär thoi voice.* (SS 2.14).

year talk ov   [yuhr TAWK uhv] hear, learn or know about, receive news of: *We naer years talk ov goeen to da oice dese days.* "One does not currently **get news** of sealing."

yellow janders   [JAWND-uhrz] jaundice. WCE from OF *jaunice* from *jalnice* from *jaune* yellow.

yer, yeer   [YEHR], [YEER] your (possessive adjective) singular and plural, as in *yer car, yeer ouse* ("house of you all"). See list under **Small Words** in introduction. Note WCE Wiltshire *yer*, Wexford Yola *yer*.

yere   [YUHR] here, near the speaker, opposite of **dere**.

yeroe   [YEHR-oh] ear. WCE, from Devon *yurole*.

yerrin   [YEHR-ihn] a reef point (used in "reefing in" or folding a sail on a spar); an earing.

yes, b'y.   "Okay," "Is that so?," "Aw, that's too bad," "I don't believe you," with context and intonation.

yesday   yesterday. Also *yest'day*.

yeur   [YUHR] year, years: *Dey bes nar seal dese foiv yeur.* "There have been no seals during the past five **years**." Also **twowvemont**.

yoi!   [YUEH] Here! Over here! (shouted aloud for attention). Note **yere**.

you, yous   [YOO], [YOOZ] stressed forms of **ya, yiz** "you." South. See **Small Words** pronoun list on page 25.

–, you.   vocative term of emphatic focus on the listener: *Yer punt is full o' wadder, **you**! / Ya goin fer a run da once, **you**?* (see endnotes, notes 2, 7).

you'm   [YOOM] you have: *You'm got a noice stigger dere, b'y.* "**You have** a hefty load there, friend." See **'m.** Note WCE, East Devon *Yeu'm za pirty as Tirzah...* (SS 4.4).

young fat   young seals or "white coats." See **bedlamer**.

Z

z-   occasional NE dialectal initial **s-** as in *zome, zon, zound, zou'wester, zupper*, etc. for some, son, sound, etc.

zad   [ZAHD] zed, zee, letter "Z." Brit. From FR *zede* from Latin and Greek *zeta* from Hebrew *zayin* "weapon" (from its Hebrew letter shape, ז).

Standard English

NE items in **bold** refer to the Newfoundland English wordlist.

A

a, an   *a* [AH], [AY], [UH]. *A emmet runned op er leg.* "**An** ant ran up her leg."

Aboriginal peoples   Several Indigenous cultures have inhabited Newfoundland island since the last glacial retreat: Maritime Archaic Palaeo-Indians (5000–3000 Before Present), Groswater and Dorset Palaeo-Eskimos (3000 BC–1000 BP), Recent Indians (2000 BP) possible descendants of the Maritime Archaics and ancestors of the Beothuk and possibly of the Labrador Innu (Montagnais). The Mi'kmaq made longtime seasonal visitations before Bay St. George settlement in 1700s.

acceptable   *noice* [NUEHS], (*d'*) *bess koin* (*ov*) [BEHS KUEHN]. *T'was a noice crowd at church.*

accident   *misfarchun.*

accordion   *carjel, cardeen, squeeze box.*

accursed   *bluddy.*

across   *adurt.*

act like, imitate   *take affer.*

actually   *b'roights* [buh-RUEHTS].

"Adam's apple"   *a kinkarn* [KEENK-arn], *weasand.*

adorn greatly   *titivate.*

again   *agin* [ah-GIHN].

against   *agin* [ah-GIHN].

agree!, I-   *Roight on! Proper ting!* Expression of enthusiastic agreement.

agree with   *go long wid*: *Free beer? Oi'll go long wid dat!*

agreement   *cardin*: *E noddeed cardin.* "He nodded **in agreement**."

agreement   *s'more t'was*: response in agreement. *Oi tinks t'is affer rainin. –S'more t'was*, *b'y.*

ailing, temporarily   *laid op*

alert, energetic   *yarry*. Note **early rising**, this listing.

all, everything   *evyting.*

alleviate, ease   *slack av. D' rain **slacked av** b' duckish.* "The rain diminished by dark."

already   *op t' now, **aaready**.*

always   *aaweez/aaveez.*

am, are, is   (continual action) *bes* [BEEZ]: *Jim **bes** paintin es skiff evy chance e gets.* "Jim paint**s** his skiff at every opportunity."

am/is/are not   *id'n* [EHD-n]: *Oi **id'n** jannying dis Christmas.* "I **am not** mummering during this Christmas."

am, are, is   See NE **is**, **'s**. See NE **'m**. Note NE **bes**.

amusing, very-   *as good as a concert.*

anchor, oldtime-   *killick*

and, but   *an*: *Sam come t' d' scuff, **an** got too sousht t' dance.*

angry retort   a *back answer, **yap**.*

annoy, to-   and frustrate, *crossackle.*

annoyed, be-   and frustrated, *vexed, tarmenteed, **real put out**.*

ant   *emmet.*

any, one   *ar'n*: *Me racket's broke. Got **ar'n?*** "My snowshoe is broken. Do you have one?"

any, either   *arr*: *Arr duff een d' pot?* "Is there **any** pudding in the pot?"

anyway   *gardless, **ataa*** [ah-TAW].

apron   *barvel*, also *barbel, barb.*

arctic tern   a *turr* (a table food sea bird).

argument, loud-   *tear op, row, set to.*

armful of dried fish   a *yaffle*. See NE **faggot**.

armful of fire wood   a *stalligans, turn.*

as customary   *loike ya wud*: *Oi seen she comin an, **loike ya wud**, oi says 'ullo.*

aspen tree   *aps, apse* [AHPS].

at all   *ataa* [ah-TAW].

attack, assault   *put d' boots to.*

attempt, apply for   *try out fer*: *Maxine **tried out fer** hairdresser a' d' trade skoo.* "Maxine enrolled in a hairdressing course at the occupations training school."

attracted to   *struck on*: *Jack bes real **struck on** Sally fom Chance Cove.*

attractive   *not a bad bit noice*; a positive reaction to something, as: *Da' skiff's **not a bad bit noice**.* "That skiff is quite attractive."

aunt   *aunt* [AHNT], [AHNʔ]

Autumn   *Fall.* Previous Brit. usage.

avoid   *sloo, veer av, shift* [SHEEF] *oer.*

awkward   *gowdy*   [GOW-dee].

axe handle   *elf.*

B

baby carriage   *pram.*

baby's pacifier   *dumb tit, dummy tit, dummy, nuk.*

back of head   *po, pole.*

back of neck   *scruff* (of a cat, person).

back to, with one's-   *back on to*: *Vy was **back on t'** da opm door.*

backward(s)   *backfarmist* [bahk-FAHR-muhst]; *She doos evyting **backfarmist**!*

bad hair day   *besom een d' fits.*

bad luck   *bad cess.*

bail   *to dip.*

bailing bucket   *a piggin, spudgell.*

baker's bread   *baker's fog* (a disparaging term).

barely, nearly not   *an so ardly*: *E got back t' shore drectly, **an so ardly**.* "He returned to shore eventually, **but almost didn't**."

barrel   *covel* (for water), *puncheon.*

barometer   (*wedder*) *glass.*

be, is, are, am   See NE **bes**.

be a helper   *go dog fer* (someone).

beach, shoreline   *lanwash, lanwatch, lamwatch.*

because, due to   *see'n (dat/as), on account ov, bein as*: *E let oi een **see'n as** oi knows es fadder.* "He admitted me **because** I know his father."

bedbugs *bedflies* [BAYD-floyz].

before *op t', fore, eed ov, afore.*

bellow, shout *to blear*: *D' gommy bleared at d' top ov es lungs.* Also **bawl out**.

begin with, to- *f' starters*: *D' magistrate give en a tirty-dollar foine jus f' starters.*

big, huge *gert, ger*: *E buildeed a gert big ouse.* "He built a **huge** house."

big meal *scoff.*

birthday custom *grace faace, d' bumps.*

black cormorant *shag.*

blueberry *hurts, ground hurts.* Also **black hurts, blueberry hurts, mathers, English blueberry**.

blizzard, final *Sheila's Brush*, a final wintry mid-March blizzard.

blow (an auto horn) *barmp.*

blow nose loudly *to konk.*

blunderer *a pissarse, pissass.*

boat *banker, bumboat, dory, punt, rodney, schooner, skiff, smack, trap skiff.*

boatload of fish *a put.*

bob along *to dob*: *O Jerry dobbed along shore.*

body position *crump*: *E got een a bad crump unner da ouse.* "He found **himself in a cramped position** under the house."

bogland *d' barrens*, as in *on d' barrens.*

boot preservative *drubbin* (oil and tallow).

boot-repair line *tacker.*

boot, sealskin- (conifer bark-tanned) *bark boot.*

bosom of shirt or upper chest: *craw.* See NE **kronk**.

bother *chafe* [CHAYF]: *Dippin d' dill bes a chafe.* "Bailing the bilge is always a **bother**."

bounce *glance* [GLAHNS] *(av).*

bow space (of a boat) *cuddy, for'd cuddy.*

boy, young- *shaver.*

bread *loaf, bun, bannock.*

bread (stovetop –) *touton.*

bread loaf end *a (h)eel.*

bread mix *barm*

bread, trappers'- *flummy, stove cake*.

broken ice *ballycatter, bellycanter*.

broken *broke*. *Es leg was broke*.

broom *besom*.

brown *blay, duckedy-mud colour*.

buoy, net- *keg/kag*; small wooden cask used as a fishnet or cod trap float.

bundle of dried fish *yaffle, faggot*.

butcher as in to clean game for table food, *clayn* (rabbits), *panch/paunch* (moose).

butter (dairy–) *good budder, table budder*.

buttercup *gillycup, gilleap*.

C

camp stove *bogie* [BOH-gee].

can *tin* as in *a tin ov peas*.

cane *stick, wawking stick*.

can imagine (said ironically) *seems t' see*: *Oi seems t' see she gettin married t' Tom*. "I **think it unlikely** she will marry Tom."

can maybe do *moight* [MUEHT].

cantankerous *crousty* [KROWS-tee].

capable (of) *wu'd'n put't pas*: *Wu'd'n put't pas Abel t' steal me boots*.

care, take- *moin*, as in *Moin wher you puts ya feet, b'y*.

cargo ship *sack ship* (that also carries wine, *sack*)

carry, drag *lug*. *E lugged d' dory op d' bawn by essauf*.

caulk *chinch* (between planks of a wooden boat, seams of a log house).

cause to feel dispirited or ill *take d' good out ov–*

ceiling *loffen* [LAWF-fuhn].

centipede *earwig* (not an insect; see NE **earwig**).

certain, sure *garnteed*: *Mary bes d' bess cook on d' shore*, **garnteed**.

chaise-longue *daybed*.

chatterbox *prate box, chewmouth*.

chattiness *chew*: "*Dat Mabel, she got some* **chew**. *Can't shut she op ataa! A real chewmouth, she is*."

characteristic of *…aa oer.*

chewing tobacco *dark cake* (a strong, heavy variety).

child's stick game *tiddly, flick d' stick, piddly.*

chimney sparks *flankers.*

chives *chibbles.*

choke, strangle *jole* [JOHL]: *Oi wud a' joled 'n f' stealin fom me rabbit slips.* "I would have **strangled** him for stealing from my rabbit trap line."

cigarette *a fag, a smoke.*

claw *to scrawb.*

claws, talons *tanners, tannels.*

clock, watch *toimepiece.*

cloudberry *bake apple.*

clumsy fellow *a bostoon, chucklehead.*

clutch, hold tight *to clum.*

coastal ship *coast boat* (cargo and passengers)

coastal village *outport.*

coastal resident *bayman* (as opposed to a *townie*).

codfish *fish* (as designated by Supreme Court of Newfoundland decision, 1915). See NE **cod**.

cod fish roe *fish peas* (eaten as a delicacy); *breeches.*

cod-fishing net *a trap.*

cod-fishing vessel *banker.*

cod (dried) in casks (for export) *screwed fish, drum fish.*

coexist with *get along with.*

cold, frosty *co* [KOH], *raw.*

cold, crisp, clear *keen*: *T'was a keen day f' teelin rabbit slips.*

common sense *click nar clue*: *E a'n't got nar click nar clue.* "He has no **common sense**."

communal social See NE **garden party**.

community day *garden party*, [community name] + *Day* as in "Robert's Arm Day."

complain loudly *bostoon, blear.*

complements, suits *goes good wid.*

company of, in the- *een tack wid.*

compass directions *nard* [NAWRD] north

> *saud* [SOWD] south
>
> *ees* [EES] east
>
> *wes* [WEHS] west
>
> *nardees* [nawrd-EES] northeast
>
> *saudees* [sowd-EES] southeast
>
> *narwes* [nawr-WEHS] northwest
>
> *sauwes* [sow-WEHS] southwest

conch shell *conk*.

consider capable of *(w)ud'n put't pas*: *Oi wud'n put't pas Abe t' steal me punt some noight.*

considered as in "All things considered..."; *tween one ting an nodder...*

continue *dodge on op, –down, –oer*: *Tink maybe oi ull **dodge on op** d' road.* "I've decided I may **continue along** the street." Also *take a dodge on op d' road.* See **stroll** (this listing).

continued on *went on. Sally wud'n home, so we **went on.***

cooking pot *pipkin*.

corporal punishment *a laysin* [LAY-suhn], *trimmin*.

co-sign for, support *go good fer*.

cotton swabs *toe*.

could not *cud'n*.

could have *cud a'*.

cough (up) *awk (op)*.

crack *a brack*.

cranberry *bankburry, bearburry*. Note **squashberry**.

crane fly *daddy longlegs* (family *Tipulidae*): *Luh, a **daddy longlegs**. Rain d'mar!*

crew *ands* : *Aa **ands** is affer leavin d'* Sadie J, *cap'in an aa.* "All **crew members** have abandoned the *Sadie J*, even the captain."

criticize, tease *to ballyrag*.

crook *a slieveen* [SLEE-veen].

crooked, out of line *squish, squishy*: *Affer d' starm, d' flag po was gone aa **squishy**.*

crotch of trousers *ferks*. Note **foreparts**.

crouch *to quot* [KWAWT], *coopy* (*down*).

crush a thing flat *to squat*.

crybaby, wimp *sook*.

cut branches *limb* (*out*): *Ya got t' **limb out** lashins o' tant trees fer a taa fence.* "You must **cut the branches off** a great many tall, slender trees in order to build a tall fence."

D

dandelion *piss-a-bed*, *toddie*, *dumbledor(e)*. Also **August-flower, devil's carpet**.

dance, an energetic- a *plank'er down*.

dance energetically *to plank'er down*.

dangerous shoal *sunkers, flowers*.

dangerous iceberg *growler*.

deceived for profit *soak*: *E got **soaked** bad on dat deal*.

deceased *poor*, a sympathetic or respectful reference. ***Poor** Aunt Mable bes gone dese twenny yeur*.

deep sleep *deed t' da world* [WEHRL].

delicate as in soft, tender, easily injured: *nish*.

delicious, tasty *scrumptious* [SKRUHM-shehs].

deranged *low moindeed* [LOH MUEHN-deed], *mental*.

detained, arrested *took op fer*: *Tom was **took op fer** lobster-catchin out o' season*.

determined effort *give er*: *Take dis mallet an **give er**!* "Take this mallet and **hit it hard**!"

detract from *take away fom*: *Terry id'n one t' **take away fom** yer weddin b' showin op late*.

distressed *opstrapless, vexed, opsot, real put out*

discard, throw away *condemn*; *chuck*.

dinner (evening meal) *supper, tea*; (banquet) *scoff*.

dinner and dance *scoff 'n scuff*.

direct address See NE **b'y, o man, o trout, babby, daw, dear, ducky, girl, maid**.

disappointed *real put out, opsot*: *Da o ooman was **real put out** over me boddle o' Screech*.

disgusted   *poisoned wid*: Sis was **poisoned wid** 'm f' kickin er cracky. "Sis was **disgusted with** him for kicking her little dog."

disgusting   *gross*; (as of a person) *not fit*.

dishes, traditional   See NE **figgy duff, jigg's dinner, pease pudding**.

dishrag   *dishcloth*.

dislike   *not fussy 'bout*: Oi naer was **fussy 'bout** lobster.

disorder, disarray   *een slings*: Sadie made bread an den leaved d' kitchen **een slings**.

disrespectful   *saucy, lippy*: Grandpa naer took no guff fom **lippy** youngsters.

distinctive person   See NE **wha' is ye loike**. Note NE **some b'y**.

dizzy, foolish   *giddy*: Da wine made oi roight **giddy**.

do, does   *doos* [DOOZ] (present tense): Oi **doos** aa d' cookin an washin at ome.

do chores alone   *to fudge*. Note NE **cross-andeed**.

doesn't matter   See **unimportant** (this listing).

dog (small)   *crackie*.

dog's bark   *yap*.

doorstep   *dreshel* [DRIHSH-uhl].

dozing state   *a dwall*, as in E's een a **dwall**. "He is **dozing**."

downwind   *luard, lund*.

drafty   *airsome*.

dragonfly   *arse-stinger, devil's needle, mosquito hawk*.

draw   *to mark out*. See NE **sketch, snap**.

dress up   *to frapse* [FRAYPSS].

dried fish   *pipsi* (from Inuttut/Inuktitut, Labrador).

drink from bottle   *to swig* [SWEEG] (alcoholic beverage).

dripping   *dribbly*: Our wadder comes from a **dribbly** brook.

drive (take a short-)   *go fer a run*. Note **dodge, dart**.

driven   *drove*: D' goats was **drove** out o' d' garden.

driven to distraction   *drove*: You got oi **drove**! "You've **driven me to distraction**!"

drunk   *sousht, pluteed, af-cut*.

dry and salt cod   *make fish*.

dry evergreen   *blasty bough*.

due to See **because** (this listing).

dumpling in soup a *doughboy*.

dunk oneself *go souse*

E

ear *yeroe* [YEHR-oh].

earing *yerrin*. *Nan bes affer losin er bess set o' yerrins.*

early-rising *yarry*. Note **alert**, this listing.

effrontery, nerve *faace*: *Madge ad d' faace t' tell oi dat loie.*

either *ar'n, ar one*

electricity, spark *juice*. *She'll naer start wid nar juice een d' battery, eh b'y?*

empty *to emp* (*out*): *Emp out d' puncheon fer oi, will ya, me son?*

empty (a room) *gut out*: *Ya aves t' gut Marie's room out afore ya paints it.*

ending, halt *let-op*: *Rain, rain, an nar let-op in soight.*

engine *hengine*.

entice with bate *to toll*.

envious *covechus*.

eraser *rubber*.

evening, twilight *duckish, eel o' d' day*.

ever, at all *firs nar las*: *D' constable naer showed firs nar las* "The policeman did **not** arrive **at all**."

every; each *evy* [EH-vee].

exceedingly See **very** (this listing).

excellent *shockin good*.

excepting *clar ov, outsoide ov, cep fer*.

excessive bites (mosquitoes, black flies) *eat aloive*: *Oi bes eat aloive wid dem nippers!*

excessive noise a *racket*. Note **charm**.

excrement *caca* [KAW-kaw] (a child's word).

exposed to cold *kronk* [KAWNK], as one's throat, pridefully doing without a scarf.

extinguish a fire *to douse, dout*.

extra amount free *tilly*.

extremely, very   *fair*: *Jack was **fair** ravness affer work.*

extremely angry   *roary-oied*, *roary-oied mad*.

F

faint   *to conk out*.

fall down   *to slurp*.

fallen completely   *slauso*, *slouso*[SLOW-soh]: *Gabe went **slauso**, een d' ditch!*

fatigued   *beat out*, **fagged** (*out*): *aa fagged out*, very tired, exhausted.

fawning person   *a sook*.

fearful of   *dreads*: *She dreads d' stroife o' ween.* "She fears windstorms."

feel discomfort   *to stroik een*: *Somtin **struck een** es leg.* "He has a sudden pain in his leg."

female friend   *friend-girl* (female friend of a girl).

fib, lie   *a coffer*.

finish a task   *clew op*.

firewood   *faddle*, *brishney*, *bavin*.

fish offal   *gurry*.

fish and brewis   *brewis* [BROOZ], boiled **cod**, boiled hard bread or hard biscuit with **scrunchins**.

fish-drying platform   *flake*.

fisherman, live aboard-   *floater*

fisherman, shore-   *landsman*

fisherman's brewis   See NE **fish and brewis**.

fisherman's wharf   *stage*, *stage eed*.

fishery premises   *room*

fish pressing area   (for export) *screwing room*, *screw store*.

fish-processing area   *stage* (wharf, processing tables, gear stowage sheds, etc.), *warsh ouse*.

Fishing Admiral   (of the harbour) *me Lard*

fishing area   *banks*, *grounds*.

fit of weeping   *a cryin jag*: *Aunt Suze bes on a **cryin jag** whenaer Uncle John goes out on d' wadder een a breeze o' ween.*

fir tree (balsam)   *var*. Also *snotty var*.

firewood, small-   *keep-e-goins*, *keep-a-goins*, *kippy-goins*.

five   *foiv (fi')* [FUEHV], [FUEH]: *You can len oi fi' dollars t' payday, eh, b'y?*

flapjack, pancake   *frozie* [FROH-zee], *bangbelly, damper dog, touton, gandy, grace cake.*

floor covering (type)   *canvas, floor canvas.*

floor, ship's deck   *planchen, planken.*

fly of one's pants   (unbuttoned) *shop door* (humourous).

foggy, wet and cold   *caplin wedder.* Note **mauzy.**

fold   *lap.*

follow   *folly.*

food, a meal   *grub.*

food, trappers'   *prog* [PRAWG].

food bag   *progbag, grubbag.*

fool   *a gommil* [GAW-muhl], *gommy, gom.*

footprints   *footins.*

for   *fer, f':* *We'm got brewis f' tea.* "We have fish and brewis **for** dinner."

for sure   *dat is* (sentence-final pragmatic marker[12]): *D' fog is tick enough t' cut wid a knoife, dat is.* Note **ataa.**

fortune, riches   *far'chun* [FAHR?-chuhn].

forecasts, predicts   *calls fer* (usually weather): *She calls f' rain een d' forecast.*

fowling   *birdin,* also *gunnin.*

freckles   *summer moes, sun mole.*

freezing rain coating   a *silver thaw.*

freezing ice   *ballycatter, frore.*

"French" fries   *chips.*

French-Indian   *a jacky tar.* See NE **jackatar.**

fried salt pork   *vang.*

fried pork cut fine   *scrunchins* (a condiment in several Newfoundland recipes). See NE **fish cakes, brewis.**

friendly greeting   to male: *b'y, o trout, skipper, o man, luv* ; to female: *babby, daw, ducky, girl, maid, luv.*

from   *fom* [FUHM].

frost   *frore* [FROHR].

frozen   *froze. Me fingers was froze een d' ween.*

frustrate to anger   *to crossackle: Don' crossackle oi, er oi ull limb ya!* "Don't **annoy** me, or I will break off your limbs!"

full load   *a stigger* [STIHG-ehr].

G

gale   *breeze, stroife o' ween, starm.*

game sea fowl   See NE **birdin**.

garbage   *lob, lawb, scroff.*

gasp, yawn   *to gape* [GAYP].

get a haircut   *get faired av.*

get thin   *gone away; rake. John bes gone away t' skin an bones fom ard work. Skinny as a rake.*

get out of the way   *shift* [SHEEF] *oer.* See NE **sloo, veer av.**

ghost   *tokens, fetch.*

give attention to   *go t' work an; mus go (an). Mus go an tar me roof.*

go in costume   *to mummer, janny, jenny.* See NE **jannying**

go to bed   *to go t' couch* [KOOSH], *turn een.*

golden paint   *gelt* [GEHLT] a decorative metallic paint.

good with the bad   *talqual* [TAHL-kwahl].

good day   *G'day* [guh-DEUH].

good fellow, man   *noice b'y* (ironic expression): *Wha'? E stole yer punt? Noice b'y!*

good night   *G'deevn* [guh-DEEV-uhn].

good evening   *G'deevn* [guh-DEEV-uhn].

good afternoon   *G'deevn* [guh-DEEV-uhn].

good morning   *G'marn* [guh-MAWRN].

good old days   *dog orn days*

gossip, tall tale   *pishogues* [FIHSH-awgz], [FIHSH-uhr-awgz]; *Tokens? Fetches? Da's aa pishogues, b'y.* See NE **blather**.

gossip (person)   *a tattletale, tattle-tongue.*

gov't. assistance   *dole, doe.* See NE **dole arder**.

graceful   *suent* [SOO-ent] (as of the shape of a ship).

gravey   *sulick, grace.*

great auk   *penguin.*

greedy *covechus.*

grocery list *arder.*

guernsey sweater *a gansey*

guilt, guilty *coffer.*

Guy Fawkes' Night *Bonfoire Noight.*

H

had better See **should** (this listing).

hall *all* [AWL], [AW] (prolonged [AW]), as in a social gathering place: *church all*, "church hall."

hand barrow *bar.*

hand weigh *to eft.*

hard knot a *snarbuckle.*

has, have *got.*

has/have been *ben*: *Jack ben on d' Labrador dese tree yeur.* "Jack **has been** fishing off Labrador for three years now."

has/have not *a'n't* [AHNT]: *Oi a'n't got d' toime f' dis!* "I **have no** time for this!"

hay mound *a pook.*

hay rope *a sugawn.*

he, him *e, en, 'm*

hear, heard *year, yeard*, as in *Oi yeard en say dat mesauf.*

her *she*; *er* as in *Er lassy tea bes d' bess een Careless Cove.* Also *she* as in *E took she to church las Sunday.*

here *yere*; *yoi.*

hi/hello. *Wha's y' at?* [was-yuh-AHT] (Ans: *Dis's it.* [DIHS ihz IHT]).

hide from work *to slinge* [SLIHNJ].

hinterland *country*: *Es tilt bees een d' country.* See NE **eensoide, een d' country.**

him *e, en,'m*: *Ya gives en a boddle o' screech an e ull tell ya anyting.* "Give him a bottle of rum and he will tell you whatever you wish to know."

hind paw of seal *daddle.* See NE **fipper.**

his *es* [EEZ].

hit another's elbow *to jut.*

hit, slap *to douse, wop.*

hold for, retain *keep a–olt ov.*

hole in stage *a trunk 'ole, truck 'ole, trink 'ole* (for drawing up sea water).

holiday *toime av, aliday.*

Holy Wednesday (before Good Friday) *Spy Wednesday.*

hooligan, ruffian *carner b'y, case, ard case, jeezler, ral.*

horse *arse.*

hot weather, It is– *She's splittin d' rocks.*

house dance *a scuff.*

how *d' goin ov: Dey near knowd d' goin ov en.* "They didn't learn how he left."

humming *chin music,* as in humming or singing wordless tunes in rhythm to accompany dancing. *Cheek music.*

hungry *peckish* (somewhat–); *ravness* or *gut-foundered* (very–).

hunting sea birds *birdin, gunnin.*

hurry *to skirr.* In a hurry: *in a tear.*

hyperactive *galin* [GAY-lin], as in *Dem cats bes aaweez galin fore a starm.*

I

I *oi,* first person speaker.

ice-glazed *glitter* [GLIHD-dehr] ice-glazed surface after freezing rain.

icicle *oice candle, conkerbill.*

identical *xac same* [ZAHK SAYM].

idiosyncrasy *got d' fashion: She got d' fashion ov readin een bed.*

if, whether *eef, , eef'n.*

imminent *comin on (now)*

immature herring *mudjurine* [MUHD-jer-een].

immature codfish *a peel, tomcod, tommycod.*

impertinent *saucy, lippy, brazen.*

impertinence *guff, sauce, brazenness.*

in, into *een.*

in any case, at all *ataa* [ah-TAW]: *Some rain! Can't get outdoors ataa!*

in bed *een bunk* (due to illness or sloth).

inboard motor a *make'n'break* (an early one-cylinder type).

infected *ampered*: *D' men on da wadder offen gets **ampered** fingers.*

infected fingernail *a **witlow*** [WIHT-loh].

initiate (as of a "new" Newfoundlander) ***kiss d' cod*** and other various tasks; see NE screech-in.

insult *crack*

intend to *dreaten* to: *Susan **dreatened t'** ang out cloz eed ov d' rain.* "Susan **intended to** hang clothes out to dry before it rained."

intense black *tawniers* [TAWN-yerz].

interrupt, prevent *shag* [SHAYG] *Dis wedder ull **shag** our plans f' d' day.*

intoxicated *af-cut*, *sousht*, as in *sousht t' d' two oies.*

irritable *broody, contrary, crousty, crookeed, cranky.*

is that so! (expression of unbelief) ***Gwan!***

isn't that so? *eh b'y*? (Central), *idn it? innit? T'day's fishin **id'n** much t' live on, eh b'y?*

isolated hill *a tote, tolt.*

it appears, seems *b' d' looks ov it*: *A breeze is on da way, **b' d' looks ov it.***

it happens. *Da's it, b'y* (fatalistic expression)

it is *t'is* [TIHZ].

it is not *t'ain't*: ***T'ain't** a gunshot away.* "It is not fifty yards away."

it is not *t'id'n.*

it was *t'was.*

J

January 6 *Teak Day*, Old Christmas Day.

jaundice *yellow janders.*

joker, wit *card.*

jump ice pans *to copy, tally.* See NE ***O Christmas Day.***

just *onny, is aa. T'is nar starm, **onny** a few blossoms, **is aa.***

just completed *affer, be affer*: *Alice **bes affer** bakeen some lovely pies.*

K

kettle, camp- *(o) slut, piper.*

kindling *splits, faddle, brishney.*

kitchen cupboard *dresser.*

knowing, attentive *known.* Said of unusually familiar dogs, horses or other animals.

L

Labrador tea *Injun* or *Indian tea, crystal tea.*

lacking *ard op fer, stuck fer: Young Davie is **ard op fer** a job o' work.* "Young Davie **very much requires** employment."

ladies' panties *stepeens* [STEHP-eenz].

lagoon as at a river mouth: *barsway* [BARZ-way].

lake, pond *pond.*

lamp, kerosine– *flirrup* [FLUHR-uhp], *tellylamp, laddin lamp, stand lamp.*

lance *lanch* [LAHNCH] (to relieve infection).

large wooden barrel *puncheon* [PUH-chuhn]. See NE **covel**. Note NE **puncheon tub**.

later *affer.*

laundry day, good- *day on.*

laundry soap *rinso. You needs d' rinso f' bad stains.*

lavatory (men's) *pump ouse.*

lazy *slack.*

lazy fellow *slack arse, angishore.*

leak *lake.*

lean *to cant.*

leather punch *hawl, awl.*

leather top boots *logans.*

leaves, edible– *greens* (cabbage, turnip, dandelion), *turnip tops.*

lend, support *toide oer,* as in *Me fadder **toideed** oi oer t' payday.*

lever *prise* [PRUEHZ]; *to **prise** (**op**)* to open (as the lid of a tin).

lewd female *skank.*

line with hooks *bultow.*

liquor, bulled- *swish.*

loan   *to len*: *T''is airsome t'noight.* **Len** *oi y' gansey?*

lobster trap ends   *eeds* [EHDZ].

longing for   *(fair) gone fer*: *We'm fair gone f' some brewis.* "We **long for** fish-and-brewis."

Look there!   *Luh!*

loon   a *loo.*

low trees   *tuckamore.*

lunch   (mid-day meal) *dinner.* Note **supper, scoff.**

M

madly, extremely   *da wensy* as in *bile da wensy,* "boil madly"; *go da wensy,* "move very quickly."

mainland Canada   *opalong* (specifically Ontario).

marble   *alley* [AHL-lee], a little marble or glass sphere used in children's *allies* or *chip-chip* games.

marsh, bog   a *mish.*

meal, large-   *feed.* Note *scoff,* banquet.

mean   *scutty.*

mean person   *a scut.*

menstrual period   *on d' rags* (explicit reference).

merchandise for fish   *truck* (barter payment).

merely, simply, just   *s'aa* as in *Oi knows d' place see'n as oi blongs dere,* **s'aa.** "I know about the place **simply** because I am from there." *Ya wants t' tarment d' poor b'y,* **s'aa.** "You **just** want to aggravate the unfortunate boy."

mess   a *clobber.*

misbehaving child   *article,* also *li'l article.*

mischief   *devilment, badness.*

mischievous   *idle.*

mishap, accident   *misfarchun*

misty and warm   *mauzy* [MAW-zee] (weather). Also *muggy.*

mitten, work-   *cuff,* a fingerless protective work mitten.

mix   *mang* [MAYNG]: *She manged op d' grub on account we's so ravness.* "She threw together a meal because we are famished."

moist mud   *pug,* as found in a bog.

molasses sauce   *coady, cotie, yankee budder.*

molasses tea   *lassy tea*. Note **lassy loaf**.

months of the year   See NE **monts**

mooring rope   *a painter*.

moors   *d' barrens*, as in *on d' barrens*

morning sea mist   *loom*.

morning   *marn*: [MAWRN] *een d'marnin*, "in the morning, tomorrow morning."

mosquito   a *nipper*

mouldy, stinking   *fousty* [FOW-stee], *smatchy*.

mouth   *gob, faace* [FAAYS].

move (something)   *shif* [SHEEF] (past: *shifteed*).

move about   *to trapse, swarv* (unnecessarily and annoyingly).

mug, cup   *noggin*, usually of enamelled metal. Note **bannikin**.

mummer   *janny, jenny*.

mutiny   *to manus*.

my   *me*: *Oi got me car painted tawniers*. "I had **my** car painted black."

myself   *mesauf* [mee-SOWF]. See **Small Words** in introduction.

N

nag about   *arp on*: *Da wife 'arped on me long air so oi got en cut*.

narrow passage   *tickle* (of inshore navigation).

narrow rocky lane   *drung, drong*.

narrow   *narry*; *to narry* (to make narrow)

native of, from   *blong*: *Jamis blongs to Careless Cove*.

native species   Only 14 known mammal species are or were native to Newfoundland island, including black bear, beaver, caribou, red fox, lynx, pine martin, muskrat, otter, meadow vole, and 3 bat species. See **Newfoundland wolf**.

naughty   *idle*.

nearly   *noigh* (*on*), *goin on*, **andy to/bout**, *aamos* as in "nearly a week."

near to, (very-)   *ome to*: *Granfer's shop bes roight ome to es ouse*. Also *longsoide*.

negative words   *no, not, naer, nar, nar'n, bain't, id'n*. Note use of double negatives, as in *E ull naer get nar ooman wid nar dollar een es pocket*. "With **no** money he will **never** get a wife."

neither   *nar'n, nar one*

never   *naer* [NAH-ehr]: *Skipper naer bes ome long enough t' see es faace.*

nevertheless   *stio fer aa* [STEE-oh fuhr aw]. *A wunnerfo starm, but stio fer aa, dey got back safe.*

New England   *Boston States.*

Newfoundland dishes or garnishes   See **ard tack; bangbelly; blony; brewis; cheeks; chibbles; chips; chips, dressin, 'n' gravy; coady; cod tongues; carboo moss; damper dog; figgy duff; fipper pie; fish cake; fish peas; flummy; frozie; jigg's dinner; kipper; lob sauce; oyster leaf; park buns; peas pudding; scrunchins; touton; troifle; yankee budder.**

Newfoundland Railway   *Newfie Bullet* (train)

Newfoundland rum   *Screech*, a name brand Jamaican rum.

no, neither   *nar*: *Dere bes nar cloud een d' skoy.*

none, neither one   *nar'n.*

nonsense   *blather.* See NE **pishogues.**

not   *a'n't, bain't, t'id'n, naer*

not bad!   *not 'af bad!*

notice   *to make notice ov.*

not to mention   *naer moin* [NAH-ehr MUEHN].

no way! not likely!   *Loike ducks!* (child's language)

numb with cold   *scrammed* (usually one's hands).

numbed (muscles)   See **pins and needles** (in this listing).

O

obliged   *beholden.*

occasional   *odd, scattered*: *Da odd trouter catches a scattered meal on dis pond.*

occasionally   *ontoimes.*

ocean, on the–   *on da wadder.*

ocean's roar   *rote* (foretells a storm).

odd gloves   *belly'n'back(s).*

of, from   *ov* [OHV], *o'* [UH]. Note **fom.**

off-shore, shipboard   *on da wadder/ wa'er.*

often   *offen.*

oil *aal* (machine-); *grace* (cooking-, garnish).

okay *aaroight* [aw-RUEH?].

old seal *doter*.

old *o* [OH].

old woman, wife *da o ooman* [DOO-mahn].

open *opm* [OH?-uhm], *o'm* [OH?-uhm].

opportunity *look-een*, as in *get a* **look-een**: *Oi went fer d' job but stio fer aa oi didn' get a **look-een!*** "I applied for the job but nonetheless had no **chance**."

or *er ('r)*.

orange *arnge* [AHRNJ], the fruit.

original baseball *rounders*.

out of fashion *(aa) gone out*: *Dat cloz is **aa gone out** now*.

outfit, equipment *fit-out*.

overcharged *soak*: *E got **soaked** bad on dat deal*.

P

pain, sting *to smert*; *struck een*; *to foine*.

paint *slack* (a lime and water solution previously used as an exterior paint).

pan of ice *clamper*.

pancake *bangbelly, damper dog, frozie, grace cake*.

pant heavily *pank*.

party *a toime* [TUEHM], *breaker-down, get-t'gedder*.

party shed *d' shed*

pass me... *and oi*...[AHN DUEH]. ***Pass oi** d' salt*.

past, difficult- *pod auger*, as in *d' **pod auger** days*.

patch of woods *dring, droak*.

patch on a boot *a teeveen*.

patience (trying-) *blue een d' faace*: *Aunt Sally talked oi **blue een d' faace***. "Aunt Sally's gab **tried my patience**."

pawn off *pawn av on* (in the sense of deceptively transfering an unpleasant chore to another): *Dey **pawned** dem ard jobs **av on** oi*.

pay (in a deliberate or exaggerated manner) *plank down*.

penis *bird* (child's word).

period of *spurt ov* (as in *a spurt o' bad starms*).

periwinkle snail *wrinkle*.

person unidentified *wassname*, *buddy*, *wassesname/wassesfaace* (masc.), *wassername/wasserfaace* (fem.).

phlegm *glander*: *O Tom got d' flu an awked op a glander*.

phone *ring op*.

photograph *to snap, to sketch* (*av*). See NE **mark out**.

photograph *a snap*. Note NE **sketch**.

picnic *bile-op*. See NE **mug-op**.

piglet *bonnif*.

pickled pig's hock *crubeen*.

pinch together *to squat* (as a finger, a tin can).

pins and needles (muscles numbed by inactivity) *asleep, dunch*.

pitcher *jug*.

pitcher plant *fisherman's basket, Indian-cup*.

pitiable appearance *sorry soight*.

playhouse *cobby (ouse)*.

pleased *proud*.

please yourself *feel yer boots!*

plenty, lots *lashins* [LAH-shuhnz], *loike flies, maggoty wid*.

pliers *pinchers*.

plug for a cask *a spile* [SPAIL].

plunge into water *to go souse/souso* [GOH SOWSH/SOWSH-oh].

pond, lake *pond*.

poor man's meal *chaw an glutch*

porpoise *puff pig*.

porridge *gruel, mush*.

posterior, derriere *arse*.

posts *strouters* [STROW-derz]; *shores*.

potato *tatie* [TAY-dee], *pratie* [PRAY-dee].

potato side dish *tatie/tater salad*

pothole *gulche*

poultice, homemade- *breed poultice*

prankster   *a devilskin, devil's limb, jackeen.*

predicament   *noice fix*: *You'm een a **noice fix** wid nar painter f' d' punt.*

prefer, rather   *just as soon*: *Oi **just as soon** not go t' work t'day.*

prepare and do   *go t' work an*: *Mus **go t' work an** fix me roof.*

preposterous   *retarded* (Note: <u>not</u> a reference to the mentally challenged).

pretending (to)   *make out*, as in *E was jus' **makin out** e was hurteed.* "He was **pretending** injury." Also *gamogue*.

prevent, interrupt   *shag* [SHAYG]. *Dis wedder ull **shag** aur plans f' d' day.*

previously   *one time.*

procrastinator   *a slackarse, slackass.*

prospect, outlook   *look-out.*

proud person   *a gilderoy* [GIL-duh-rueh].

provided (for)   *sot op; found.*

ptarmigan   *partridge* [PAHRʔ-reej].

pudding   *duff, figgy duff.*

pull from water   *aul* (check nets or traps): *Dey **auled** der traps.*

pulled back tightly   *scunned back*; *Jane's hair was **scunned back** wid a ribbon.*

purchased   *boughten* [BAWT-uhn].

purse   *hand bag* [AHN bahg].

push aside   *to shuff* [SHUHF]; ***shuff av*** to push away from, as a boat from the wharf

put out (fire)   *douse*

Q

quick brief visit   *a dart*, as in *take a **dart** down d' wharf* "make **a quick visit to—**"

quarrel   *a row* [ROW], *tear up.*

R

railroad   *railway.*

raise, lift, hoist   *ist* [AIST].

raise, raised   *eave op, ove op*, as by frost.

rascal   *case, ard case*; rascally boy: *a jackeen, a devilskin, devil's limb.*

react forcefully   *come (roight) aboard ov* (someone).

reaction, bad-   *kick bout*: *Dere's a wunnerfo kick bout Matty's moonshine.*

Really! No kidding!   expression of surprise, ***Pom moy so! Gwan!***

Rear Admiral (of the harbour)   *me Lady*

received training   *went een (t' be)*: *Aunt Vy's son went een t' be a priest.*

recognize, see   *to lay oies on.* *Oi naer laid ois on 'm fore dis.* "I didn't **recognize** them."

redo   *toime back*, as in *Eef oi ad me toime back…*"If I could **redo** my past…"

regardless   *ataa* [ah-TAW].

regional dialect   *talk*: *Dey aves a dif'rent talk een Snail Cove dan we people.* See also *flat talk, slang, accent.*

relax, rest   *take er easy* [TAYK-ehr AYZ-ee]: *Oi ull take er easy affer oi poiles op enough foirewood fer d' winter.*

rely or depend on   *go on*, usually used with negative: *Ye can't go on da wedder forecast.*

remember, recall   *moin*, as in *Oi do moin when dere was more cod on d' go.* "I **recall** when there was more cod fish available."

remind   *put een moin ov*: *Wha' [WAW?] you said jus' put oi een moin o' Fadder Jones.* "Your remark **reminded** me of Father Jones."

reprimand   *loine (s.o) ov*: *Aunt Maggy loined en ov fer walkin on er wet floor.* Also *come board o', go board (ov), tongue-bangin.*

resemble, look like   *turn affer.*

restless   *fidgety* [FIHJ-uh-dee]. Note *idle.*

rest (from work)   *a spell. Peter took a spell fom cleavin splits.*

retain, hold on   *keep a-hold ov.*

retort   *back answer, yap.*

revengeful   *spitey* [SPUEH?-ee].

rhythm instrument   *ugly stick*

rinse   *rench* [REHNCH].

rock-pile blind   *a gaze* (from which one hunts game birds).

rocky beach   *bawn, barren, fish beach.*

roof covering, a-   *tar felt.* See NE **tar, pitch**.

rosefish *a spratt.*

rowboat *dory, punt, rodney.*

rowboat seat *tawt.*

rude *ignorant* [EEG-ruhnt].

ruin *to* **come agin**: *Devilment aaweez* **comes agin** *a hangishore.*

rumour has it that *cardin to*: **Cardin to**, *e bes aaready married to nodder ooman.*

S

sale by auction *a vandue* [VAHN-doo].

saliva, excessive- *wadder panks* [WAWD-dehr pahnks].

salt fish (washed) *wadder arse.*

same, identical *xac same* [ZAHK SAYM]

sand-bar, lagoon *barsway* [BARZ-way].

saved *sove op*: *Suze* **sove op** *ten dollars.*

scan carefully *scun* [SKUHN].

scattered *abroad*: *E wopped me bite* **abroad** *d' planken.* "He **scattered** my share of money **on** the floor."

school *skoo. Li'l Jargie naer missed a day o'* **skoo**.

school grade level *book*: *Wha'* **book** *you een now, Jargie, eh?*

scissors, shears *snips.*

scraped, abraded *scrawb, scrob*, or *scrope* (one's skin).

sea, on the–, at– *on da wadder.*

sea birds *shell birds.*

sea urchin *oar egg, orz egg, whore's egg, hozzie egg.*

seal *a swoile.*

sealer's blanket *kirby, curvey.*

seal hunting *swoilin.*

seal's forepaw *fipper* [FIHP-pehr]; See NE **daddle**.

sealskin boot (dress boot) *bark boot.*

searching for *be affer.*

seaweed *dulse.*

second of a pair *d' feller to*. **D' feller t'** *me odder sock.*

secure footing *purchase*: *E got good* **purchase** *on d' clumpers an stayed droy.*

see-saw *weigh-de-buckedy*.

sense well-being *to feel mesauf, yersauf, etc.*: *Oi id'n feelin mesauf t'day.* "I **feel out of sorts** today."

served (meal) *took op.* *Oi'll ave yer brewis **took op** drectly.*

set a trap *to teel* (usually for rabbits).

settler, pioneer *a livyer; planter*.

sexual drive *nature*; *Young Davy's **nature** ull come agin en some day.*

shallow depth *shoal*, as of water.

share *a bite*, as in *me bite* "my share."

she, her *she*: *Aunt Dot? Oi give **she** a toimepiece fer er birt'day.*

sheltered *lun(d), lundy*.

ship See *NE* **boat**.

shiver with cold *to biver, bibber, snacker*.

shoal *bank, ground*. Note **shoal**.

short shower, flurry *a dwoy*.

short distance *a gunshot* (about 50 yards or 46 metres).

short fire log *a junk*.

short thread *ravel*.

should, had better *mus*: *Oi mus' wroight dat down fore oi fergets en.* "I **had better** make a note of that or I will forget it."

Shrove Tuesday *Pancake Night*.

silly trick *a gamogue* [gahm-AWG].

single girl *a maid*.

size up *to gunny* (something).

skeleton *a rames* [RAYMZ].

skin a seal *to pelt, sculp*.

slab of ice *pan*. See NE **copy**.

slap of the hand *a wop* [WAWP], *douse* [DOWSS].

sleep paralysis *da o hag*.

sleepy *groggy*.

sleepy eye deposit *sleep*.

slice of bread, thick– *Labrador sloice*.

slow sailing *jogging*.

sly person *sly conner*.

small breaking seas *lops* [LAWPS].

small amount of *a gob ov.*

small pieces *flinders* [FLIHN-derz].

small bit *a soign.*

small rounded hill *a knap* [NAHP].

small leak *a peeze*; *to peeze, weep.*

small slim fir tree *a wattle* [WAWʔ-uhl].

small woods shack *a tilt.*

small dog name *pish.* Note NE **cracky**. Also *crackie.*

smoker's pipe *a dudeen.*

snack with tea *a mug-op.*

snow flake *a blossom.*

snowshoe *a racket, skin racket.*

snowshoe plaiting *babbish*

so (to that extent) *dat, da'.*

soft sea ice *slob* (cannot be walked on), *lolly.*

soft sound *a gig* [GEEG]: *O Pish bes some good dog, naer a gig out ov en.* "Pish is a good dog, very **quiet**."

sole of sock *a vamp*

sometimes *ontoimes*: *Ontoimes d' toide comes oer da wharf.* "**Sometimes** the sea floods the pier."

song or lyric (traditional) *come-aa-yer* [kuhm-AW-yuhr]

soon *bumbye, drectly, da once. Goin home da once?* "Are you going home **soon**?" Also *now da once,* "very soon."

soot *smut.*

so that/in order that *ferto* [FUHR-duh].

southerly *sudard.*

sore, infection *a amper.*

sown roughly *scunned.*

speak with as in "wishes to–" *wants a word wid.*

speed, reckless *full tilt* (*een*): *First toime a' da wheel, e went* **full tilt** *een a loight po!*

spoil, about to– *smatchy.* See NE **fousty**.

spoiled, gone bad *blowed,* as of canned or bottled foods.

spring cleaning   *ousecleanin toime. Ousecleanin toime evyting bes aa op een slings.* "During **traditional spring cleaning** everything is in chaos."

sprinkling   *a scatter* (of snow, flour, etc).

spruce beverage   *calabogus, spruce beer.*

squeak, creaking   *a scroop, a whizzle.*

squeaky   *scroopy.*

stacked cod to dry   *wadder arse.*

stay, remain   *to boide* [BUEHD].

stay out all night   *to jake.*

step inside   *to duck een.*

steer a vessel   *scun.*

still river water   *a steady.*

stink, bad smell   *funk.*

stomach   *puddock* [PUH-dihk].

Stop that!   *Knock av!*

storage shed   *a store.*

stormy   *darty. Me son, t'is mad rough an **darty** out t'noight!* "Buddy, it's **stormy** out tonight!"

stow tightly   *to chinch, stog*: *D' li'l nipper **stogged** es faace wid chips.* "The child **filled his mouth** with french fries."

straight   (unmixed rum or whiskey) *neat.*

straight, aligned   *fair, faired op, strayt* [STRAYʔ].

straighten, align   *fair op*: *Fair op y' skirt, girl. Ya looks loike a streel!* "**Straighten** your skirt, girl. You look slovenly."

strait   *strayt* [STRAYʔ].

strangle   *jole* [JOHL].

street   *strayt* [STRAAYʔ] (prolonged [AY]).

stroll   *dodge op, –down, –oer*; *marl*: *Tink maybe oi ull **dodge op** d' road.* "I've decided that I may **go for a stroll** up the street."

strong, healthy   *clever.*

stuck, settled   *lodged*: *Joe ad a herrinbone **lodged** een es weasand.* "Joe had a herring-bone **stuck** in his throat."

student's note book   *scribbler, exercise.*

stupid   *stun*: *Ac' stun an y'ull be put back een skoo.* "If you act **stupid** you will fail a grade in school."

stupid fellow   *bostoon, chucklehead, oonshick, stun po.*

stutter   *stoppage*: *E got a stoppage een es speech.* "He **stutters**."

such a thing   *da loike*: *Oi naer done da loike!* "I did not do **such a thing**!"

suicide door   *mother-in-law door*

superstitions   See NE **pishogue**.

supper   (as in "banquet") *scoff*. Note **dinner, scoff, feed**.

supported   *took op fer*: *E took op f' Joany stio fer aa she was wrong.*

suppose   *low* [LOW]: *Oi lows e made a far'chun.* "I suspect that he made a fortune."

surely, for sure   *garnteed, sure (an)*: *Sure, an she bes d' bess cook on d' shore, garnteed.*

surface   (as of fish) *to breach.*

surprise cake   *guess cake.*

suspenders   *bracers.*

swallow   *glutch* (especially with difficulty).

swearing   *blaggard.*

sweater   *garnsey, gansey, jumper.*

swell up   *plim*: *D' boat plimmed op aa out o' shape affer he bes on shore aa winner.*

sweltering   *close* [KLOHS].

swindle   *soak*: *E got soaked bad on dat deal.*

scissors   *sithers* [SIHDH-ehrz] (a folk correction).

T

tablet, personal   *(chaulk) slate*, a school student's erasable work pad.

tack   *sparble.*

tall and slender   *tant* [TAHNT] (trees, poles, masts).

tall fence pickets   *longers* [LUHNG-erz]. See NE **strouters**.

tar (heated til thin)   *pitch.*

tarring brush   *tar mop.*

tea   *tay* [TAY], as in **mug o' tay**. *Stir tay wid a knoife, stir op stroife.*

tea kettle   *piper.*

tempting   *moreish* [MOHR-eesh] (said of food): *Mmm, dis duff is moreish.*

tender (boat)   *bumboat.*

thanks   *tanks, tank you.*

thaw   to *unthaw* [awn-TAW] as ice to water.

the, this   *d', dis: D' dulse covered d' bawn affer d' breeze.* "The seaweed covered **the** beach after **the** gale"; *Tom come ome da weyk.* "Tom came home **this** week."

their   *deyr.*

there   *dere.*

therefore, thus   *so soigns.*

these; for (time)   *dese: E ben deed dese ten yeur.* "He has been dead **for** ten years."

they, them   *dey, dem, em*

thick   *tick.*

thick soup   *a lob sauce.*

thin and boney   *rawny.* Note NE **rake**.

thingamajig   *wassname, chummyjigger.*

thud, bang   *tump* [TOOMP].

tree bark   *rind* [RAIN].

thole pin   *towpin.*

three   *tree.* See NE **nummers**.

throat   *weasand* [WEE-zuhn]. See NE **kinkarn**.

through   *trou.*

throw, toss, discard   *chuck, foire away.*

tin cup   *bannikin.* Note NE **noggin**.

tiny piece   *a peck.*

to; in order to   *to, t'.*

toadfish, sculpin   *gruffy, scopim* [SKOHʔ-uhm].

tobacco   *baccy* [BAHK-kee], plug tobacco (for chewing) or loose tobacco (for pipe).

toilet (overnight portable-)   *chamber pot.*

tolerate, accept   *go. Oi can't go er brewis.* "I can't eat (**tolerate**) her fish-and-brewis."

tolerated discomfort   *a sufferin comfort.*

tomorrow   *mar, d'mar.*

tongue blister   *pip.*

too-small cod   *a roast leggie* (filleted and roasted as is). See NE tom cod.

town resident   *a townie* (specifically of St. John's).

traditional hat   *salt 'n' pepper cap.*

tree without bark   *a whiting.*

tree roots (dried)   *crannicks.*

trending now   *on d' go.*

trivial possessions   *gilguys* [GIHL-geuhz].

troublemaker   *a ral.*

tumble over   as in head over heels: *arse-oer-keddle.*

twigs for kindling   *brishney, faddle.*

twilight time   *duckish, eel o' d' day.*

two weeks   *fortnight* [FAHRT-nueht].

U

unclear opportunity   *someting nodder.*

unconscious   *co junk. E trippt an knockt esauf out co junk.*

uncooperative   *contrary, crookeed, crousty, cranky.*

undecided   *on two moins.*

uncommited person   *nunnyfudgen*

uncouth person   *skeet*

under   *unner.*

understand   *to fadom (out), twig.*

uneven ground   *pumbly.* See NE **bawn.**

unimportant   *no odds, aa d' same, aa 'loike: Ar difference, t'is no odds, aa 'loike.* "It is **unimportant, doesn't matter.**"

unjustified   *not called fer.*

unkempt female   *a streel.*

unleavened   as in baking, *dunch, dunchy, dunce.*

unless   *widout.*

unlucky person   *a jinker.*

unmanageable (person, engine)   *cranky*

unreasonable   *cracked*. See NE *mental*.

unsatisfactory   *pisspoor*.

unsuspected   *unbeknownst*: **Unbeknownst** *to me, d' maid was married*.

unsweetened tea   *switchel* [SWICH-uhl].

upset, anxious   *opsot* [ohp-SAWT]. Note NE **vexed**.

upwind   *luff, winard*.

useless thing/person   *scroff* [SKRAWF], *lob*.

V

vacation   *toime av, aliday*.

veranda, deck   *bridge*.

very   also "exceedingly" or "excessively": *some, **wunnerfo**, fair, mad, aavo, **preddy, roight**, terrbul, **shockin**: Sure e was **wunnerfo** ravness at d' table.* "For sure he was very hungry at the table."

very satisfying   *some good*.

vessel   See NE **boat**.

W

wad of tobacco   *a quid* [KWIHD] (chewing tobacco).

waking nightmare   *o hag*   (sleep paralysis syndrome).

warn   [DRIH?-uhn] *dreaten. She **dreatened** en t' come ome sousht agin.* "She **warned** him not to return home drunk again."

wart   *a hurt*.

was not, were not   *wud'n*: *Sally **wud'n** home, so we went on*.

wasn't always   *usen't*: *Daniel **usen't** t' be af-cut aa d' toime.* "Daniel **wasn't always** partly drunk."

wasp   *a wop* [WAWP].

waste time, to-   *more toime den 'nough*.

water bucket   *draw bucket*.

water carrier   *wadder nipper*.

water sounds   *squish*.

water, the ocean   *wadder, wa'er: She's a wunnerfo day on d' **wadder**.* "It is a pleasant day to sail on the **ocean**."

weak spot in sea ice   *swatch*.

weather for, the-   *day on: Wha' a **day on** cloz!* "It is **a very favourable day** for drying laundry outside."

wedding attendants   *broidesb'ys, broidesgirls, faddergiver*

weep, cry   *bawl.*

we have   *we'm*: *Da weyk* **we'm** *boideed* [BUEHD-eed] *home.*
"This week **we've** stayed home."

well done   *knocked.*

whale   *grumpus* [GRUH-puhss].

what   *wha'* [WAW], [WAW?].

what did you say?   *Wha'? Sorry? Beg pardon?* [PAHRD-ehn].

what is/are-   *wha's* [WAWS], as in *Wha's o Jimmy so mad bout?*

what's-his-name   *buddy, wassesname, wassesfaace; chummy.*

what's-her-name   *wassername, wasserfaace; chummy*

when, whenever   *when, whenaer* [ween-EHR]

whiskey, hot-   *hot toddy*

who are you?   *Who owns you?* "Who are your parents?" (as to a child).

why   *wha'...fer* as in *Wha' you paintin dat cheer* **fer?**

why?   *Wha'fer?* as in *Y' paintin dat cheer? Wha'fer?*

wife   *da o ooman*

will   *ull. Dey ull come ome drectly.*

wimpy, peevish   *sooky.*

wind storm   *a breeze (o' ween), starm.*

windowshop   *to twack, ping.*

witty   *droy.*

woke up at -   *naer blowed t' -.*

woman is pregnant   *rock een er killock*: *Mary's got a rock een er killock.*

wood shavings   (for lighting a fire) *bavin.*

wooden soup ladle   *mundle.*

working alone   *cross-andeed* [AHN-deed]. Note *fudge.*

would   *ud, wud. Dey ud be ome cep f' da stroife o' ween een da Gulf.*
"They **would** be home but for the gale in the Cabot Strait."

would have   *ud ι ', wud a'.*

wrestle   *to rompse* [RAWMPSS].

Y

yard; backyard *garden*; *backgarden*.

year, years *yeur*, *twowvemont*: *T'is nar seal d' yeur.* "There are no seals this **year**" (a countable measure of time, distance and amount may drop its plural -*s*. after *da* or a number).

yes *aar*.

yesterday *yesday*.

you *ya, yiz, you, yous/ye* depending on singular, plural, stressed or unstressed; see pronoun list under **Small Words** in introduction.

you have *you'm* [YOOM]: *You'm got a noice stigger der, b'y.* "**You have** a hefty load there, pal."

young seals *young fat*, "white coats," *bedlamers*.

your *yer, yeer* [YEHR], [YEER] (see possessive modifier list under **Small Words** in introduction).

yours *yers, yeers* [YEERZ], [YEHRZ] See possessive pronoun list under **Small Words** in introduction.

Z

zed, zee *zad* [ZAHD].

Endnotes

1. www.canoe.ca/JamMovies/ArtistsM/moore_julianne.html
2. "Les pécheur [sic] basques furent souvent éprouvés par les rigueurs du climat de Terre-Neuve. Echcvete, déjà cité, parle de nombreux bâtiments du Guipùscoa pris dans les glaces pendant l'hiver de 1577 et de la mort en conseqience de 540 marins dans le port de Lutus Sombrero." (Harrisse, Henry. *Découverte et évolution cartographique de Terre-Neuve et des pays circonvoisons*. London: Henry Stiles Son & Stiles, 1900.) The tentative assumption is that "Lutus Sombrero" was situated in Placentia Bay. The passage in question is cited in footnote 4 on the same page (LXI) of Harisse's section on "Les Basques" of his *Découverte et évolution cartographique de Terre Neuve*, which says: "4 Il y a bien à l'entrée de la baie de Plaisance, sur la côte Sud de Terre-Neuve, une localité nommée depuis longtemps le cap ou la montagne du Chapeau rouge; mais nous n'avons pas encore rencontré de "Chapeau jaune (lutus sombrero?[*sic*])." A ce propos, notons que Francisque-Michel dit que "le nom de Chapeau rouge est sûrement de l'hôtellerie où les marins de Bordeaux venait conclure leurs affaires, op.cit., p. 341": "It is there at the entrance to Placentia Bay, on the South coast of Newfoundland, a place called for a long time Red Hat cape or mountain; but we have not yet come across 'Yellow Hat (lutus sombrero?)'. In this regard, note that Francisque Michel said that 'the name of Red Hat is surely the hostelry where Bordeaux sailors came to conclude their business', op.cit., P. 341" ["op.cit." referring to a previous citation on the same page: "Documents de Vargas Ponce, Arca de Noé" of the latter 1500s]. Cape Chapeau Rouge is today a landmark and local heritage site at the entrance to, and inside the boundary of St. Lawrence on the south coast of the Burin Peninsula.
3. "Modern English is a direct descendant of the language of Scandinavians who settled in the British Isles in the course of many centuries, before the French-speaking Normans conquered the country in 1066," Jan Terje Faarlund, University of Oslo, Joseph Emonds, Palacky University, Czech Republic (2012), www.york.ac.uk/language/news/events/talks/special-lectures/emonds/ and morgenbladet.no/2015/07/kontroversiell-teori-serios-debatt
4. "Allegedly" only because the author did not personally experience the prohibition, being enrolled in other courses at that time; fellow students and subsequent acquaintances remember with indignation.
5. www.cbncompass.ca/opinion/columnists/2012/10/23/

the-royal-readers-3105192.html, "Enrico" in comments section.

6. "Sampling attitudes to dialect varieties in St. John's" by S. Clark, 1982: despite high dialect loyalty, subjective opinion affirmed usage impeded social status.

7. In a brief televised interview, a local witness to the American Arrow Airlines air disaster at the Gander International Airport in 1985 who reported hearing "*a big tump b'y*" confounded both the US reporter and her network's transcribers! (See **tump, b'y**); personal observation.

8. Cornish **English** is a West Country dialect of English. Cornish **Celtic** is an extinct language, related to Welsh and Breton, enjoying a renascence as Revived Cornish.

9. Otherwise known as *lexis, syntax, semantics*, and *phonology* in formal language studies.

10. Brown, Ivor. *I Give You My Word*. London: Jonathan Cape Ltd., 1945.

11. Map suggested by a detail of the "Imperial Federation Map of the World Showing the Extent of the British Empire in 1886," 24 July 1886, Walter Crane (1845–1915), File 09_03_000082, Norman B. Leventhal Map Center, Boston Public Library; in the public domain.

12. *Pragmatic markers* are emotive and expressive little words or short phrases that grease the wheels of spoken conversation and so relate to the discourse itself, not to the topic of discourse. Pragmatic markers in colloquial Standard English include as *vocatives* the indefinite pronouns in direct-address commands ("Call a doctor, **somebody**! **Anybody**!") and the 2nd person pronoun, ("**You**, turn it down!"), and certain nouns in casual, running speech ("Hey, **guys**, what're we doing tonight?"), but never the **non**-imperative 2nd person pronoun in word-final position as in Newfoundland English: *Oi's shocked, you*. Compare Northern Bavarian *Allmächd na, du,* "I am shocked, you" or Polish, *Ty klamczuchu!,* "**You** liar!" Hungarian, *Te geci!* "You (pejorative noun, lit. ejaculatory fluid)!"

13. *Voiceless glottal stop* in linguists' jargon, sounded as a very short, abrupt "uh" for "t" between vowels as in dialectal *bu'er* [BUHʔ-uhr] "butter"; see also [ʔ] under PRONUNCIATION KEY.

14. Dent, Susie (2007), *The Language Report: English on the Move, 2000-2007.* Oxford University Press.

15. "...language shifts under economic growth and globalization, rather than the loss of speaker populations themselves, represent the major underlying process of recent declines in speakers....Economically developed regions, such as North America and Australia, have already experienced many language extinctions, most probably due to the negative impact of economic, and associated political and educational, developments." *(Global distribution and drivers of language extinction risk,* London: Proceedings of The Royal Society B, 2014).

16. *London Cant*, the vernacular of the mostly urban English lower classes as set out in a 1699 dictionary by an unknown antiquary who took the pen name, "B.E. Gent"; see **Further Reading**.

17. "It has been speculated that the rolling 'rrr', a distinctive element of the speech of the West Country of England, has been associated with pirates because of the West Country's strong maritime heritage, with for many centuries fishing the main industry (and smuggling a major unofficial one), and where there were several major ports. As a result, West Country speech in general, and Cornish speech in particular, may have been a major influence on a generalized British nautical speech." -en.wikipedia.org/wiki/International_Talk_Like_a_Pirate_Day

18. As rendered in a full-page ad in American computer magazine *Byte*, February 1982 issue, p. 193: "Ah-ha! Eureka! All-riiight!"

19. The annual world class *Targa Newfoundland* is the only premium motor-sports road rally event of its kind in North America. Each September 200 international competitors from as far as Australia race a five-day 2,200 km course through seventy outports of eastern Newfoundland island. The Targa events during 2001–2011 added over $110 million to the provincial economy (*The Telegram*, 06 Aug., 2011).

20. Reid Newfoundland Company Passenger Train No. 1 in January, 1900, was entirely torn from the tracks. Gap gusts blew 100-ton rail cars off the tracks until 1939 (see **human wind gauge**). Even today, with no place to turn around, as many as 15 big rig trucks are ditched yearly. Winds sometimes requires official closure of the roadway to let three trucks through side by side at 10 km/h, the heaviest on the outside. The worst southeast winds are hurricane Category 2 and may be increasing due to climate change.

21. "Newfie" first appeared in a 1942 dictionary of slang. The last dictionary mention of "Newfie" as "offensive" was the *Gage Canadian Dictionary* of 1983 and the *Random House Unabridged Dictionary* of 1987. Alberta's ban on "Newfie" personalized licence plates ended 2008.

22. From *Le Petit Nord or Annals of a Labrador Harbour*, a 1920s account of life at the Grenfell Mission, St. Anthony, NL, by Lady Anne Grenfell, wife of Sir Wilfred Grenfell.

23. "(2) In the province of Newfoundland, a resident of the Province may, without a permit and during the period commencing on September 1st and ending March 31st, hunt murres for human food only." Migratory Bird Treaty Act of 1918, 1949 amendment (www.mun.ca/serg/turr hunt.pdf).

24. Newfoundland politician Henry W. LeMessurier composed "The Ryans and The Pittmans" from a sea shanty of the 1600s and 1700s. It has been sung in various forms around the world and featured in

1800s ballads and in novels and latter 1900s television and movies. However, the song, like other potential examples of Newfoundland literature, was published only in SE, never in any traditional NE dialect. The chorus in NE:

We ull rant an we ull roar loike true Newfoundlanders,
We ull rant an we ull roar on deck an below
Widout we sees bottom eensoide d' two sunkers,
Den straat trough d' Channel t' Toslow we ull go.

25. "D' Juloy Droive" or "An D' Band Played Ode T' Newf'n'lan" (all to the tune of "And the Band Played Waltzing Matilda")

Now, when oi was a young feller wid nary a care,
    oi fished fer me grub on a banker.
Fom frore on d' Labr'dor to d' grizzly Grand Banks,
    b'y, oi lugged me o grub bag aa oer.
Den een nointeen fiddeen, aur King Garge says, "Me son,
    you bess not be a slacker, dere bes work t' be done."
So dey gived me a tin at, an dey gived me a gun,
    and oi dodged me way av to da waar.

An d' brigade band played Ode t' Newf'n'land,
    whoile aur ship shuffed av fer d' sea.
An trou aa d' cheers, d' flag-wavin an tears,
    we made sail fer France and Marseilles.

Affer Gal'p'li oi moinds Juloy Firs een 'sixdeen,
    ow aur blood stained d' mud an da wadder.
An ov ow, een dat hell dat dey caad Beaumont-Ham'l,
    loike swoiles on da oice we was martyred.
Jerry Hun, e was yarry, unbeknownst to we b'ys.
    E rained we wid bullets, shells blinded aur eoyes.
An be terdy minutes gone, we was swatted loike floys.
    Aamos blowed we back ome to d' Narrows.

An d' band played da Ode t' Newf'n'land
    whoile we stopped t' bury aur slain.
We buried aurs, an dem Huns buried deyrs.
    Den she started en at en agin.

An dose dat was loive, b'y, we troied to survoive,
    een dat mad wurl ov blood, death an foire.
An fer noigh on twowv weyks, oi kep me sauf aloive,
    whoile round me d' carpses poiled oigher.
Den a gert German shell knocked me arse oer kettle,
    an when oi woke op een d' Reg'ment 'ospital,
An seen what she ud done, dere was near worse poor martal.
    Naer knowed dere bes worse tings dan dyin.

Naer more oi'll be out on d' barrens,
    near more on da wadder oi'll be.
Fer t' fish dem Grand Banks, a man needs es shanks.
    Naer more luggin me grub bag fer me.

So dey gaddered da wounded, d' crippled, d' maimed,
    an dey shipped we back ome to da Avalon.
D' shell-shocked, d' blinded, d' limbless, d' lame,
    dose proud wounded eroes ov Beaumont.
An when aur ship pulled tween d' Narrows oi cud see,
    and looked at da place wher me legs used t' be,
Oi tanked Christ dere bes nar soul dere waitin fer me,
    t' grieve, t' marn, an t' pity.

An d' Brigade Band played Ode t' Newf'n'land,
    whoile dey carried we down d' gangway.
But nar soul dere cheered. Dey jis stood dere an stared.
    Den dey turned aa deyr faaces away.

An so now, evy Lebent, on me bridge oi jis sits,
    an oi watches d' parade pass longsoide we.
An oi sees me o comrades, ow proud bes deyr march,
    aa took op een deyr dreams ov o glory.
Da o men marches slowloike, aa bent, stiff an scarred,
    d' long fergot eroes fom a long fergot waar.
An dem young people says, "What be dey marchin fer?"
    An oi says t' mesauf d' same question.

But d' band plays da Ode t' Newf'n'land,
    an da o ands stio answers d' caa.
But yeur affer yeur, more o men be not dere.
    Bumbye nar'n ull be marchin ataa.

"As loved au fadders, so do we love,
    Where once dey stood, we now stands."
An o ghosts might be yeard
    whoile dey marches by d' Cenotaph.
"We loves dee, God guard dee,
    God guard dee, Newf'n'land."

©Russell Bragg
November 2015

Further Reading

The following are suggested for investigative or comparative reference, but do not necessarily represent or support all assertions or opinions expressed in this work.

Amano, Tatsuya, et al. (2014), *Global distribution and drivers of language extinction risk*, London: Proceedings of The Royal Society B 281: 20141574.

Anon. (1862), *Song of Solomon, in Twenty-four English Dialects*, London: H.I.H. Prince Louis Lucien Bonaparte.

Barkham, Selma Huxley (1989), *The Basque Coast of Newfoundland, Plum Point*: The Great Northern Peninsula Development Corporation.

Barnes, William. (1886), *A Glossary of the Dorset Dialect with a Grammar...*, London: Trübner & Co.

Clark, Sandra (2004), "Newfoundland English: phonology" in Bernd Kortmann (ed.), *A Handbook of Varieties of English*. 2, Berlin: de Gruyter.

Clark, Sandra (2010), *Newfoundland and Labrador English*, Edinburgh: Edinburgh University Press.

Davis, Norman (1965), *Sweet's Anglo-Saxon Primer*, Oxford: Oxford University Press.

Devine, Patrick Kevin (1937), *Devines's Folk Lore of Newfoundland in Old Words, Phrases and Expressions (Their Origin and Meanings)*, St. John's, NL: Robinson & Co. Ltd.

Evans, Arthur B. and Sebastian (1881), *Leicestershire Words, Phrases, and Proverbs*, London: Trübner & Co for the English Dialect Society.

Gent, B.E. (1699), *A New Dictionary of the Terms Ancient and Modern of the Canting Crew...*, London: William Hawes, Ludgate Street.

Grenfell, Anne, et al. (1920), *Le Petit Nord; or, Annals of a Labrador Harbour*, Boston: Houghton Mifflin Company.

Grose, Francis (1811), Lexicon Balatronicum: *A Dictionary of Buckish Slang, University Wit, and Pickpocket Eloquence*, London: Printed for C. Chappel.

Halliwell-Phillipps, James Orchard (1850, 1887), *A dictionary of archaic and provincial words, obsolete phrases, proverbs and ancient customs, from the fourteenth century*, Vols. 1 & 2, London: John Russell Smith.

Hernández, Nuria (2011), "Personal Pronouns in the Dialects of England," PhD thesis, Universität Freiburg im Breisgau, Germany.

Howe, Stephen (1996), *The Personal Pronouns in the Germanic Languages*, Berlin: de Gruyter.

Hughes, Geoffrey (1991), *A Social History of Foul Language, Oaths and Profanity in English*, Oxford, UK: Basil Blackwell, Inc.

Janes, Percy (1970, 1976), *House of Hate*, Toronto: McClelland & Stewart.)

Lobov, William, et al. (2005), *The Atlas of North American English*, Berlin: de Gruyter.

McAllister, Stephanie (2010), *The Newfoundland Poetry Anthology: Dialect Literature as Carrier of Cultural Identity*, Toronto: University of Toronto Press.

McArthur, Tom (1998), *The English Languages*, Cambridge: Cambridge University Press.

Mohr, Melissa (2013), *Holy Shit, A Brief History of Swearing*, New York: Oxford University Press.

Nares, Robert (1888), *A Glossary, Or, Collection of Words, Phrases, Names, and Allusions...in the Works of English Authors...*, London: Reeves & Turner.

Noseworthy, Ronald G. (1971), "A Dialect Survey of Grand Bank, Newfoundland," St. John's: Memorial University of Newfoundland.

Poole, Jacob (1867). *A glossary, with some pieces of verse, of the old dialect of the English colony in the baronies of Forth and Bargy, county of Wexford, Ireland* (W. Barnes, Ed.). London: J.R. Smith.

Scott, Peter J. (August 1987), "Common Names of Plants in Newfoundland," *Regional Language Studies, Newfoundland*, Number 11, St John's: Memorial University of Newfoundland.

Story, G.M., et al. (1982), *Dictionary of Newfoundland English*, Toronto: University of Toronto Press.

Wagner, Susanne (2004), "English Dialects in the Southwest: morphology and syntax" in Bernd Kortmann (ed.), *A Handbook of Varieties of English*. 2, Berlin: de Gruyter.

Weyers, Christian (2009), "Basques Traces in the Toponymy of Newfoundland and Various Coasts of Atlantic Canada," Dresden: Technische Universität Dresden. York University: Proceedings of the 23rd International Congress of Onomastic Sciences.

Willson, Beckles (1897), *The Tenth Island*, London: Grant Richards.

Wright, Joseph (1898), *The English Dialect Dictionary*. London: Henry Frowde